About the Author

Tom Kelly's interest in murder stories began when he was a reporter covering murder trials in Louisiana and in Washington, D.C. During his twelve-year stint with the *Washington Daily News,* Kelly covered some of the murders discussed in this book. He is now an editor/ senior writer for *Canada Today/Au'jourd'hui* and has written for *The Nation, Nation's Business, The New York Times, The Washington Post,* and *The Washingtonian.* He is currently at work on a book entitled *Kay Graham and The Washington Post.*

Contents

MURDERS
Washington's Most Famous Murder Stories

By Tom Kelly

 WASHINGTONIAN BOOKS

This book is dedicated to Marguerite Lelong Kelly, the mystery woman in my life.

Book Design: Ed Schneider
Photo Editor: Linda Altshuler

Published by Washingtonian Books
1828 L Street, N.W.
Washington, D.C. 20036

Picture Credits

John Burwell, 20, 28, 44, 62, 102, 112
International News Photos, 66
Library of Congress, 7, 19, 22, 26, 30, 32, 33, 34, 36, 48, 50, 52, 54, 75, 76, 79, 81, 84, 87, 89, 94, 96, 101, 106, 109, 110, 114, 119, 120, 126
Chevrolet, 60
Robin Moyer, 58
United Press International, 10, 11, 15, 40, 41, 43, 68, 70, 71, 128, 129
U.S. Signal Corps, 49
Wide World Photos, 8, 12, 13, 123

Introduction

MURDER IS AS AMERICAN as apple pie.

In the country's first two hundred years more Americans died suddenly and violently in what might be called private transactions than in wars.

This devotion to private enterprise has both negative and positive aspects. We are embarrassed (and should be) when we consider that we kill one another much more often than do, say, the French or British. On the other hand we have never had official, government-sanctioned, civil blood-letting such as the judicial excesses after the French Revolution or even those of the reigns of Henry the Eighth, Bloody Mary, Oliver Cromwell, or Victoria Regina.

The inclination toward the violent resolution of life's little problems was born with the Republic—there were few murderers (or at any rate few who murdered white men and women) among the Colonists. Only 40 persons were convicted of murder in Pennsylvania between the Dutch settlement in 1624 and the writing of the Declaration of Independence, but the new citizens of the United States changed all that. Americans kill after provocations that would make a Frenchman shake his fist or an Englishman write a letter to the *Times*.

Murders are educational in that they reflect the customs and passions of time and place. If you want to know how your forebears lived and what moved them to emotional display, read the transcripts of 19th-century trials. You will find that we do not live in an unprecedented age of violence. The streets of Washington were just about as safe in 1976 as they were in 1876, a fact reflected not by official statistics (there were none then and today's are no more trustworthy than a lawyer's tears) but by trial testimony and old newspaper accounts that give a hundred incidental glimpses of the ambience of the times. Women who traveled alone in the 1870's and 1880's, for example, frequently carried pistols, dainty models, purchased readily at downtown stores. Gentlemen were as easily served. The gent who shot Garfield bought his five-shooter at a gun

1

shop across from the Treasury Department and, on the proprietor's advice, practiced shooting it in a public wood a couple of blocks from the White House.

Then, as in recent times, politicians were inclined to give Washington a bad name, but the crime capital of the United States has always been west of the Potomac. In the 1850's Los Angeles County, with a peak population of 8,000, had 44 murders. To meet that level of havoc today, Washington, D.C., and its environs would have to have an annual total of some 1,600 homicides. (The District had 235 in 1975, the area as a whole less than 300).

Old transcripts and newspapers also give us more homely information—about the food people ate (heavy; mutton for breakfast), the clothes they wore (bulky; broadcloth in July), the books they read (pious; tomes of purple sermons), the pastimes they enjoyed (participatory; euchre in the parlor), and the tasks and avocations that filled their hours (they spent much time sitting in parks and they traveled frequently and slowly—the train from the District of Columbia to Baltimore could take several, dreary hours. Communications were leisurely—people wrote long letters back and forth with the facility with which teenagers now use the phone).

Murders are traditionally classified as crimes of passion or greed, but passions change and greed takes new forms at different times in different places. People killed in 1870 or 1910 or even 1960 for reasons that are now out of fashion. In 1870 a young Marylander—a most hard working, law-abiding, upright young man —killed his sister's seducer in broad daylight before a score of witnesses. He was, of course, acquitted as soon as the jury sat down and cast its ballots. He was behaving as the community expected him to. He was, like many a murderer, a social conservative.

The murders in this book are the Nation's Capital's murders (some take place outside the city's bounds, but they all have Washington connections). A murder in the District of Columbia is often essentially different from one committed in Las Vegas or Baton Rouge. Washington is the city of ambitious, middle-class people. It has never suffered gang warfare nor the depredation of a Billy the Kid or a Pretty Boy Floyd. But the passion for respectability has moved many Washingtonians to kill, and greed in the Nation's Capital is more apt to take the form of an uncontrollable desire for a government appointment than for a diamond as big as the Ritz. General Sickles, who killed his wife's distinguished lover in Lafayette Square in 1859, came close to combining the basic Washington motives—he was preserving his political and social positions as well as his marriage. Even Larry Lord Motherwell, the carpenter who seduced and occasionally killed impressionable women, was so enamoured of respectability that he enlisted as a morning-coated usher in striped pants at President Eisenhower's own church and posed as a nuclear scientist with an apartment at the Army War College.

This emphasis may suggest that Washington murderers are so careful of appearances that their handiworks are as tedious as the keynote speech at a DAR convention. The opposite is true. As De Quincy pointed out long ago, the true student of murder is not concerned with a footpad bludgeoning a passerby but with the malefactor who sets out to disguise his actions and gain his goals by complex and devious means. DeQuincy was, of course, English and English murders, though relatively rare, are often marvelous. The English are so thoroughly middle class that they would rather slip arsenic into the afternoon tea than display the emotions inevitable in a shootout. For much the same reason (hypocrisy is too strong a word), Washingtonians can make marvelously devious scoundrels. One, a proper bureaucrat engaged in social uplift programs, hired two of his benighted clients to kidnap, rape, and murder his wife, assuming, incorrectly, that no one would connect him with the crime. He was, naturally, caught because of his absurd ingenuity and was convicted. The conviction placed him among the less fortunate malefactors; half of the killers in this book got off—most of them freed in spite of overwhelming evidence. In most of the cases from the last century, the killers escaped their just desserts, and they escaped because they were respectable and because they killed persons to whom they had been properly introduced. Respectable people never kill strangers. Most often they kill husbands or, when the man with the gun is the husband himself, the seducers of wives.

The most persistent mark of these Washington murderers, next to respectability, is incompetence. It must be acknowledged that we can not study the motives and techniques of the truly successful, the murderers who buried their crimes as well as their victims, but the available records do suggest that the Washington murderer has, perhaps, been too much influenced by the non-consecutive quality of the Federal bureaucracy, where causes often have no effects and actions no consequences. The majority of our killers seem to have had a childish belief that no one would notice the corpse or, if anyone did, that he would assume that the departed succumbed to *cholera morbis* or had been struck by lightning.

Still, many of our protagonists have gotten away, literally, with murder, and they have been aided and abetted by lawyers. For every successful attorney who triumphs by pure legal logic, there are five who specialize in emotions, bias, sentimentality, and histrionics. Their tactics are defended with the time-worn proposition that it is better that a hundred guilty go free than that one innocent person be convicted. The point is irrelevant— it is more improbable that improper stratagems ever delivered one of the unguilty; it is undeniable that they have often freed the guilty.

But the point of this book is not that our system of justice fails but that it works surprisingly well. If one were to consider the net results of all the cases herein in terms of the letter-of-the-law, one would have to conclude that justice was often ill-served. But laws are made by Congressmen and other unreliable parties and are seldom custom-tailored to fit a citizen's needs. The jury that acquitted young Mary Harris when she shot her lying seducer in the marble halls of the Treasury Department knew beyond doubt that it was indeed her fair hand that pulled the trigger. They also believed that a law that did not provide for recognition of her superiority over her victim was a law best ignored. There was a great attachment in the 19th century to the "unwritten law"—betrayed husbands, betrayed maidens and, in some instances, brothers of betrayed maidens were entitled to at least one free shot.

From this broader view point, there are only three cases considered here in which we would say substantial justice was denied.

The first one was Chief Eastlake, who shifted the blame of his wife's murder to his earnest mistress, a Miss Knox. Miss Knox got 20 years, the Chief got transferred to the Washington Navy Yard.

Mrs. Wharton, who almost surely poisoned a couple of members of her immediate family as well as a house guest to whom she owed money, really deserved to hang. She escaped the rope because gentlemen jurors in those days were simply unable to convict women of respectable connections of anything more henious than a social faux pas.

The other failure of justice occurred in the 20th century when Beulah Limerick, the Whoopee Girl, died before she really had a chance to live. She had tried too hard, poor child, to have a good time with too many men. She was a loose, loose young woman but as generous as a summer breeze—she had a line tattooed across her lower tummy, "Pay as You Enter" but that was only a joke. Her death, as it turned out, was, accidentally, the perfect crime. It was not that the police had no case or no suspect. They had too many cases against too many men. When they brought them all to court they canceled each other out.

Beulah's case is as instructive as it is sad. As we suggested earlier, the purpose of this book is not to indulge you in vicarious violence and gore (tune in on prime-time TV if that's your interest) but to put you in touch with the hopes, dreams, frustrations, confusions, and disasters of very real people, including both victims and killers, who tried to cope with the world's tribulations in the rooming houses, mansions, and on the streets of Washington a decade, two decades, five decades, or a century or more ago.

Tom Kelly
September 15, 1976
Washington, D.C. 3

Larry Loses One Lady Too Many

WHEN THE LAWYER asked Larry if he'd ever hit Mrs. Putney, Larry said: "Oh, Heavens no."

Larry Lord Motherwell was a striped-pants usher at the National Presbyterian Church and sometimes he dressed up as a Navy captain, or pretended to be a missile scientist, or a high, mysterious government official, or a foreign correspondent.

Most often he pretended to be a Ph.D.

Really he was a carpenter and a lady killer.

He was a soft-voiced man who seldom cursed and hardly drank, and if he had a fault it was a tendency toward murder and lying.

His first wife, Dorothy, left him, suddenly, and his second died, suddenly, in the bath.

And Mrs. Pearl Putney, 72 and silly, thought he was going to marry her until he drove her to a mountain pine grove in California and threw her away.

Larry was tall and soft and handsome and an inconspicuous ornament on the Washington scene in 1950, when he was living in a cooperative apartment on Porter Street with his second wife, Sarah.

One day, perhaps by chance, he opened his door to put out the garbage when Mrs. Putney opened hers to do the same.

They introduced themselves over the cantaloupe shells and coffee grounds. Soon she was giggling like a schoolgirl.

Mrs. Putney was the widow of Professor Alfred H. Putney of American University and the State Department. The professor had died in 1929, a bad year for everybody. Mrs. Putney, a young 42, was left with her aging mother, Ida Dabrohua, and a small fortune. Small fortunes were worth a lot immediately after 1929, and Mrs. Putney's remained intact. She also had some jewelry, a chamois bag full of diamonds, Spode china, sterling silver, Persian rugs, and an occasional invitation to an embassy reception in memory of the professor, who had been an authority in international affairs.

But it wasn't much fun during the thirties and forties. So she was enchanted when she met Larry over the garbage.

He was a mere 32, she 65. Her mother

was still hanging on at 85. Larry, as he called himself, was busy working his way up in the world. He did not do it in a nice, straightforward fashion. For one thing, his name originally was not Larry Lord Motherwell. It had been Frank Eugene Caventer and he had gone into District Court and had it changed. He told the court he had been raised by an aunt and uncle named Motherwell, though he had not. His mother, who raised him along with his father, had been a Motherwell. Anyway, Frank Eugene switched.

He became a "doctor" the same way he became a Motherwell, by desire, but without going through any formalities.

He got rid of his wife Sarah as casually.

On November 7, 1953, Sarah was found dead, face up, in the bath. Larry Lord called the police. He told them that he had been out for a couple of hours and had returned to find the corpse. Sarah had been a healthy young woman. The Deputy Coroner, Richard M. Rosenberg, ruled she had drowned, accidentally, possibly after an attack of "pancreatitis." Pancreatitis is the inflammation of the pancreas, an organ that squirts digestive juices into the stomach. Its connection with accidental drowning, if any, is not clear.

Mrs. Putney reacted emotionally to Sarah's death—she told Larry that she was adopting him as a brother. Thereafter he called her "Sis" and her mother "Mama."

Sometimes he would kiss one or the other on the cheek or forehead. "They seemed to like it," he said.

If Mrs. Putney entertained any romantic thoughts about her neighbor in 1953, they were at least premature. Two weeks after Sarah's death, Larry was busy renting an apartment in Frederick, Maryland, for himself and a girl named Sally. Sally, who had left her husband, was apparently under the impression that she was to be the next Mrs. Motherwell. She was wrong.

Larry was moving around a bit socially. President Eisenhower was a member of the congregation of the National Presbyterian Church, the premier Presbyterian church of the land. At that time, it was housed in an impressive Romanesque edifice just off Connecticut Avenue

Motherwell was seized in Las Vegas in January some seven months before Mrs. Putney's remains were found in the Great American Desert.

near N Street—its tall, square bell tower visible for miles. Larry joined the church and became a Sunday morning usher, wearing striped pants and swallowtail coat. The other members of the congregation were under the impression that he was an engineer.

He also told stories about himself around Porter Street. He told George Cawthorne that he was an atomic scientist with an apartment at the National War College.

When there was a rumor, possibly started by Larry, that the shade trees of Porter Street were about to be chopped down, he said he would ask the Secretary of the Air Force to intervene. When the trees survived, the gentle folks of Porter Street celebrated with an ice cream party and Larry was the man of the hour.

Larry was not a real mover and shaker. He was not even much of a carpenter. Mostly he was a playboy and a conductor of what came to be called "Motherwell's Guided Tours."

After Sarah died and Sally faded away, Larry married a nice young telephone operator, but she did not occupy his complete attention. He took one of his wife's fellow operators off to Florida, where they got an apartment. He told the girl that he was a man of such official importance that a special government guard called "The Dagger" watched him, unobtrusively, twenty-four hours a day. The girl, who did not suspect that Larry was a wrong number, was devastated when she got a telegram one day saying he was dead and his ashes had already been scattered over the Everglades. It was signed, "The Dagger." He turned up a bit later and told her the telegram was a mistake. The ashes had belonged to his twin brother. Then they set off for the west, driving through Marysville, California, on their way to Reno. Dr. Motherwell, as he signed himself on the motel registers, told her he intended to get a

The Weather

Today—Becoming cloudy and rather windy with rising temperature, high 38 degrees. Clearing tonight, low 25 degrees. Tuesday—Fair and colder. Sunday's temperatures: High, 25 at 3:50 p. m.; low, 13 at 8:35 a. m. Details, B2.

The Washington Post
and Times Herald
FINAL

82nd Year .... No. 45   Phone RE. 7-1234   Copyright 1959 The Washington Post Co.   **MONDAY, JANUARY 19, 1959**   WTOP Radio (1500) TV (Ch. 9)   TEN CENTS

Motherwell Seized in West

Sought Here In Missing Widow Hunt

Found in Nevada Motel With $2000 And a New Auto

By Alfred E. Lewis and Alfson B. Bailey
Staff Reporters

Larry Lord Motherwell, object of a Nation-wide search in connection with the disappearance of Pearl Ida Putney, 72, a wealthy Washington widow, was held yesterday in Las Vegas, Nev.

Motherwell, 42, a Washington construction worker, also is wanted by police in Frederick, Md., for questioning about the discovery in a Frederick pet cemetery of the body of a baby girl believed to have been Motherwell's daughter.

Las Vegas Det. Lt. Bill Hand said Motherwell was picked up in a motel in the Nevada city where he had registered Jan. 12 under the name "Art Rivers."

Handlon said Motherwell, who had $2000 in cash in his pockets when he was picked up, quietly admitted he was Motherwell but would tell police nothing more.

For Frederick Police

Motherwell was being held in Las Vegas at the request of Frederick Police Chief Charles Main, who said he was satisfied that Motherwell had demanded an attorney.

Main and Frederick County Sheriff Horace M. Alexander would fly to Las Vegas today to question Motherwell about the disappearance of the infant girl's body Nov. 29 during an investigation into the disappearance of Mrs. Putney.

3024 Porter st. nw., has not been seen since she and Motherwell were traced by police to a motel in Marysville, Calif. Aug. 25 after they had shared a leisurely cross-country auto mobile trip from Florida.

Washington police said Mrs. Putney was believed to have been carrying more than $20,000 in cash and about $30,000 to be used to purchase a

Las Vegas police said Motherwell was being held under a security felon. They reported Motherwell had also been entered on the arrest book as a fugitive from Maryland.

Counter on Case

No charges have been placed against Motherwell by Washington or Frederick police. Main, who held a conference last night with Sheriff Alexander and State's Attorney Edwin F. Nikirk in Frederick, said he may institute proceedings for a warrant and the return of Motherwell to Maryland after talking to him in Las Vegas today.

Motherwell's detention came

See BABY, A3, Col. 1

Tabloid's Articles On Queen Halted

LONDON, Jan. 18 (AP)—The tabloid Sunday Pictorial announces today it is not going to publish any more episodes in its controversial new series, "The Queen in Her Castle."

The Pictorial published the first installment of the series by William Charles Ellis, for nine years superintendent of Windsor Castle, last Sunday.

But three days ago an interim injunction was issued on Queen Elizabeth's behalf in the High Court, restraining Ellis—from breaking an agreement he is said to have made not to give information about the royal family for publication in the press. A decision on whether the ban is to be made permanent is due Tuesday.

Hunt Halted For Vanished Family of 4

Weather Forces Postponement in Virginia Search

The weather yesterday forced police to call a temporary halt to their week-long search of the woods, lakes and lonely roads of Louisa County, Va., where a family of four disappeared without leaving a trace.

County Sheriff Willis E. Proffitt said the area's dense underbrush made it impossible for even a helicopter to give a clue, and foot investigators have almost given up hope.

FBI agents continued an intensive search. But a spokesman here said yesterday that "absolutely nothing" had been discovered to throw light on the case.

Some authorities have said the family must have been kidnaped, but may have learned of ward for information leading to recovery of the missing persons has been offered by a friend.

The offer for information on the Jackson family—Carroll V. Jr., his wife, Mildred, 27

The missing family lives in Apple Grove, Va. Their parents found abandoned a week ago on State Route 609 near Mineral, where the Jacksons were last seen on a visit to Mrs. Jackson's parents.

Los Angeles Is Choice of Democrats

Committee Picks City as Site of 1960 Convention

NEW ORLEANS, Jan. 18 (AP)—A hard-bargaining Democratic Party committee today chose Los Angeles as the site for the Party's 1960 national convention.

Three other cities — San Francisco, Philadelphia and Miami Beach — were in the final running. But the committee declined to give any information on how the final voting or competition within the committee went in a move to prevent controversy.

Chicago and New York also sought the convention.

The action by the Site Selection Committee means Los Angeles will get the convention although it must be approved by the Democratic National Committee. The parent group's approval is considered routine and is expected at a Feb. 27-28 meeting in Washington.

New Arena Offered

A similar Republican Party committee, meanwhile, planned to meet in Des Moines, Iowa, Monday and Tuesday to pick bids from the same six cities that sought the Democratic Convention.

Los Angeles also could have the edge on other cities in attempts to get the Republican convention. The television radio industry particularly is urging that both parties meet in the same city to simplify the technical problems in the case.

Camille Gravel Jr., chairman of the Democratic Site Selection Committee, said his group considered 30 to 40 factors in making its choice.

A main consideration for Los Angeles apparently was that city's new sports arena to be completed in May, with 17,000 seats and surrounding facilities. Los Angeles also put up a $500,000 cash offer and additional lucrative extras.

Other determining factors, Gravel said, were seating available space in and near the convention amphitheater, convention offices, caucus rooms, eating facilities and food supplies, accessible hotel facilities and transportation.

All Offered Cash

Like Los Angeles, the cities of San Francisco, Philadelphia and Miami Beach put up offers. New York offered $300,000 cash and Chicago $250,000. All the cities offered additional inducements.

A fight before the full Democratic National Committee was promised on behalf of Chicago by Mayor Richard J. Daley. He said he will appear at the Democratic meeting in Washington Feb. 27.

Meanwhile, Chicago also rates concentrated upon preparing a strong pitch for the summer, when the very pleasant agenda of the Republican Convention Site Committee in Des Moines.

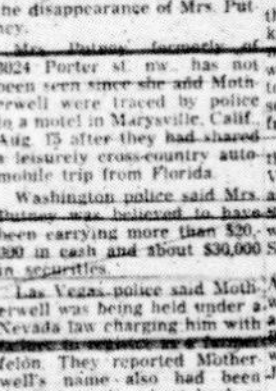

LOOKING FOR A HOME?

Turn to Washington's biggest market place for homes, the Classified Section of The Washington Post and Times Herald, publishing more District and Suburban Homes-for-Sale advertising than any other Washington paper.

Today's Index

28 PAGES—2 SECTIONS

A-20 Pages—General News, Editorials, Sports
B—18 Pages, Arts News, Women, Classified, Comics

	Page		Page
Allsop	A13	Merblock	B15
Appel Ch	A13	Horoscope	B15
City Life	B1	Keep Well	B14
Crossfeld	B7,12	Kilgallen	B7
Comics	B14-17	Movie Guide	B12
Crossword	B17	Music	B12
Dar Line	B16	Obituaries	B12
Dixon		Pearson	A17
Editorials	A15	Sokolsky	A15
Events Today	B7	Sports	A16-19
Fed'l Diary	B1	TV-Radio	B6
Financial	A15	Wendt	B3
		Women	B4-5

President Frondizi of Argentina

President Arturo Frondizi of Argentina, pictured in his office in Buenos Aires, is scheduled to arrive here Tuesday. One of his chief aims is to seek closer economic ties with the United States.

Harvester Strike Ends For 37,000

New 3-Year Pact Ratified by Vote of 90% of Workers

CHICAGO, Jan. 18 (AP)—Rank-and-file members of the United Auto Workers Union voted today to end their two month strike against International Harvester Co.

Seymour Kahan, international representative of UAW's Harvester department, said members of 33 locals scattered over the country voted overwhelmingly to accept a new three-year contract, the ratification vote was conducted during the weekend.

Kahan said 37,000 striking production workers will return to their jobs in 15 Harvester plants and 10 depots and warehouses Monday.

Kahan said reports showed about 90 per cent favored acceptance of the contract. At least one local—817 in Louisville, Ky.—with 700 members—voted to reject the agreement. About 11,200 of the workers are employed in four plants in Chicago and about 6800 in plants in four Illinois cities—Canton, East Moline, Rock Island and Rock Falls. Others are employed in seven plants in Memphis, Louisville, Fort Wayne and Indianapolis, Ind., Springfield, Ohio and Stockton, Calif.

Also involved in the strike were workers in Harvester parts depots and warehouses in eight other cities.

Stevenson Warns U.S. Must Reclaim Ideals

By Milton Viorst
Staff Reporter

Adlai E. Stevenson warned last night that the conviction, he said, are Communist dedication and sacrifice and the belief that the "great purpose" and "humanity in a matter of indifference because the easy option.

He said the tempo of Soviet faith is "sluggish" while American faith is "sluggish." Stevenson termed as address an examination of our collective conscience. He said "there is no more urgent day than to discover why we have failed . . . to get back into the race . . . .

Stevenson termed his address an examination of our collective conscience." He said "there is no more urgent day than to discover why we have failed . . . to get back into the race . . . to recapture the leadership . . . to set to work the ultimate energies of free society."

Adlai Stevenson honored in ceremony following his Constitution Hall address. Page B4.

The two-time Democratic presidential candidate addressed the first A. Powell Davies memorial address last night at Constitution Hall. The lectures are named for the outspoken liberal theologian and minister who was minister of All Souls Unitarian Church here until his death in 1957.

An audience of 4000 heard Stevenson, who was applauded.

We seem unaware," he said, "that freedom dom has to be remade and re-earned in each generation of man."

In the Soviet Union which Stevenson visited last summer, the very prophetic matic political leaders seem to believe profoundly in the future . . . .

"We have offered aid not to help others but to shield ourselves. We have reacted to countless Soviet initiatives, and have thus doing very nicely.

Communist Office Closed In Argentina

Government Acts As Frondizi Leaves For Visit to U. S.

BUENOS AIRES, Jan. 18 (Reuters)—The Argentine government tonight closed Communist Party headquarters after declaring a general strike which stopped all transport for a few hours and street cars for travel in the Argentine capital.

The government also closed down the editorial offices of the Communist newspaper La Hora and recalled military reservists and canceled leaves.

The declaration that strikes were illegal meant that strikers would not be paid for days off they were idle and that they were subject to dismissal without severance pay.

Bank and commercial employees joined the strike which now includes every union but railway workers.

The upsurge of discontent brought Argentina to a political crossroads just as President Arturo Frondizi left for a two-week visit to the United States as guest of President Eisenhower.

Frondizi is due in Charleston, S. C., Monday and in Washington on Tuesday.

The provisional president of the Senate, Jose Maria Guido, temporarily will be in charge of the government.

The call up of reserves and the police and armed forces for

See FRONDIZI, A13, Col. 4

Mikoyan Bars 'Free' East Berlin

Tells TV Hearers Counter-Offers Are Unconvincing

By John Scali
Associated Press

Soviet Deputy Premier Anastas I. Mikoyan last night rejected as "impossible" any thought of merging East and West Berlin into a single free city.

But he vigorously renewed Russia's demand that West Berlin be converted into a free city, contending this is needed to keep the area from becoming a possible hotbed of war.

The 63-year-old Soviet leader defended Russia's plan to end four-power Berlin rule during an hour-long interview on the NBC-WRC television program "Meet the Press."

Without reiterating from the Kremlin's stand, Mikoyan answered a barrage of questions about Communist policies in Hungary, Germany, Asia and inside the Soviet Union. He moved his replies with charges the American press "imagines" things about Russia and spreads untruths.

Speaking from a Washington studio heavily guarded by police, Mikoyan made these main points:

• Russia favors new diplomatic talks with the West even though he said American leaders have failed to offer him a "constructive counterproposal" during his meetings with them. He has conferred with both President Eisenhower and Secretary of State John Foster Dulles, among others.

• Premier Nikita Khrushchev is not trying to build a Stalinist-type dictatorship for himself. Soviet decisions are made not by one person, but by a group.

• American forces abroad from Formosa to ease tensions. Russia has "no reason to restrain the Chinese (Communists) because we regard them as loyal very restrained.

• Vice President Richard M. Nixon, or any other top American official, would merit the warm reception if he were to visit the Soviet Union.

Mikoyan always did not leave Lebanon voluntarily, but were forced by the American public opinion to withdraw.

• Russia's intervention in the United Nations because, Mikoyan said, the United States controls "a voting machine" in the international

See MIKOYAN, A5, Col. 2

Mission Paper Seized in Congo

LEOPOLDVILLE, Belgian Congo, Jan. 18—Belgian authorities here seized this week's edition of Horizons, a weekly newspaper edited by Africans and published by the Catholic mission, it was announced today.

The edition contained a program for the Congo, drawn up before the recent Belgian government declaration of future independence for the colony, the authorities

U.S. and Russia Nearing Agreement On Exchange of 300 Top Scientists

By Edward Gamarekian
Staff Reporter

A United States-Soviet agreement to exchange top-level scientists is now nearing completion.

Negotiations between the U.S. and Soviet National Academies of Sciences—the top group of scientists in each nation—have been under way since steps are extended reaching in time," the speaker said.

The exchange is being worked out under the Lacy-Zaroubin agreement of early 1958. The scientists to have a free choice of whom they will visit and within the limits on merit of course.

The exchange will vary from short to extended stays, and each scientist is expected to be announced within a week or two.

was set up to advise the Federal Government. It is supported by grants for individual projects it carries out for the Government and private organizations.

The Soviet Academy is supported entirely by the government.

This exchange was initiated by the National Academy of Sciences, which recently visited U.S. Academy President Detlev Bronk to Russia last fall.

Scientific exchanges have taken place in the past but these were arranged by universities, foundations, and private, non-profit societies.

The Truth About the Teamsters

Fear of Bridges Forced Employers To Seek Labor Peace Under Beck

By Bernard D. Nossiter
Staff Reporter

Second Article in a Series

Dave Beck "has all the copybook virtues as befits a self-made man in the best Horatio Alger tradition."

So wrote a New York reporter as late as November, 1953.

Indeed, underneath the stapstick of union dues buying Beck this dozen diaper there is something awesome in the spectacle of his rise and fall. For Beck teetotaler, did climb from poverty to head the Nation's largest union to become president of the Washington University's regents and become one of the few union leaders to count president Eisenhower as a friend.

But Beck's is no Greek tragedy. His failing to grief through hot and fatal flaw. Beck is a grotesque combination of greed, dishonesty, vanity and hypocrisy. His $14 custom-made (union bought) tie was part of a self-made situation of respectability, the lacquer of the middleclass carpet cleaner, his mother Mary, had to work in a laundry. The family did no better after moving to Seattle when Dave was 4.

Young Beck left high school in his junior year and worked alongside his mother at fourteen for 10 to 12 hours a day. Then

'Copter Is Stork For Island Baby

A three-week expectant was flown by helicopter last night from her isolated home on Smith Island in the Chesapeake Bay to Crisfield (Md.) Hospital.

Two hours after her arrival, Harold Evans, wife of a waterman, gave birth to a 6-pound 4-ounce son. Hospital officials said the young mother is "doing very nicely."

Norfolk Coast Guard headquarters called for the helicopter from Patuxent River Naval Air Station after Coast Guard patrol boat day proved unable to reach the snow-bound island. Crisfield Hospital said the case was unique in its history.

President Eisenhower as a pure and simple corporate executive. More than 20 years ago, he told a reporter who visited his Seattle headquarters, "I run this office like a business—just like the Standard Oil Co. Our business is selling labor."

Beck was born in Stockton, Calif., in 1894. His father, Lemuel, was a poverty-ridden divorce in Reno and make her his bride. When he got there he changed his mind. There was a bigger game back in D.C.

Back in D.C., he began paying close attention to Pearl. On October 10, 1956, he sent her a bouquet of red and white flowers which she found "beautiful." On October 17 he took her for a ride to Frederick and showed her "Motherwell's Mountain," a landmark known by that name to no one but him.

Once he called Pearl to say he'd just had a 40-minute interview with the Queen of England, who was visiting the White House. He said he'd given her a smooch.

Pearl got a little suspicious when he told her he was going abroad on a secret mission and she ran into him downtown the next day. But she pushed her suspicions aside.

Her mother died in 1957 at the age of 93. Almost immediately Larry noticed that she "seemed like a new woman."

"There were changes in Sis," he said later. "And I grew worried as the months went by." She began taking dancing lessons from a young man at the Arthur Murray studios on Connecticut Avenue.

On one embarrassing occasion she was carrying the trash out when the bag broke and ale cans and bottles cascaded to the pavement.

"Wine and gin bottles, I think," straight-laced Larry said later.

It was his considered opinion that "she was haunted in this apartment. She said 'Mom' was looking over her shoulder all the time."

By June 1958 he was determined to take her away from all that—it was time for another Motherwell Tour. He proposed marriage.

First, there would have to be a divorce. They would drive west, to Reno, then return to live, happily, in Sarasota, Florida. They would hardly want to be burdened on the way with possessions and bank accounts left behind. They advertised Pearl's 1953 Pontiac for sale. A. Page Lockart, a tax auditor with the District Government and a man with a cold, appraising eye, answered the ad. Mrs. Putney asked $500. A. Page Lockart was suspicious since the car obviously was worth more. So he offered $450. Larry

Larry Lord Motherwell.

suggested they split the difference and the sale was made—for $460. Mrs. Putney introduced Larry as "my brother, a retired admiral."

They advertised Mrs. Putney's cooperative apartment at 3024 Porter Street, and a lady named Rosemary Chaplin made a bid. The bid was below the asking price but it was accepted. Miss Chaplin said there seemed to be a sense of "urgency." Mrs. Putney introduced Larry as "Dr. Motherwell, my stepbrother."

She introduced him to her real half-brother, Castro Dabrohua, of Winnetka, Illinois, as Lt. Commander Motherwell, recently of the USN.

As June drew to a close, Larry and Pearl went to the Union Trust Company to cash checks and close her savings account of $6,009.60. In all they withdrew a total of $24,204.25 from her three accounts.

They advertised jewelry and glassware for sale and Henry Wilson, a dealer, came to bid. Pearl was reluctant and finally only sold him a few things for $20. She put the rest, her rugs, china, antique furniture, silver and, perhaps inadvertently, her diaries for 1956 and 1957 in storage in Lexington, Maryland. The time had come to depart and some $60,000 had been turned into cash or negotiable paper.

Mrs. Putney was eager and willing. She believed Larry was a doctor of some sort, a retired Naval officer of some rank, and a missile expert. She believed he was going to divorce his third wife and marry her. They drove through North Carolina, Georgia, Louisiana, Texas, New Mexico, and on to Marysville, California. Marysville is a nice town in the mountains. Larry had been there once before with his long distance operator. Larry and Pearl arrived on August 14, 1958.

Miss Noreen Facer, the desk clerk at the Town House Motel, remembers him but not her. He seemed pleasant and nice. Others saw her and remembered her as a little old lady. It was the last time anyone except Larry admits to having seen her alive. Two days later Larry was at the San Francisco International Airport, sending a telegram to Pearl's brother, Castro Dabrohua. It was signed "Pearl" and Larry said she had prepared the message. It said she was going to marry an old friend named D'Avious and they were going to Mexico on the D'Avious yacht. He spelled it "yaht." He spelled ceremony "cerimony." He spelled Dabrohua "Duabrahua."

Janice Hampton, the Western Union clerk, said pleasantly, "Are you the man to be congratulated?" And Larry said, "No, I'm sending this for my aunt." He waved vaguely behind him, but no aunt was identifiable in the throng. Larry flew back to Washington and picked up his wife and child, and they all flew back to San Francisco. Then the three Motherwells drove, leisurely, back to Washington, where Larry paid off the $2,000 balance due on his car and deposited another $2,000 in a savings account at American Savings and Loan.

Castro Dabrohua was suspicious. Pearl's postcards seemed strange. The telegram announcing her approaching marriage to D'Avious was stranger still. His name, her maiden name, Dabrohua, had been misspelled. He had never heard of anyone named "D'Avious." Weeks passed, and no further word came from Pearl. Mr. Dabrohua, a mild man but determined, called the Metropolitan Police Department and insisted that they concern themselves with his absent sister.

Captain Michael Mahaney, of the Missing Persons Bureau, did. He dropped in on Larry at his Lyman Place apartment and left word that he'd like to have a chat. A few days later Larry came to headquarters. He told Captain Mahaney he'd last seen Pearl in Corpus Christi, Texas, where she was traveling with and engaged to marry a small man with a thin, waxed moustache. When Captain Mahaney called Larry again a few days later, Larry was gone.

Detective Gertrude Goettel came back from vacation in October and Captain Mahaney assigned her to what was now the Putney/Motherwell case.

Miss Goettel found that Larry's second wife had died abruptly in the bath, and she found that shortly thereafter, on June 19, 1954, Larry had taken their retarded daughter, Heather, out of the Takoma Park nursing home where she had lived since birth. Larry told Mrs. Ella Hinkson, the proprietor of the home, that he was putting the infant in the Squibb Institute in Florida. Miss Goettel found there was no Squibb Institute in Florida. She went to Frederick, one of Larry's favorite locales, and found in the records that Larry had buried a box containing a "beloved pet dog" in a Frederick pet cemetery on June 20, 1954—the day after he took Heather from the home.

Miss Goettel got the Frederick police to dig up the box.

Inside were Heather's bones and a few toys. Larry had his sentimental side.

Larry was far gone from Frederick. After leaving Captain Mahaney a couple of months before, he had changed his name and gone south. He looked up an airline stewardess, an old acquaintance, in Florida and gave her a big bag full of not-very-valuable trinkets. The trinkets had belonged to Pearl.

He then took a plane for Cleveland.

He found a seat next to a slender, brown-haired practical nurse who was returning from a Florida vacation.

"I'm Arthur Rivers," he said, sitting down, and he went on to say he was a foreign correspondent with the United Press and he'd just been up in the hills with that then daring rebel, Fidel Castro. The practical nurse was, unfortunately, fascinated. They landed but she did not come down to earth. They became engaged. He gave her a garnet necklace set in gold. He gave her a cameo. He took them both out of a chamois bag. Mrs. Putney's bag. Mrs. Putney's necklace. Mrs. Putney's cameo.

He could not marry her at once, he said, since he was a spy as well as a foreign correspondent, and the government insisted he remain single until after his next, and last, dangerous assignment abroad.

He bought a new car in Detroit for $2,600, a Plymouth station wagon, paying for it with crisp $1,000 bills.

The nurse slipped him $600 for expenses and they left Cleveland in November—about the time Miss Goettel was digging up Heather's bones.

They took the usual tour, to California by way of Florida, and then rented an apartment in Laguna Beach. It was now early December and time to say goodbye. He told the nurse that duty called; he was off on his secret dangerous assignment to the Far East.

He went instead to Las Vegas and checked in at the Baghdad Motel.

He was soon the toast of the Baghdad —Arthur Rivers the correspondent, this time returned from 20 years in China, Burma, and India. He was, by happy coincidence, now doing a series of articles on motels. Roland Bliss, the Baghdad manager, was impressed.

After a few days he checked out, saying he was off to Europe on assignment.

Poor Pearl Ada Putney was last seen alive leaving a motel in Marysville, California, on August 15, 1958.

He went instead back to the not very practical nurse, who loaned him $2,000. Then back to the Baghdad where he told the enthralled people at the motel coffee shop that he had been hastily recalled from Europe to cover Fidel Castro, who was about to take over Havana.

He usually slept late and had breakfast at the coffee shop, and he reported that the wild joy of Las Vegas was getting him down. He had been going, he said, to parties for Jack Benny and other persons of great luminosity.

In the afternoons he'd drop in at the Last Frontier Village Rock Hollow Lapidary Shop, where he would chat with the owner, Marian Cannon, 32, about the finding and polishing of stones. He suggested that they visit a remote canyon to hunt rocks and she has since been glad she declined. He left the Plymouth at Earl Neff's garage to have it tuned up.

Meanwhile Captain Mahaney's cries of alarm from Washington, D.C., were being heard across the land. The Las Vegas paper, noticing that Motherwell had been a frequent visitor in the past, ran his picture in the Sunday paper.

Miss Cannon, the rock dealer, and Mr. Neff, the auto mechanic, each saw it and called the cops.

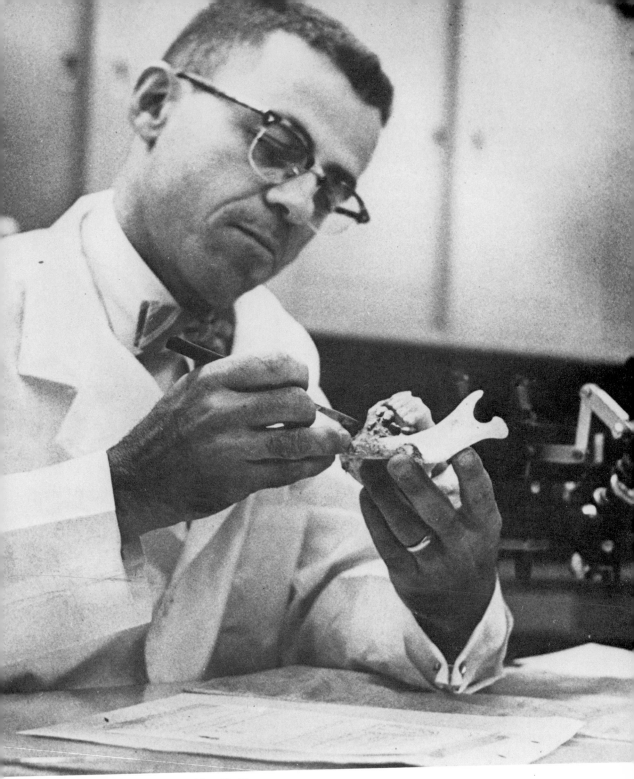

The last of Mrs. Putney was identified by criminologist David Burd. The lower jaw and denture was found near Downieville, California.

Mike Whitney, of the Las Vegas police, came to the Baghdad and took him away on January 18, 1959.

"He paid his bill the way he always did, with a $100 bill," Mr. Bliss said. "But his hand was shaking so hard he could hardly hold it."

He had $1,600 in his pocket—the last of the nurse's $2,000—and God knows what in the back of his head.

"Yes, I'm a con man," he told Mike Whitney, "but not for profit. Sometimes I'm a liar and I impress people."

Chief Charles V. Main, of Frederick, and Sheriff Horance Alexander, of Frederick County, came and got him, and they all drove back east in the Plymouth.

In February, the Frederick Grand Jury, incredibly, refused to indict him for the murder of Heather, and Motherwell, incredibly, was free again.

He got out of town in the nick of time.

On February 25, Mrs. Alma Freeman, picking pine cones in Turner's Canyon, off State Route 49 near Sierra, California, stumbled over something white.

"I mistook it for a puffball but a little girl who was there picked it up and brought it to me and I could see it was some kind of a skull. I took it to our cabin and showed it to my husband."

Pearl Putney had been found at last.

Under-Sheriff James F. Hill would search the two-acre pine grove and find a lean-to made of stones and sticks and bark against a fallen log, and under it he would find human gray hair and the outline of a human body. He would find a dozen bones, scattered, including a leg and a pelvis. He would find traces of an old bonfire, with scraps of burnt leather and cloth and a piece of metal from a shoe.

The search for Larry Lord Motherwell began again.

It took six months.

At the end of the summer, FBI Special Agent John Ogden walked up to him at the Atlanta airport and tapped him on the shoulder. Larry said he was Craig D. Foster and, sure enough, inside his briefcase were papers that seemed to show that Craig D. Foster was the owner of a Cuban steel firm worth $6.5 million. Special Agent Brian F. O'Shea looked through Larry's quarters at an Atlanta

Larry, here looking at least mildly discouraged, paid his Las Vegas motel bill with $100 notes, but his hand shook as he pulled them from his billfold. The man in the motel room doorway is a Las Vegas detective.

After his Las Vegas arrest the bland carpenter was brought to Frederick, Md., to face incidental charges that he murdered his retarded, infant daughter. The county, in a burst of economy, avoided a costly trial by letting Larry go.

rooming house and found a Social Security card and a driver's license made out to Allen Michel Dubar and the draft of a letter, signed Dubar, to the State Department, asking how he could go about getting a passport to study abroad. Special Agent John J. Cotter found a pawn ticket for a handful of diamonds. They had been pawned for a mere $250. They were Mrs. Putney's diamonds, gone from her chamois bag.

The governor of Georgia signed papers permitting the State of California to call him to account and Larry was off once more to the Golden State.

The trial began February 15, 1960, in Downieville, the seat of Sierra County.

The county had 2,400 inhabitants; Downieville had 350. The courtroom had 40 seats. There were two cafés that closed after dark, at 5:30 PM each day. Downieville is at the bottom of a steep canyon and the sun goes down at four o'clock. Once, in gold rush days, Downieville had the longest bar between St. Louis and San Francisco, but now in the late evening the only sound of life was the gurgling laughter of the Downie and the Yuba rivers as they come together in the middle of town.

The state agreed to pick up most of the trial expenses and a special deputy attorney general, Lynn Compton of Los Angeles, was named to lead the prosecution. Judge Warren Steel was on the bench.

Motherwell moved into the tiny jail, read books on the history of California, and ate meals prepared by the sheriff's wife, Mrs. W. Dewey Johnson. Mrs. Johnson helped out in one of the two cafés and Larry got the same food as her other customers. Attorney John Regis, of Washington, took over the defense.

Edward Moon, who called himself a semiretired laborer, was the first one picked for the jury, and he got to be foreman. Two other men and nine women were picked over the objection of Attorney Regis, who said he felt that was too many women.

Motherwell told reporters he was 41 years old, which was probably a lie. He said he had been born in Jefferson County, Pennsylvania, which may have been the truth.

The prosecution called 60 witnesses, flying most of them in from Washington, which cost the State of California a lot of money.

The defense called two: Mrs. Putney's half-brother, Castro Dabrohua, who'd also been called by the prosecution; and Larry Lord Motherwell, or whatever his name was.

Larry, gentle and bland, said Mrs. Putney had engaged him as a driver to take her across the country on, as it were, "one last fling."

He admitted they had registered at motels as "Dr. and Mrs. L. L. Motherwell." The "Dr.," he said, stood for Driver, and they had shared rooms because "she was afraid to be alone at night."

She had told him, he said, she slept better sitting up so she had slept in a chair and he in the bed wherever they stopped.

All was friendly but on the up-and-up, he said, until they got to New Orleans, a town that is liable to bring out the worse in anyone.

"It was past midnight when she returned," Larry said, recalling the carnival city. "She was slightly tipsy. I was on the bed reading a magazine. She plopped herself across the bed and gave me a very demonstrating kiss. She said, 'How's my man.' I smelled alcohol. I was taken aback and began to talk to her about drinking. She said she was really beginning to live. I finally got her into a chair and quieted her down."

The worst was yet to come. As was the custom she went into the bathroom to get ready for bed but this time, Larry said, she left the door ajar. And instead of putting on both a nightgown and a robe she put on just the gown.

"She said it was new and asked if I thought it was pretty. I was embarrassed and told her to put on her robe, which she did."

He also told her, he said, that this sort of thing must never, never happen again.

And it didn't either, he said, until one night, August 14, in Marysville, California.

They had driven, he said, from Las Vegas, and had checked into the Town House Motel in Marysville. He had gone to dinner alone and he was back in the room when she returned. She was "tipsy" once more.

"I was taken aback."

Once more she tried to seduce him.

"Mrs. Putney wanted me to kiss her. She disrobed to the extent of being 'shady.' She made a few vulgar comments. She told me I was being paid enough to know she was a woman, a woman alive and, in her opinion, attractive, that I wasn't such an angel that I didn't know she was a woman."

Motherwell said he did then the only thing a sensitive man could do—he checked them both out of the hotel, even though it was two or three in the morning.

14

Larry Lord Motherwell mournfully sits in a Las Vegas jail.

It was his story that they then drove, not to Turner's Canyon, but to San Francisco, where she announced that she intended to marry an attentive older man, a Mr. D'Avious, and they parted friends. The name D'Avious was, perhaps, his most original invention. A search of phone books in all the cities and towns involved failed to produce a single person of that name and a California expert on names said he had never come across it in years of research.

Larry's lawyer, John Regis, called Pearl "a little old lady with sex on her mind," who'd hatched a "diabolical plan" to lead Larry astray.

The jury did not believe it.

They found Larry guilty of first degree murder, and after another full trial as required by California law, they voted 11 to one for the gas chamber and then when one jurior, a lady, stubbornly refused to concur, 12 to zero for life. Larry stood white-faced. "It's not what I expected," he said.

A higher court later cut the charge to second degree murder because the trial judge had failed to let the jury know that second degree was a possibility.

As a second degree murderer, Larry was eligible for parole in 1965.

Trial Judge Steel, however, had expressed the hope at the time of the conviction that the parole boards of the future would resist the temptation to turn Larry loose too soon since there were still little old rich ladies abroad in the land.

The parole board was never tempted.

In 1965, just about the time he was ready to apply for parole, Larry, working as a dental assistant polishing the teeth of a fellow prisoner, flipped over with a fatal heart attack.

Which was surprising.

Who would have thought Larry had a heart.

15

A Whoopee Girl Dies

BEULAH LIMERICK WAS HER name and her life was a limerick too, in five dirty, sing-songy lines.

There was a young girl in the Crash,
Whose youth was thrown away with
the trash,
A sad little rounder,
A Whoopee Club founder,
A playgirl without any cash.

She was 19 in 1930, a dreadful year to be 19. She was an usher at Poli's Theater (Poli's would die in the Great Depression too), a slim girl with sullen, bee-stung lips and silly whoopee socks. She did the Charleston and drank bathtub gin, but the roaring, singing twenties were out of breath and out of money.

She lived at 6th and East Capitol, amid the disapproving middle-class, until the cold economic winds blew her to a stark and rickety frame house out by the dump, at No. 18 19th Street, Southeast. Her brother, Vernon, and her boyfriend, Richard Reed, lived there, too.

She died on New Year's Day, 1931, a

day and a year of hangovers.

Richard, a slender reed for a girl to lean on, got up at 4:45 AM that day and went to her bare, basement room to light the potbellied stove. Richard went early to work at a Benning Road filling station— any job was a good job in 1931.

He said later that Beulah was alive when he left.

Vernon got up at 8:30 AM, and when he looked in on his sister she was dead.

He jumped in his Model-T and went to fetch his mother, Mrs. Dorothy Limerick, who lived down by the railroad tracks, at 116 North Carolina Avenue, and mother and son called Casualty Hospital, at 7th and Massachusetts, a small institution known as the Slaughter House by youngsters who played on its weed-grown tennis court.

An intern, a Dr. Green, found Beulah on her cot, stretched out on clean sheets, her arms folded across her flapper's chest, her boyish bob neatly combed, her pouting lips neatly rouged. It was 10 AM.

Her mother was in charge. She told the doctor that Beulah had a history of hemorrhages and he found blood flecks in her mouth. But there was no blood on the white pillow case, and Dr. Green remembered the pillow case and the sheets, he said later, because they were the only clean things in the house. He signed the certificate, death from hemorrhages, and a man from the W. W. Deal Funeral Home, at 816 H Street, Northeast, came and took the body.

That evening, an under-undertaker was dressing it when he noticed a depression, a neat bullet hole, in the back of Beulah's head, neatly plugged with Beulah's hair. He called the police.

The *Washington Post* said the next day that the "Police got off to a belated start on what promises to be one of Washington's most perplexing murder mysteries." The promise remains fulfilled.

The best men on the homicide squad went to work—Waldron, Flaherty, Tally, Sweeney—through the night, grilling Mrs. Limerick and Vernon and Vernon's other two sisters, Reed, and a dozen friends and acquaintances. The *Post* reported that they "detained" Mrs. Limerick and "locked up" Richard, the live-in boyfriend, and one William E. Paddy, who had taken Beulah to a New Year's Eve dance at the public hall in Capitol Heights. They had their first clues and first suspects.

It was the start of an avalanche. Soon the police would have more suspects than squad cars, more clues than night sticks.

Among the clues was the tantalizing fact that Beulah had once been married to a Maryland farmer named Earl Aitcheson and that marriage had been annulled on December 11, 1930, three short weeks before her death. But the marriage had occurred back in 1925, when Beulah was but 14, and it had lasted only a few months. Earl had let her go with no apparent regrets. Why the belated annulment? It seemed possible that Beulah's mother was hoping for another marriage for Beulah.

There was the clue of the immaculate pillow. Intern Green insisted that Beulah's carefully coiffed head lay on a spotless pillow case. The detectives who arrived much later insisted that there was no pillow case, merely two decrepit sofa pillows. Who took the pillow from the bed?

The grim new year of 1931 opened with "Jazz" mingling with "Prayers" and with Beulah Limerick, age 19, dead from a bullet hole in the head.

There was above all, Beulah's leather-bound diary—a blend of sadness, sex, and a young girl's dreams. There were too many names in the diary. Beulah had been a girl of too much experience, of shallow sophistication. Across her tummy, it was said, the words "Pay As You Enter" were tattooed. Beulah couldn't quite believe in the story-book romance of Mr. Right, but she would have liked to believe in it.

". . . Met several new ones, I wonder how much I care for . . . . is really darling. I believe he's ace high now. I wonder how long it will last. . . ."

She knew from an abundance of experience that it wouldn't last long. "Oh well, enjoy life while you can is my motto," wrote Beulah, who lived in an unheated shack, who danced at dirty public halls, who made believe until she died.

She lived in a clumsy fairy tale. Beulah, in her diary, was a club woman, a traveler for pleasure, the darling of celebrities, a girl who sipped cocktails with dashing young men.

She had traveled; with a girl named Iona Dewey, she had hitchhiked to Gridley, Kansas. And they had hitchhiked home again.

The club, alas, was the Sky High Whoopee Club, which Beulah founded, a band of jobless young men and restless girls, gathering in cheap, rented halls, for dances at which everyone got drunk on rotgut and the boys got in fights.

She knew one celebrity, of a sort, a radio personality at a suburban station who sponsored Whoopee Clubs. "He sang his new song for me," she wrote and, pathetically, "Gosh, I hope our Club is a success."

From the mass of men, one at first emerged, and with him came a dazzling set of clues.

Private Robert F. Langdon, of the fifth precinct, was the patrolman on the beat

The Washington Post is the only Washington newspaper publishing the reports of The Associated Press every morning, for home delivery, call National 6163.

The Washington Post.

NO. 19,922   ENTERED AS SECOND-CLASS MATTER POSTOFFICE WASHINGTON D.C.   WASHINGTON: THURSDAY, JANUARY 1, 1931.   COPYRIGHT, 1930, BY THE WASHINGTON POST CO.   THREE CENTS.

Weather—Cloudy and colder this afternoon and tonight; somewhat partly cloudy. Temperature—Highest 52; lowest, 31. Details on Page 2.

CAPITAL GIRL MYSTERIOUSLY SLAIN

RAIL COMBINE FANS ANOTHER ROW IN G.O.P.

Fess and Couzens Bandy Words, Supporting and Attacking Hoover.

OHIOAN SEES HELP FOR UNEMPLOYED

Michigan Senator Avers Actions of President "Most Unethical."

SEES INTIMIDATION OF COMMERCE BODY

Willard Says Consolidation Will Be Completed in Few Months.

By EDWARD T. FOLLIARD

AT ODDS ON RAIL MERGER PLAN

Senator Fess (left), who rushed to the defense of President Hoover after Senator Couzens had issued two statements yesterday attacking the Chief Executive for his stand on the proposed railroad merger.

NEW YEAR CROWDS SEE $35,000 BLAZE

Flames in Maddux Hotels Office Basement Cause Second Alarm.

DENSE SMOKE CLOUDS FALLS INTO SLUMBER

JOFFRE LINGERING AS OLD YEAR DIES

Marshal Amazes Doctors by Demanding That He Be Shaved.

CONSENT RULE UNDER FIRE BY UTILITIES BODY

Seeks Modification on Ground Power Firm's Profit Excessive.

COMMISSION ALLOWS NEW RATE SCHEDULE

Slight Revisions Are Made Only in Commercial Classifications.

JAZZ MINGLES WITH PRAYERS AS 1931 DAWNS

New Year Is Welcomed by Gay Parties and Meditation.

HOOVERS TO SHAKE HANDS OF CITIZENS

More Church Services and Celebrations on Program of Capital Today.

Settle Died by Poison; Suicide, Naval Report

Deadly Fluid Said to Have Been Near White House Aid's Body; Police Tell of Lieutenant's Auto Hitting Four Persons.

BULLET WOUND IS DISCOVERED AT MORTUARY

Death by Violence Is Not Revealed Until Hours After Demise.

INTERNE OF HOSPITAL ISSUED CERTIFICATE

Brother and Roomer Held as Police Investigate Puzzling Case.

DANCE ON MONDAY PRECEDED SLAYING

Gun Used in Killing Is Still Missing; Authorities Hide Theories.

BUSCH WEALTH HEIR IS KIDNAPED IN CAR

Armed Man Captures Boy, 13) While Youngster Is on Way to Party.

POLICE SEARCH STARTS

$3,100 BANK HOLDUP COSTS THREE LIVES

Guard and Depositor Killed by Hail of Shots From Hooded Bandits.

FLEEING 'SUSPECT' SLAIN

Rain U.S. Lacked in 1930 May Be 25 Years Arriving

But Forecaster Mitchell Believes Nature's Habit of Evening All Scores Will Assert Itself and All Needs Will Be Supplied.

Calvin Coolidge Says:

The year 1930 has been a sharp reminder that men can not escape from the command that they shall earn their bread by the sweat of their brow. We can not, for long reap when we have not sown. We can not hold what we do not pay for. The law of service can not be evaded or repealed. Nor is it yet in the power of man under any system of government we can adopt or any organization of society he may form to make this a perfect world. But the ability to take the best of things, to secure progress, to learn from adversity is not to be disparaged or ignored.

The creative energy of nature is not diminishing but increased by the fallow season. Mankind requires a time for taking stock, for the recuperation, for gathering energy for the next advance that is the significance of the New Year. We take a new inventory to see what we have, we take new bearings to see where we are, we can correct our conduct by new resolutions. After all the allowance for error and relapse, such a course guarantees improvement. Perhaps the best resolve to live so that next year new resolutions will be unnecessary.

(Copyright, 1931.)

Progressives in Senate May Force Extra Session

All Semblance of So-Called Harmony Expected to Disappear When Congress Reassembles; Appropriation Bill Delay Is Forecast.

By CARLISLE BARGERON

near 19th and A. He was on duty the night Beulah died.

Later, when the murder was discovered, he volunteered to stand guard in the basement bedroom, beside Beulah's empty cot. And while he was busy—and he was busy indeed, as we shall see—the police were getting some interesting second thoughts from Mrs. Limerick and one of her married daughters, Mrs. Julia Bywaters. Had Beulah been afraid of any particular man? Yes, the ladies now recalled. Beulah had been very much afraid of a certain policeman, Private Langdon, to be exact. Private Langdon had dropped in, uninvited, on Beulah, asleep in her basement cot. He had accused her of "misconduct" and told her that he knew the name of everyone who went in and out of the house. He had once boasted to Beulah (Mrs. Limerick said) that he had "bumped a woman off."

Captain Edward Kelly and the squad proceeded to the Limerick house where Private Langdon was on guard. Earlier the police had searched the small, ill-furnished building and had found one .38-caliber pistol and a .25-caliber shell in the ashes of Beulah's stove. Since death was caused by a .25, the shell had more significance than the gun.

When Captain Kelly joined Private Langdon, however, he learned that Langdon had been conducting his own little search and had been fantastically successful. He had found another .25-caliber shell, this one in a coffee cup in the kitchen. And he had found a .25-caliber slug under the rotten floor, beneath Beulah's cot. The squad was impressed, though not, perhaps, in just the way Private Langdon had intended.

Langdon was a man, to be fair, who would impress a number of people—a cop who looked like a cop should, tall, broad of shoulder, stern of eye, jutting in the jaw. Out of uniform he favored broad-brimmed hats, turned down all around, long heavy overcoats, and a manner of studied portent.

Someone remembered that Langdon himself owned a .25-caliber pistol. The homicide men went to his home at 12th and Oates, Northeast, and found not one but two. The police, with the notable exception of Private Langdon, were de-

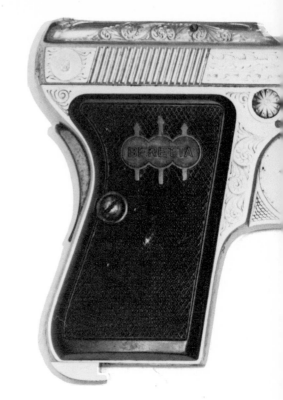

lighted. They promptly announced his arrest.

Inspector W. S. Selby said portentiously that there had been no shell in that coffee cup when he had searched the place 24 hours earlier. Another spokesman said that it was "the unusual discovery of the shell together with Langdon's alleged annoying of the dead girl which caused his arrest."

The next day, in a resounding anticlimax, the police's ballistic experts found that neither of Langdon's two .25 guns had fired either the fatal shot or the slug found in the floor, or the shell in the ashes, or the one in the coffee cup.

Langdon, after further questioning, told a new tale.

He had, as a matter of fact, been in the immediate vicinity of Beulah's basement about 2 AM on the fatal night. He had seen a man leave the premises. He had shadowed him to Bland's lunchroom at 14th and East Capitol Street. He had done so, he said, because he thought the man might be on his way to a speakeasy. Speakeasys, as everyone knew, were against the law. The man turned out to be William Paddy, who was already locked

Although a number of the suspects had guns, the .25-caliber one that killed Beulah was never found.

up and who had admitted bringing Beulah home from the Capitol Heights dance about 12:30 AM. He had not, however, said anything about hanging around until 2 AM.

Langdon said that after trailing Paddy, to no great effect, he had returned to Beulah's place at 4 AM and had shined his flash through the glass of her door. He had seen her, he said, apparently safe within, her head covered by her blanket, her feet sticking out toward the potbellied stove. That, said Langdon, was the last time he saw Beulah, dead or alive.

The police kept Langdon in custody, but a certain zip had gone out of their case.

They kept Paddy on hand too.

Vernon, Beulah's brother, also in custody, was allowed to attend her funeral at Deal's, under guard. He "sobbed convulsively," the press reported. Then the spotlight suddenly shifted to Philadelphia.

The police got a telegram saying an "exhibit golfer" there, named Ted Martin, had been closely associated with Beulah the previous summer and that he *knew something about her death.* Martin, a mere twenty years old, was picked up, and sure enough his wallet was stuffed with clippings about the murder. He admitted the association with Beulah.

Meanwhile, back in the District, the cops returned to Langdon's house and found a whiskey still with three 52-gallon barrels of rye mash and a half-gallon of "alleged rye whiskey." (It had been hidden in the basement behind a wooden partition.) They also found three more guns, making a total of twelve. None of the new ones were .25 caliber. Langdon said, when asked, that he had so many guns because he had "once aspired to become a ballistics expert."

And up in Philadelphia, golfer Martin confessed that he had given the police the tip himself. "I wanted to get publicity to increase my golf instruction classes. It was a great stunt, but I didn't think it would end this way."

Surrounded by confusion, the police moved rapidly and decisively. They turned the whole case over to the coroner's jury. The coroner's jury began an inquest at the handsome chapel-like morgue on Maine Avenue. The audiences were so large that they had to move it to the District Building.

Fifty-two witnesses were called. The press said they would testify to "startling and hitherto unpublished facts." They did testify, and some of the facts certainly had been unpublished and a few were mildly startling.

Mrs. Limerick—the mother—admitted that she had persuaded her son Vernon and Beulah's boyfriend Paddy to lie about Beulah's last fling. The two gallant men had first told police that both had escorted Beulah to the Capitol Heights dance and that Paddy had left her at her door.

Mrs. Limerick said that she had asked the boys to fudge the truth because she was afraid that the insurance company that had issued a policy on Beulah's life might not pay off if it found out that she "ran around and drank."

Private Langdon gave the jury a detailed account of the wild behavior he had witnessed from time to time while peeking through Beulah's window. The press said the details were "unprintable" and the coroner asked the ladies present to leave the room during the recital. He had to ask them twice.

The most startling development, perhaps, came from Martha Bargfrede, Beulah's close friend and secretary of the Sky High Whoopee Club. Martha said that the day after the murder, the Limerick family had told her that a gun had been 21

Police questioned five of Beulah's boyfriends. A sixth suspect, the cop on the beat, was detained two days later. (Insert) Beulah was rich in boyfriends but poor in everything else, and her basement bedroom was furnished with bare essentials.

found in the stove and had warned her to keep her mouth shut. Martha, in the course of a highly dramatic performance, also denied that her husband, George, had "violently remonstrated" with Beulah after she and Beulah had stayed out all night whoopeeing it up.

Martha said Beulah's real problem had been her mother. "I told her," Martha said in the argot of the time, "if I had a mother like that I'd go jump in the lake."

After Martha finished, the cops arrested her and her husband, George, apparently just for the hell of it. They released them in a couple of days and the inquest went on despite the complaint of the District Commissioners that the crowds were dirtying up the District Building.

After the last witness had his say, the coroner's jury had its—and it was just as bizarre as all that went before.

It reported that Beulah "came to her death by means of a gun shot wound, hemorrhage, and shock" and that Private Langdon, Richard Reed, William Paddy, and Vernon Limerick should all be held for the Grand Jury. The four men, the jury said, "had sufficient guilty knowledge" to warrant this.

It didn't say how these four, whose interests were at obvious odds, could be jointly involved in a single murder.

The police, who perhaps would have been willing to start all over again, announced that they were looking for a brand new suspect, Edwin McIntyre, a friend of Beulah's, who had suddenly left the city the day after the murder. McIntyre promptly gave himself up and said that he had left town to go to southern Maryland to look for work. He hadn't found any.

Life in 1931 was haphazard for the jobless hungry young. McIntyre, with a warm cell and three meals a day, told the cops "that he would be glad to be under arrest until the matter was cleared up."

22

On January 20 Donald E. Boyer, a milkman from Chestnut Farms Dairy, said, somewhat belatedly, that between 4 and 4:30 AM on the morning of the murder, while he was delivering milk some 150 yards away, he had heard a pistol shot and had seen a blue roadster speed away from behind the Limerick residence, a story he had been telling to customers at Bland's lunch room near Holy Comforter Church for several weeks before the police heard about it.

And then the police themselves turned up a clue, perhaps the most solid clue in the whole case. They had methodically opened and searched the sewers all the way across Southeast, at every corner, from Beulah's house at 19th and A to her mother's house at 116 North Carolina Avenue. And in the last sewer, the one by the mother's home, they found 11 .25-caliber bullets and part of a .32-caliber revolver.

But at this point who could say what the clue meant. Any evidence that pointed at one man was balanced by something that pointed just as fiercely at another.

The Grand Jury met and, as instructed, considered the evidence against Langdon, Paddy, Reed, and Limerick and then, as it had to, it ordered them all set free.

No one but the guilty yet knows who killed Beulah Limerick. No one knows who folded her hands across her chest and tried to hide the murder by plugging up the hole in her head.

Perhaps it doesn't matter. The thing that killed Beulah, basically, was the sick sad world in which she lived for a very few years. It didn't treat the other members of the Sky High Whoopee so very well either.

The year 1930 was a bad one, with scant supplies for gracious living. Somebody had carefully arranged Beulah's hair, but the police, searching that miserable house, couldn't find a single comb.

23

The Slow And Lingering Death Of James Abram Garfield

THE TIME: early summer of 1881.

THE PLACE: the city of Washington, population circa 200,000 (one quarter black, one tenth foreign born). The city's only industry is government and the hotels—the old Willard, the Riggs House, the Arlington, the Ebbitt—and boarding houses are full of people seeking government jobs. The front pages of the *Washington Post* and the *Evening Star* carry listings of those named to clerkships and special notices of those appointed to higher posts—A. C. Phillips is to be Receiver of Public Moneys at Harrison, Arkansas, and Jerome B. Hawley is to be Gauger for the Territory of Arizona. There are also reports of persons in danger of being removed from office—General Carmer has replaced Mr. Paine as Chief Clerk of the Agriculture Department; but Alonzo Bell, Assistant Secretary of the Interior, has told the *Post* reporter that he has "not resigned," that he has "no intention of resigning," that he does not think he "will be requested to resign," and that he does not "desire to resign."

Otherwise, the front page news tends to be parochial: the YMCA has been locked out of its quarters at Lincoln Hall for refusing to pay the rent, increased from $900 to $1,200 per annum, and ex-Senator Christiancy has accused his wife, Lillie, of committing adultery with one Edil Giro, a Spaniard, on Christmas Day. Most things of significance (including the nexus of Mrs. Christiancy and Giro) seem to occur on, or within a few blocks of, Pennsylvania Avenue.

The Avenue runs from the foot of the Capitol past the open fields surrounding the Smithsonian Building, the White House, and within sight of the unfinished Washington Monument. To the south is a smelly canal, alive with mosquitoes, winding close to the White House along B Street (the future Constitution Avenue). Members of Congress go home in the summer; other officials who can leave town do—the heat of July, August, and September is constant, overwhelming, and unremitting with temperatures as high as 104.° It is difficult to sleep at night.

Those still in town spend their leisure hours in the parks—half of the city's area is taken up by parks, streets, and the grassy circles at the intersections of the avenues. Seven railways enter the city, each with its own terminus. The most conspicuous is the Baltimore and Potomac Railroad depot at 6th and B streets (the site of the future National Gallery of Art). Its tracks, partly covered by sheds, extend south across the open fields of what will some day be the Mall.

The assassin, Charles Guiteau.

THE PRINCIPALS IN ORDER OF THEIR APPEARANCE:

CHARLES C. GUITEAU: A small, odd, unappealing man, occasionally dapper, fond of blue suits. He is, in his own phrases, a "lawyer-theologian" and a "Stalwart of Stalwarts." He cheats landladies and is most anxious to be America's consul in Vienna, Paris, or somewhere.

ANNE BUNN GUITEAU: His unfortunate wife.

JAMES ABRAM GARFIELD: President of the United States—easy going, friendly, high-spirited, and in excellent health. He is not, perhaps, altogether honest: He was named during the Credit-Mobilier scandal as one who took a small bribe—some $390. A sturdily loyal Republican, he was a member of the commission that certified that Hayes, the Republican, had won all the contested states in the presidential election of 1876. This loyalty brought him a steady if not swift sequence of successes. He was minority leader of the House for a decade and was named to the U.S. Senate in 1880. The Party that year was split between factions; the "Stalwarts" wished to elect Ulysses S. Grant to a third term, and the "Half Breeds" wished to elect James G. Blaine. Garfield was the compromise candidate and was barely elected, with a plurality of only 7,000 votes. He made Blaine his Secretary of State and (perhaps absentmindedly) named another "Half Breed," William H. Robertson, Collector of the Port of New York. The "Stalwart" leaders, Roscoe Conkling and Thomas Platt, both of New York, resigned from the U.S. Senate in protest. They then began a campaign to have themselves reappointed by the New York State Legislature. (Senators were not popularly elected in 1881.)

CHESTER ARTHUR: The Vice President, a cautious Stalwart.

JAMES G. BLAINE: The Secretary of State, the leading "Half Breed" and a future candidate for President. (He will run in 1884 against Grover Cleveland and will be defeated when one of his supporters, a Protestant clergyman, calls the Democrats the party of "Rum, Romanism, and Rebellion." It is a phrase that will rally millions of Catholic immigrants to the polls.)

MRS. WILLIAM S. GRANT: A cheated landlady.

AQUILLA BARTON: A black hackman who waits in vain.

PATRICK KEARNEY: A brave policeman.

DR. BLISS: A garrulous and self-important physician who believes in the curative powers of whiskey.

THE ENSEMBLE, ON STAGE AND OFF: Robert Lincoln, Secretary of War; Mr. O'Meara, the proprietor of a gun shop; Alexander Graham Bell, inventor of a bullet-detecting device that does not work; Mr. Jennings, the eminent engineer; and the Gentlemen of the Press.

A DAY IN 1867: Charles Guiteau meets Anne Bunn, 16, a telegrapher, at the library of the Women's Christian Association in Chicago. She is impressed by his piety. They marry in 1868.

A LESS HAPPY INTERLUDE SOME YEARS LATER: Guiteau, who has a meager income, is self-indulgent. He wears $75 suits and stays at the best New York hotels. When his wife protests his plan to skip without paying a bill, he locks her in the hotel's hall closet all night. After he contracts a social disease, she divorces him and returns to telegraphy.

ONE AFTERNOON IN 1876: Guiteau, once more in Chicago, is annoyed when his sister, Mrs. George Scoville, asks him to remove some wood from her driveway. He chases her with an ax.

THE EARLY WINTER OF 1880: Guiteau believes, or at any rate preaches, that Christ's Second Coming occurred in 70 AD. His lectures on the subject are poorly attended. He decides to hitch his wagon to a star and follows Colonel Robert Ingersoll from town to town in upstate New York and New England, attempting to rebut the celebrated atheist's contention that there is no Hell. Ingersoll speaks to crowded halls, but Guiteau on his best night, in Syracuse, clears $5.

AUGUST 6, 1880: Guiteau switches to politics and composes a stump speech in behalf of Ulysses S. Grant. When Garfield's nomination becomes certain, he changes the title to "Garfield and Hancock" (the Democratic candidate is Winfield Scott Hancock) and hands out copies to 200 Republican leaders meeting at the 5th Avenue Hotel in New York City. He sends one copy up to Garfield in room 35. The speech is never delivered, by Garfield or anyone else.

THE CAMPAIGN: Guiteau is in constant attendance at Republican headquarters. He sees vice-presidential candidate Chester Arthur privately at least ten times and feels encouraged by the attention he receives. He sends Garfield a note saying he plans to marry a rich wife and would like to be appointed consul in Vienna. After the inauguration, he comes to Washington to pursue his dreams.

AT THE WHITE HOUSE: The White House is easy of access. Guiteau visits daily, sometimes pretending to be a newspaper reporter, and he sends frequent notes to the President: "I regret the trouble you're having with Senator Conkling. You are right and should maintain your position. You have my support and that of all patriotic citizens. I would like an audience of a few moments." The President does receive him, once: "As soon as General Garfield was at leisure, I stepped up to him and gave him my speech. Of course, he recognized me at once. . . . I told him I was an applicant for the Paris consulship . . . . and I left him reading the speech and retired. . . ."

He writes numerous letters on White House stationery, and a White House aide, Colonel Crook, objects: "You seem to make yourself at home here and to be laying in a supply of stationery."

"Do you know who I am?" Guiteau replies. "I am one of the men who made Garfield President."

APRIL: Guiteau calls on Colonel Robert Ingersoll to ask him to endorse his application for a consulship. The colonel is startled by his impudence but is polite when Guiteau tells him, untruthfully, that he is a friend of General Logan.

MAY 18: Guiteau begins to have doubts about his future. "I retired about eight o'clock, greatly depressed in mind and spirit from the political situation. An impression came over my mind like a flash. That if the President was out of the way, the whole thing would be solved."

MAY 20: He moves to Mrs. Grant's boarding house at 921 14th St., Northwest, giving the President and Secretary Blaine as references.

MAY 22: He visits the State Department to importune Blaine. Blaine loses his temper. "Never speak to me again about the Paris consulship. Guiteau says he believes Garfield is ready to give him a job. Blaine, like a true politician, retreats. "Well if *he* will . . . ," he says, implying that it's all up to Garfield now.

MAY 23: Guiteau writes a last letter to Garfield that begins, "I am trying to be your friend," and warns that unless the President rids himself of Blaine "you and the Republican Party will come to grief. He receives no reply.

JUNE 1: His decision becomes firm. "It kept growing upon me, pressing me, goading me. At the end of two weeks my mind was thoroughly fixed as to the necessity for the President's removal and the divinity of the inspiration. . ."

JUNE 6: He goes to O'Meara's Gun 27

Shop at 15th and F Streets and asks to see a .44 British Bulldog pistol displayed in the window. O'Meara tells him the price is $10. Guiteau asks him to hold it for him.

JUNE 8: Guiteau borrows $15 from his cousin, George Maynard, and returns to the gun shop, buying the Bulldog, a box of cartridges, and a woman's penknife. He pays an extra $1 for a bone handle, since it occurs to him that bone will show to better advantage than wood in a museum showcase. O'Meara tells him he can practice shooting in a woods by the river, near the White House. Guiteau practices and then walks over to Lafayette Park where he sits on a bench and calls to the guard at the west gate, "Is the President in?"

JUNE 12: He attends Sunday services at the National City Christian Church on Vermont Avenue, having heard that the President will be there. He sits in the back, but cannot get a clear shot at Garfield, who is up front. After the services he checks the side windows to see if it is possible to shoot the President from outside the building.

JUNE 18: He reads that the President and his wife, Lucretia, are going to Elberon, New Jersey. Mrs. Garfield, familiarly known as "Crete," has been ailing. The plan is for the President to take her to the resort town and then return. Guiteau goes to the Baltimore and Potomac depot intending to kill the President. He does not. "Mrs. Garfield looked so thin and she clung so tenderly to the President's arm, that I did not have the heart."

JUNE 20: The President returns and Guiteau is waiting at the station. He approaches, gun in pocket, but again does not shoot. "It was such a terribly hot, sultry day." He decides to consider this venture a rehearsal.

JUNE 25: He pays a visit to the huge, somber, red-stone city jail on the Anacostia river. The jailors allow him to peek through the doors, and he is pleased at the accommodations.

JUNE 30: Garfield, in a reflective mood, asks Robert Lincoln to tell him the details of his father's assassination. Lincoln obliges.

JULY 1 (morning): Having been dunned by Mrs. Grant, Guiteau slips away from her boarding house without paying

Guiteau spent an extra dollar to get a bone handle on his .44 British Bulldog pistol so that it would look more impressive in a museum showcase.

and checks into the Riggs House. (Evening): He lurks in Lafayette Park and watches Garfield as he leaves the White House, walks up Madison Place at the edge of the park, and turns into Blaine's house on 15th Street. He sees the President and Blaine emerge, "in the most delightful and cozy fellowship possible— just as hilarious as two young school girls. It was a very hot, sultry night, and I was tired and wearied by the heat, so nothing was done about it then."

JULY 2: The President is to leave today for the North. Guiteau rises at five o'clock and takes a stroll in Lafayette Park, then returns to the hotel for breakfast at seven. At nine he takes a horse car up the Avenue to the depot. He tells a hackman, Aquilla Barton, who is parked on B Street, that he will pay him $2 for a quick trip to the Congressional Cemetery. (The Cemetery is a short distance from the city jail.) Barton is to be ready to gallop as soon as he emerges from the building. Guiteau then goes inside, leaves two packages of papers at the newsstand, and pays 20 cents for a shoe shine. Mrs. Grant, meanwhile, has prepared a classified ad for insertion in the *Washington Post*:

"Wanted—Charles Guiteau, of Illinois, who gives the President and Secretary Blaine as references, to call at 921 14th Street and pay his board bill."

THE IGNOBLE EVENT TAKES PLACE:

THE PRESIDENT RISES BRIGHT and cheery and, on a dare from his son Harry, leaps over the bed.

It is time to leave the hot miasmas of Washington. This Saturday morning he and the boys are going north. He will deliver the commencement address at Williams, his old college, they will go yachting on the Hudson, and then they'll join Crete at Long Beach, New Jersey.

Half of the Cabinet—Secretary and Mrs. Hunt, Secretary and Mrs. Windom, and Postmaster James—is going with him.

Colonel Jamieson, solemn and fussy, is the first at the depot—he is in charge of logistics. He stations himself at the train gate and directs the members of the party and their baggage to the presidential car. Garfield's sons, Harry and James, ride up the Avenue in a carriage; the President and Blaine (who is seeing him off) follow in a coupe. The boys leap from the carriage and run into the depot. The President leans from the coupe and calls to Patrick Kearney, the depot policeman, "How much time do we have?" "About ten minutes, your honor," Kearney replies.

The President alights—a handsome man, tall, trim, and bearded. He is too warmly dressed in coat, trousers, and waistcoat of mixed gray stuff, and a high, square hat. He and Blaine stroll arm-in-arm through the B Street entrance into the ladies' waiting room. The open chamber, lined with rows of benches, is almost empty. A lady attendant stands to one side and a short dark man in a black suit, a crisp white shirt, and a broad-brimmed black hat waits by the entrance to the main hall.

The President and Blaine chat merrily, moving past the empty benches. It is almost cool here, under the high ceiling. The man in black comes to meet them, but neither Garfield nor Blaine seem to notice. The man stops four feet away and draws a heavy pistol from his pocket. He points it at the President's heart . . . and fires.

The President still does not seem to notice—he takes another step. "My God," he says. "What is this?" The bullet has gone through the sleeve of his coat. The assassin fires again, turns abruptly, jams the pistol into his pocket, and walks rapidly toward the 6th Street exit. Blaine starts after him, calling, "Rockwell, where is Rockwell?" Colonel Rockwell, a presidential aide, is nowhere around. Mrs. Sarah V. E. White, the ladies' room attendant, runs to the President, who is stretched on the floor, and cradles his head in her arms. The floor is covered with blood. The President's son Harry runs up sobbing, tears streaming down his face. The President coughs up phlegm and blood, and whispers something to the crying boy.

The assassin changes his course, now walking toward the B Street entrance where the hackman waits. Officer Kearney grabs him in a hug, pinning his arms to his side.

"It's all right," the man says to Kearney. "Keep quiet, my friend. I wish to go to jail."

The men and women from the presidential party stream into the ladies' waiting room, Colonel Jamieson in the lead. Someone shouts: "He shot the President —arrest him."

The assassin is still calm. He stands rigid in Kearney's grip.

"Yes, I have finished Garfield—Arthur is President. I am a Stalwart."

Kearney reaches in the man's pocket and pulls out the big five-barreled pistol. The depot janitor goes for the police. The room is filling up with people from the streets. The assassin grows nervous. The Metropolitan Police arrive and Kearney hustles him out, to B Street and a van. He is taken at a gallop to the police station.

"I think I know him," Blaine says to Jamieson. "His name is Ditteau."

The President lies in a spreading pool of blood. He is lifted painfully, put on a mattress, and carried to a small room on the depot's second floor. People push their way in, and the air turns sour; it is difficult to breathe. Dr. Bliss arrives, the first physician on the scene. He is sixty years old, bald, with flowing gray sideburns, and an air of self-importance—the embodiment of medical pomp. Bliss says the President must be taken to the White House at once. An ambulance is summoned.

The depot is now a surging mass of noisy people. Fire Chief Cronin, Police Officer O'Connell, and two other men carry the President down the stairs on a stretcher. The shoving, pushing crowd makes it difficult to get him into the ambulance. He is conscious but quiet and very pale. The ambulance horses gallop down the Avenue with a dozen mounted policemen ahead, clearing the way around the Treasury and through the west gate of the White House.

Cronin and his helpers carry the President upstairs to his own room on the southwest corner of the second floor. It is pleasant and airy, with bird's-eye maple woodwork, and hung with drab silk. The bed is by a window in the west wall and the President can look out and see the Potomac's sweet, clear water. He complains of a pricking sensation in his feet. Dr. Bliss summons a number of other doctors, as if there were safety in numbers: Dr. C. M. Ford, Dr. D. L. Hunting-

ton, Dr. N. S. Lincoln, Dr. Robert Reyburn, Dr. Basil Norris, Surgeon General Wales of the U.S. Navy, and Dr. C. B. Patterson. Surgeon General Barnes of the U.S. Army, who attended Lincoln in his final hours, is the senior physician.

The pricking sensation in Garfield's feet suggests strongly that the bullet touched the spinal column. The President's pulse is very rapid. He is still conscious and he speaks occasionally. There is a medical consultation at 2 PM. The physicians say that if the bullet hit the

bladder or the intestines, the patient is doomed. If it missed those vital organs, he will "recover without a doubt."

The President receives visitors—his Cabinet and Colonel Ingersoll. He tells them that he is certain Guiteau is crazy. "No one but an insane person could have done such a thing. What could he have wanted to shoot me for?" The Cabinet leaves. Robert Lincoln says aloud, "My God, how many hours of sorrow I have passed in this town."

In Long Branch, New Jersey, General

The splendid engravings of the illustrated newspapers were always dramatic but not always accurate. The ladies' waiting room at the depot was almost empty when the fatal shot was fired, and the assassin was seized by one policeman rather than by two civilians and what here seems to be a soldier.

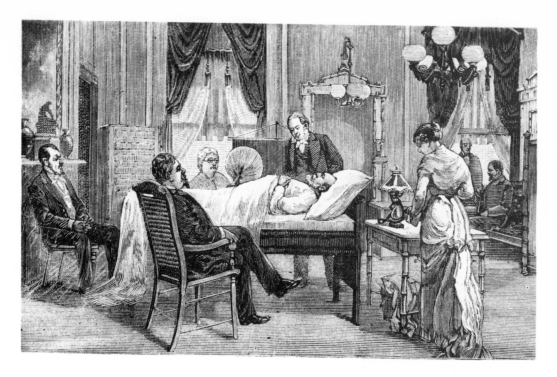

The White House sick chamber was clean, well lighted, and cool. What may have been the world's first private air-conditioning unit kept the temperature in the seventies except on the hottest days. The dying President was never alone, as squadrons of doctors, office holders, relatives, and friends moved in and out of the room during the long, hot summer.

Swaim, an old family friend, walks into Mrs. Garfield's sitting room and sits down.

"I have some rather bad news to tell you, but I guess you are enough of a philosopher to bear it bravely."

"What is it?"

"Well, the President has met with an injury."

"How serious is it?"

"It is pretty serious but not fatal."

"How did it happen?"

"He was shot some way, by accident I guess, handling a pistol or something."

Mrs. Garfield looks at General Swaim for a long moment and says, "No he wasn't."

A special car is sent to Long Branch and Crete, her daughters, Mollie and Lullie, and Mrs. Rockwell come home. They slip into a carriage at the depot and are driven through the Smithsonian grounds to the south front of the White House, away from the Avenue, to avoid the crowds. The Avenue is in turmoil. Police and government officials gallop up and down, carrying messages and spreading rumors. One mounted messenger at the Treasury Department tells people that the President is dead. An angry crowd gathers at the police station, and Guiteau, at his own urgent request, is removed to the jail on the eastern outskirts of the city.

Secretary Lincoln orders out two artillery companies, one to guard the White House, the second, which will camp a mile east of the Capitol at Lincoln Park, to supply guards for the jail. The British minister, Sir Edward Thornton, who is returning to England and who had been at the White House saying a formal goodbye the day before, calls again to offer his wishes for recovery. The Japanese minister arrives with an interpreter. The stock market drops five points. In late afternoon the Honorable Samuel Shellabarger emerges from the White House to say there is "absolutely no hope."

At 11 PM there is better news. The President's pulse is down from 126 to 116. The doctors believe they have found the bullet. It is in the liver, they say, and they know how to reach it. All the symptoms are now favorable. Dr. Bliss draws urine from his patient with a catheter and the temperature drops to 99°. Dr. Bliss says there is an improvement in respiration and he attributes it to the administration of champagne. He has a pleasant exchange with the President.

Garfield: "Tell me, what are my chances?"

Dr. Bliss: "I now think that there is a very good chance for your recovery."

Garfield: "Well I will take that chance."

The Cabinet spends the night at the White House, sleeping on sofas.

The first edition of the *Star* is almost jubilant: "The Good News Today—The President Alive and Better—Encouraging Bulletins from the Sick Room—Favorable Signs—The Physicians Hopeful."

The next morning, Independence Day, a new alarm is sounded: "Suspense! Change For the Worse in the Night." But on July 5th all is well once more: "Good News, A Reassuring Bulletin—His Condition Decidely More Favorable This Morning."

Bliss picks four more medical associates—Dr. D. Hayes Agnew of Philadelphia; Dr. Frank H. Hamilton of New York; Dr. Silas Boynton, the President's cousin; and Dr. Susan Edson of Cleveland, a female homeopathist.

The eminent engineer, Jennings of New York, is called to design an apparatus to cool the President's room. He suggests a forced air device but says that the White House does not have enough electrical power. He is given *carte blanche* and the complete technical support of the Navy's engineers. The White House basement is turned into a machine room, and an ingenious system is installed. Air is forced through an iron chamber that contains 3,000 feet of Turkish toweling, hung in rows half an inch apart. The toweling is saturated with water dripping from granulated ice and salt. The fan blows the cool air through an auxiliary chamber where it is dried by charcoal, and then through a flue to the President's room. The system keeps the room's temperature in the seventies except on the hottest days.

Crete and the children visit the President every morning and every afternoon. The President takes nourishment regularly. The bulletins are unfailingly optimistic. The President makes small jokes. Alluding to a nasty letter that Ulysses S.

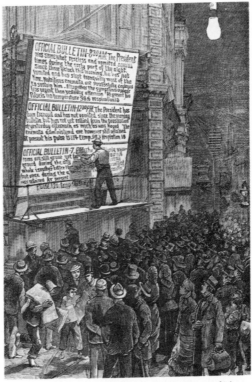

"Official Bulletins" of the President's condition were issued several times a day, often filled with trivial and irrelevant detail. As time went on they grew more and more optimistic, right up to the day of his death.

Grant has sent to a Senator Jones earlier, he says, "I wish that I could get up on my feet. I would like to see whether I have any backbone left or not." He does one bit of official work—signing an extradition paper to return a forger to Canada. The Cabinet members are barely civil to Vice President Arthur, so he discreetly stays out of sight, spending most of his time in New York.

Dr. Bliss gives himself public credit for his course of treatment: "Some people say that prayer have saved the President. They may think so. In my opinion it was whiskey."

Word comes that the Stalwart leaders, Conkling and Platt, have been defeated in the Albany legislature in their attempt to return to the U.S. Senate. Garfield is more than gracious.

"I am sorry for Conkling. I will offer him any favor he may ask or any appointment he may desire."

Alexander Graham Bell produces a mechanism to locate the bullet in the President's body. It is a form of induction balance. The doctors have revised earlier opinions and now believe the bullet to be lodged in the front of the abdomen. Garfield watches Bell's tests with intense interest. Bell says the device confirms the physicians' conclusion.

Charles C. Guiteau sits impatiently in the city jail. He is reported to be working on his autobiography, *The Life and Theology of Charles C. Guiteau, Prepared by Himself*. The papers he left at the depot newsstand have been read by the police and made available to the press, which has printed them down to the last exclamation point. They are vainglorious rhetoric. The principal one is a proclamation addressed to the White House:

"The President's tragic death was a sad necessity but it will unite the Republican party and save the Republic. Life is a flimsy dream and it matters little when one goes. A human life is of small value. During the war, thousands of brave boys went down without a tear. I presume the President was a Christian and that he will be happier in Paradise than here. It will be no worse for Mrs. Garfield, dear soul, to part with a husband this way than by natural death. He is liable to go at any time anyway. I have no ill will toward the President. His death was a political necessity. I am a lawyer, a theologian, and a politician. I am a Stalwart of the Stalwarts. I was with General Grant and the rest of our men during the canvass. . . ."

The assassin, it seems, is not a monster but merely a fool. On the 22nd day of July the physicians estimate that the President will be up in two weeks. On the 23rd he suffers a severe chill and his temperature climbs to 104°.

The President's wounds are infected and the infection is spreading through his body. A sac of puss breaks inside his mouth. The parotid gland is infected and the left side of his face is partly paralyzed. The doctors are helpless. They fuss and take temperatures and pulses and order "absolute silence," but in truth their patient is not receiving any medical treatment—he is simply getting intensive nursing care. He is fed carefully but lacks appetite. His weight drops from 210 to 135 pounds. His physicians have only the vaguest notions of the nature of his injuries, but the public is beginning to suspect that

he is mortally ill. Cyrus W. Field, the man who laid the transAtlantic cable, announces the collection of funds for Mrs. Garfield, should she soon be a widow. He himself contributes $25,000. Garfield is touched. "How kind and thoughtful. What a generous people."

Still, the bulletins of the idle doctors remain idiotically cheerful. The dreadful symptoms are sugar-coated; the President is frequently delirious but the notices on the bulletin board at the Pennsylvania Avenue gate do not mention it. Colonel Rockwell gives a guarded hint late in August. "Sometimes he is a little incoherent on awakening," he tells a reporter, "but at all other times his mind is clear as ever."

The physicians decide to move him out of the city to the ocean side in New Jersey. A wealthy Englishman, Charles G. Franklyn, offers the use of his 20-room cottage on the beach at Elberon. The preparations are extraordinary. The track at the Baltimore and Potomac depot is extended, and in New Jersey a special 3,200-foot spur is laid to the Franklyn cottage. The President is moved on September 6th, the

Elaborate preparations were made for the President's removal from the White House to a New Jersey resort, where it was hoped he would convalesce. Pennsylvania Avenue was cleared of all traffic, and sawdust was banked over the horse-car tracks, to make the passage to the train depot less jarring.

hottest day of the year.

A large American Express wagon is used as an ambulance. Sawdust is laid across the horse-car tracks where they cross the Avenue. A special car is cooled with ice boxes and screened with wire netting. It moves north at a good clip ("Let her go," the President orders), averaging 55 miles an hour, and making seven miles in five minutes north of Perryville. It makes the trip in eight hours. The President is determinedly cheerful. He waves at the crowds that line the station platforms along the way, but he is very tired toward the end. Reporters remark on Dr. Bliss' cheerful countenance as the party settles down in the big cottage by the sea. "I should think I was cheerful," he says. "Why, the man is convalescent."

The man is not convalescent. Only one doctor, Boynton, the President's cousin, is intelligently pessimistic. On September 11 the President develops pneumonia in the right lung.

On the evening of September 19th the President's old friend, General Swaim, is in the sick room.

"How it hurts here," the President says, pressing his hand to his heart.

Swaim gets him a glass of water and puts a cold cloth on his head. The President sinks back on the pillow. A half hour ticks slowly past.

"Swaim, can't you stop this? Oh Swaim."

The main artery has collapsed. The President is dead. An autopsy is performed by the resident staff.

Garfield's body comes back to Washington on another special train to lie in state. Ulysses S. Grant, the ultimate Stalwart, rides with it—and some are outraged. One hundred thousand people file past the body in the Capitol Rotunda in two days. The body is shipped to Cleveland, the Garfield's home town, and buried on September 23.

The *Post* carries a headline: "A Blundering Autopsy."

It appears that the hapless doctors missed the bullet entirely, and that it was not found until after the intestines had been removed and placed in a basin. It was not where they—and Alexander Graham Bell—had decided it must be.

It had fractured the eleventh and twelfth ribs, bored through the back bone hitting the first lumbar vertibra, severed the artery, and stopped in the pancreas. The President had been doomed from the moment he was shot. He would have bled to death on the floor of the ladies' waiting room at the depot on July 2 had not an aneurysm, a bubble in the artery's wall, formed, sealing the gash and permitting the blood to circulate. Had Garfield been shot 90 years later he might very well have lived—antibiotics would have stopped the infection and immediate surgery might have patched the artery. But in 1881 his case was twice doomed.

Chester Arthur is now President and the life and theology of Charles C. Guiteau is still going on.

Guiteau writes the new President a letter:

"My inspiration is a Godsend to you and I presume that you appreciate it. It

35

raises you from $8000 to $50,000 per year. It raises you from a political cypher to the President of the United States with all its powers and honors. . . . Never think of Garfield's removal as murder . . ."

The letter then offers some suggestions for appointments to Arthur's Cabinet, adding that "I took the responsibility of putting you and Senator Conkling into position and feel I have a right to make these suggestions."

Guiteau is vain and foolish. Is he also insane? Colonel Ingersoll thinks he is not.

"Eccentric he certainly is, but not insane from a legal standpoint. If at all insane, it is not of that character which touches his moral perceptions. His motive? Oh! The man was soured and embittered against the whole world. His life was a failure. There was nothing in the past or the present as an augury of hope for the future. He was ready to die and he determined with the malignity of a fiend to drag someone down with him, and he did it."

Dr. Edward C. Spitzka, the future president of the American Neurological Association (and living proof that not all doctors in 1881 were quacks), offers the opinion that Guiteau had been in a "more or less morbid state throughout his life" and that if he wasn't crazy he'd certainly do until crazy came along.

Guiteau is, at any rate, having a very good time. He has sought attention all his life—as a young man he tacked a poster on his wall that read: "Charles J. Guiteau, Premier of England, Will Deliver a Lecture in St. James Hall, London." He had dragged poor Anne Bunn from empty lecture hall to empty lecture hall and had published a pamphlet called "Truth—A Companion to The Bible," which sold a few copies. He had tried to start a newspaper to be called *The New York Theocrat*. Now, at last, he has his audience.

The trial begins November 14, in Washington's old courthouse, with something of a carnival air. Lemonade and cake stands are set up outside and the benches are packed within. Guiteau is represented by six lawyers, with his brother-in-law, George Scoville in the lead; but he remains remarkably outspoken in his own behalf. His choice line of defense is a syllogism: Garfield was not

killed by the bullet Guiteau fired since "three weeks after he was shot his physicians officially announced that he would recover. Therefore he was not fatally shot. The doctors who mistreated him ought to bear the odium of his death."

The fanciful argument does not take root, and many people are getting tired of Guiteau's endless proclamations. One of his guards at the city jail takes a shot at him through the window, grazing his head, and a letter writer to the *Star* suggests, ghoulishly, that he be "forced to eat two ounces of his own flesh daily until he eats himself up."

Guiteau doesn't mind. He holds daily receptions in his cell for reporters and visitors and he enjoys the holidays. "I had a very happy New Year. I had plenty of visitors: high-toned, middle-toned, and low-toned people. That takes in the whole crowd. He calls the prosecuting attorney an "old hog" and a "low-lived whelp" in court and refers to his own attorney, his sister's husband, as a "consummate jackass." On one occasion he suggests that the jury be taken out for daily walks as an

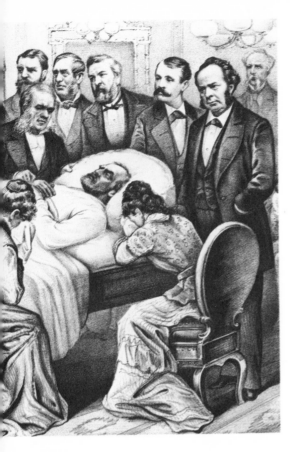

Garfield died as his friend General Swaim sat beside the bed. The purpose of this engraving is to depict everyone involved by any degree of blood or feeling. At the time of death the President weighed 135 pounds, having lost 75 pounds in two painful months.

aid to digestion and on another he announces that "an act of God will blow this court and jury out of this window if it is necessary."

Finally he addresses the jury formally, telling them that "to hang a man in my mental condition would be a lasting disgrace to the American people." He sings and recites the words to *John Brown's Body.*

It is to no avail. The jury is out for four hours and five minutes and it returns to pronounce him guilty. He is furious but soon recovers his composure. He continues to receive visitors in his cell, and he sells them his autograph for $1. On June 30 he is taken from his cell to a scaffold in the courtyard. Some 250 people are in paid attendance—some having spent $300 for a single admission. Guiteau

gives them their money's worth. First he reads the tenth chapter of *Matthew:* "And fear not them that kill the body but are not able to kill the soul," and he says he will declaim his own "pathetic hymn" unaccompanied, though it "would sound better set to music."

> I am going to the Lordy,
> I am so Glad.
> I am going to the Lordy,
> I am so Glad.
> I am going to the Lordy,
> Glory Hallelujah. Glory Hallelujah.
> I love the Lordy with all my Soul;
> Glory Hallelujah.
> And that is the reason I am going to the Lord.
> Glory Hallelujah. Glory Hallelujah.
> I am going to the Lord.

He dies at the end of a rope. He has in truth accomplished one of his avowed purposes, though not in the matter intended. He has united the Republican Party. The Stalwart faction is in permanent eclipse. It is customary to say that his act also ended the old political spoils system and brought the advent of Civil Service purity and pride. Charles A. and Mary R. Beard would write in their *Rise of American Civilization* that "the shot then fired rang throughout the land—driving into the dim and addled brain of the most hardened henchman the notion that there was something disgraceful in reducing the Chief Executive of the United States to the level of a petty job broker." Civil Service is adopted by a reluctant Congress as a memorial to Garfield, but some see this as ludicrous. Henry Adams writes: "The cynical impudence with which the reformers have tried to manufacture an ideal statesman out of the late, shady politician beats anything in novel writing."

And in truth the reform is less than complete. Ninety-five years later the spoilsmen still line the corridors of power —the politically appointed bureaucrats, GS 16's, 17's, and 18's, are still rewarded with jobs for their partisan efforts and turned out of office to make way for a new contingent when their party loses a presidential election. If Guiteau had been around to write a speech for Richard Nixon in 1968, he would certainly have been in town, hat in hand, in January 1969.

A High-Caste Chinese Puzzle

ZIANG SUN WAN DIDN'T HAVE a Chinaman's chance.

Wan was a dashing potential movie tycoon with an ulcer. He was both a mother's boy and a ladies' man, though at first glance he seemed the very model of a conscientious businessman: pince-nez glasses, suit coat, vest and watch chain, jade stick pin, spats, soft voice, and solemn round face. He was the son of a Shanghai merchant prince and a part-time playboy of the Eastern world. In December 1918, he was 21, short of funds, suffering from dyspepsia, and living in Mrs. Gertrude Bartell's boarding house in the Bronx.

His closest friend, Ben Sen Wu, age 20, with whom he'd shared a cabin on the slow boat from China, was in Washington, a student at George Washington University and third man at the Chinese Educational Mission at 2023 Kalorama Road. Wu was both brilliant and dumb. After six months at GW he was speaking English like a native of Foggy Bottom.

He was also suave, affable, well dressed, and an Episcopalian. But he had an unfortunate hobby: showgirls. He too was a playboy, a stage door Johnny lurking in the alley behind the high brick walls of the Gayety Theater, his gloved hands clutching a bouquet of roses. Showgirls are expensive, and Wu tried to balance his personal books by stealing the Chinese mission's stamp money. It was an unwise move. Dr. T. C. Wong, the mission head, and his number one assistant, C. H. Hsie, were stern men who kept an eye on the stamps. In a three-man staff, Wu was the only possible suspect. He was directly accused, and Dr. Wong confided his suspicions to the police. A detective followed Wu around for a few days but failed to stick him with the stamps.

Wu then decided on another scheme—a way to tap not the petty cash but the mission's main reserves. The mission had $150,000 in the Riggs Bank, part of the indemnity reluctantly paid by the Chinese government after the United States had helped squash the Boxer Rebellion. Teddy

Ziang Sun Wan, who was held as the alleged slayer.

Roosevelt had decreed that the money due the United States could be used to educate bright young Chinese in American colleges. The mission took charge of the money, and Dr. Wong took charge of the mission. He was a Christian and a gentleman; with Teddy and the rest of the Washington establishment watching benevolently, he had to be both.

There were few Chinese in Washington in 1918, and most were humbler folks who clustered on lower Pennsylvania Avenue and the adjacent blocks and who conducted their affairs in the back rooms of the On Leong and Hip Sing Merchant associations, known vulgarly as the Tongs. Dr. Wong was, of course, neither an On nor a Hip, but he often made his way to Chinatown restaurants since he loved to entertain friends and visiting students at dinner. His favorite was the Nanking, on 9th Street, across the street from the old Gayety. One evening after a good meal, he was strolling toward the streetcar stop at 9th and F when he was surprised to see his second assistant Mr. Wu ahead, his arm linked with that of a buxom blond. She was, he found on inquiry, a member of the Gayety

line and her name was Jeanne La Mar. Dr. Wong was scandalized. The Gayety was a burlesque house. In those days burlesque was good clean fun, the girls buxom in tights and the jokes no bluer than a cornflower. President Taft had attended the Gayety performances incognito and ladies were invited. But no chorus girl was a proper public companion for a member of the Chinese mission staff.

Young Mr. Wu was in trouble and in the process of getting in more trouble. His second scheme to finance the high life was under way, and it was both more ambitious and less intelligent than his first. He needed a cohort for it, so he wrote Wan in New York and invited him down for Christmas. Wan was in need of money and cheer—at the end of the previous summer he had taken $2,000 his doting mother had sent for his tuition at NYU and rented a storefront nickelodeon with folding chairs and had shown *The Perils of Pauline* and other primitive flicks. In two months he was broke and had a severe pain in his stomach. He treated it with his favorite remedies—strong whiskey, weak women, and apple pie. By Christmas he was confined to his own bed and unable to travel. By January he had recovered; when Wu sent a second telegram inviting him down, he came.

Dr. Wong, an old friend of his mother's, gave him a cold welcome—he had learned that Wan was not enrolled at NYU and he suspected that Wan's lifestyle was no more exemplary than Wu's. Dr. Wong administered what seemed later to be deliberate snubs. For one thing he did not take Wan out to dinner. Still, with Wan's stomach in the shape it was, he would have been a difficult dinner guest. And Wan was not in town for pleasure alone. Soon after Wan's arrival, Wu laid out his plan. Dr. Wong paid all mission bills and made all educational grants by check. He and Mr. Hsie signed and countersigned each of them. Some were for large amounts. Wu's scheme was to steal a check from Dr. Wong's checkbook, fill it out for $5,000 payable to Wu, then forge the signatures and cash it at Riggs Bank.

On January 25, Wu took the first step —he stole the check. The next day Dr. Wong noticed that it was missing. He told Mr. Hsie. They promptly reached an obvious conclusion and phoned the police and asked that a detective be sent around. Then they went to lunch at Braslau's delicatessen at 18th Street and Columbia Road. When they got there they found Wan and Wu seated at a table eating corned-beef sandwiches. Dr. Wong asked Wu why he had taken the check. Wu loudly denied doing so. The two younger men left in a huff. Dr. Wong and Mr. Hsie sat down to a somber meal. Meanwhile, back at the mission, Detective Bradley arrived from headquarters. No one was home so he left his calling card in the mail box. When Dr. Wong and Mr. Hsie returned from lunch, Wan was waiting. He announced that he had decided to return to New York the next day, and they gave him a cold goodbye.

On the morning of January 27 Wan made a conspicuous departure and took a cab to the Union Station, but instead of getting on the train he walked across the plaza and checked in at the Harris Hotel, signing the register with his true name and giving Shanghai as his home address. At noon he sent a telegram to his brother Van in New York, telling him to come to Washington. When Van still hadn't arrived by 4 PM Wan sent another, telling him to "throw your work away and come at once." Van arrived at midnight. On January 28 Wan and Wu met to discuss their next move.

On the afternoon of January 29 Wan waited until Dr. Wong and Mr. Hsie were out and then slipped into the house on Kalorama Road. A handyman named James Snead came by and banged on the door, shouting that he was there to lay a fire in the furnace. Wan called down from an upper floor that they were all going to New York for several days and wouldn't be needing his services. An hour later Kon Li, a GW medical student who lived across the street, came and knocked. He was looking for Wu. Wan slammed the door in his face.

Meanwhile Wu was at GW chatting gaily with friends. He asked two of them to dinner at the Oriental Café at 11th Street and Pennsylvania Avenue, explaining that he'd been all tied up with a visiting friend for the past week and hadn't had much chance to step out. Dr. Wong had arranged a dinner party too, one to

Dr. T. C. Wong, who was found murdered in his home.

which Wu had been conspicuously not invited. It was set for the Nanking at 7 PM and was in honor of Mr. T. C. Quo, who was departing to be the Chinese delegate at the World War Peace Conference in Paris.

Wu hurried through his meal at the Occidental and excused himself, telling his two friends that he had an appointment. He left at 7:30 PM, catching a streetcar at 14th and F. Dr. Wong's party ended too; it was discovered that one of the 13 guests was coming down with influenza. Flu was nothing to sneeze at in 1919. At 9:30 PM Dr. Wong and Mr. Hsie escorted the guest of honor to the streetcar stop at 9th and F.

Things were very quiet at the Mission House the next day.

Wu failed to show up for his classes at GW, a singular happening. An attaché at the Chinese Embassy, who was a fellow student, phoned Kon Li, the student from across the street, and asked him to check up on him. Li remembered his rude reception the day before and this time he was more persistent. When no one answered his knock, he peered through the window and saw a foot on the floor, toes 41 pointed up. He could not see who was attached to the foot. He pried open the window, climbed in, and found that it belonged to Dr. Wong, who was stretched on the rug in the sitting room, fully dressed, an overcoat concealing his head, his vest scorched. He had been shot in the chest. A brass lamp was lying nearby. It was spotted with blood. A chair was overturned. Kon Li went out through the window in search of police. With the help of a passing newsboy, he found Patrolman Bradshaw making his rounds. Bradshaw called the Tenth Precinct, and in a twinkling five detectives were on the scene.

The police went about things systematically—noting the hole in Dr. Wong's chest, a gash in the back of his head, and the spots on the lamp. They then moved on, through the house, room by room. Along the way they found two more bodies; Mr. Hsie was face down in the basement, shot once in the back of the head, and Mr. Wu, shot in the head and chest, was in the basement too, a pillow over his face. A .32 caliber revolver was on a chair three feet away.

The newspapers exploded in headlines. The *Post* announced with a splendid array of head, subhead, decks, and sub decks:

THREE HIGH-CASTE CHINESE

FOUND KILLED IN HOME:

Dead Since Wednesday,

Members of Educational Mission Here Are Shot.

MOTIVE A MYSTERY.

Dr. Wong, Director; C. H. Hsie and Ben Sen Wu Victims.

TWO WERE GWU STUDENTS.

Mysterious Tragedy in Kalorama Road Residence Discovered When Another Student Calls to Learn Why Hsie and Wu were Absent From Classes.

ASSASSIN BELIEVED TO HAVE TURNED AWAY VISITORS.

No Attempt at Robbery—Papers of International Importance Left.

Kon Li told the police and the press about the rude reception he'd gotten from a young Chinese stranger. Neighbors reported hearing a number of shots between noon and midnight Wednesday.

The police issued two bulletins: "This is the most baffling mystery in Washington's annals of crime," and "There may have been some secret known by all three

men detrimental to certain persons." Raymond W. Pullman, the chief of police, said that at first he had assumed that Wu had shot the others and committed suicide, but that he'd changed his mind after noticing that Wu was shot in the back of the head.

The *Post,* then run by an amiable drunk named Edward Walsh McLean, a man of elemental fears, suggested that there might be some kind of crazy Oriental conspiracy afoot. Referring to the victims as "Chinese of the Highest Caste" and to the putative murderers as "Chinamen," it suggested that Tong warfare had erupted in Washington.

The *Post* offered the expert opinion of Representative Julius Kahn, of California, a self-proclaimed friend of the victims, who said: "There is nothing so deadly as the hatred of Tong cliques. There is nothing that can compare with the cool, calculating way in which the Chinese gunman goes out to slay a marked man. He is a sure shot, though cowardly."

The *Post* then offered some specific theories, one being that "an assassin acting as a secret agent for some fanatical group mistook Dr. T. C. Wong, of the mission, for Dr. T. T. Wang, an important member of the Chinese parliament, who had passed through Washington some weeks earlier on his way to Paris." The *Post* noted that "Wang and Wong are identical in Chinese characters." It seemed to be saying that the assassin had looked up his victim's name in some Chinese phone book and had then gone to the wrong address.

The next day, however, the *Post* abruptly abandoned the Tongs.

"POLICE HAVE CLEW IN CHINESE MURDER," it announced. "BELIEVE THEY KNOW WHO SLEW THREE EDUCATORS—MOTIVE STILL A MYSTERY."

The clue, or clew, was a $5,000 check presented to the Riggs Bank by a young Chinese and signed, apparently, by Wong and Hsie. The bank had refused to cash it and, the *Post* said, "Officers of the bank declared to be certain" of the identity of the young man.

Two days later the headline said, flatly, "ARREST OF CHINESE SLAYERS IMMINENT," adding: "Detective Kelly brings men from New York City."

(Above) The house at 2033 Kalorama Road, N.W., where the bodies were found. (Below) The basement where Dr. Wong's body was found.

Kelly had fetched both Wan and his brother, Van, and he and half a dozen other detectives were questioning them illegally and at length. The questioning was illegal since neither had been arrested but both were kept locked up in separate rooms at the Dewey Hotel. Police Chief Pullman explained that with a verve that would have made him an ideal spokesman for later administrations: "There are no arrests and no one is held as a government witness. In either case there would be a notation on our blotters. The two men are voluntarily aiding us."

The volunteers were on duty 24 hours a day, and Wan's stomach was in awful shape. He was being fed neither wisely nor too well—a ham sandwich for breakfast plus a slice of his favorite apple pie. Between meals he was grilled in the traditional technique known as Mutt and Jeff or the Good Detective and the Bad Detective. Kelly was the good detective and a colleague named Burlingame was the bad. Burlingame would hit Wan with a coathanger and stomp from the room shouting that if he had to take much more of Wan's audacious behavior he'd kill him. Then Kelly would shake his head sadly and advise Wan to tell all for everybody's sake since he didn't know how much longer he could restrain Burlingame. In theory Wan would break down and confess. In practice Wan and Van steadfastly denied knowing anything of interest. They smiled a lot and were excessively polite, but they insisted that the triple murders were mysteries to them. The headlines, however, remained optimistic: "TANGIBLE EVIDENCE OBTAINED, Suggests early solution of baffling case." By February 4, six days after the killings, the *Post* said with a flourish: "ARRESTS IN TRIPLE TRAGEDY DUE TODAY." On the fifth, it backed away to "FAIL TO PROVE GUILT, Police lack evidence for arrests, CANNOT FIND $5,000 CHECK, Detectives believe both it and letter have been destroyed."

The *Evening Star* ran a picture of the Dewey Hotel where, it said, "two Chinese are held in murder case," and the police denounced the *Star* for "noncooperation." The *Star* said primly that it had found the hiding place on its own and it hadn't promised to keep it a secret.

It is possible that the unwelcome attention spurred the police to conclusive action. On the evening of February 9 the cops took Wan and his brother out of the hotel and hustled them over to Kalorama Road. The next morning the *Post* announced that "POLICE REHEARSE CHINESE MURDERS IN MISSION HOUSE." The story reported that "for several hours the police by means of various lights and other methods took the two men through the scenes supposed to have been enacted on the night of the murders." From room to room, up and down the stairs, the tour took 12 hours, from 7 PM to 7 AM. In the end Wan confessed.

"Wong and Hsie Murdered by Wu; Wan Killed Wu, Explanation of Chinese Tragedy Given by Elder Brother," the *Post* said. The explanation was interesting if peculiar: Wan had come to the Mission House that fatal Wednesday (he said) to discuss the "best means of obtaining money" with Wu. Murder (he said) was far from his mind. Wu came and they discussed money. Then Dr. Wong came and Wu abruptly shot him dead. Wan was horrified. After a while Hsie came and Wu shot him too. Then Wu told Wan he wanted him to take the bogus check to the Riggs Bank and cash it. Wan refused. They quarrelled. Wan, who'd seen Wu in action, decided he'd move first. He took the revolver from the kitchen table where Wu had carelessly left it, walked into the furnace room, and shot Wu in the back of the head.

The tale had its limitations. It did not explain, for example, who had taken the check to the bank *after* the murders but before the bodies were found. It obviously wasn't Wu, and even by Wan's own account that would seem to narrow it down to him or his brother, Van.

On February 19, Wan and Van were finally allowed to meet the press—they were displayed in their cells while the reporters watched from a respectful distance. "Wan and Van offered no protest," the news account said. "Both appeared in good spirits. They have enjoyed games, especially cards. Each is an inveterate smoker of strong cigarettes." As the newsmen watched, Detective Stringfellow produced a pack of cards and did indeed start to play a game with the brothers.

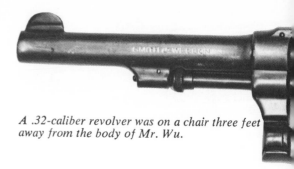

A .32-caliber revolver was on a chair three feet away from the body of Mr. Wu.

He reported to the patient press the next morning that the game had gone on until 1 AM, at which point Wan had eaten a slice of apple pie and gone to bed.

The brothers were rushed to trial. Van was the principal witness. Van said that he had come to Washington in response to his brother's summons and that he knew absolutely nothing about the murders or the forgeries. He even denied going to the bank, though the Riggs people said they recognized him. He said that while he was at Union Station, two young Chinese, who introduced themselves as Mr. Wang and Mr. Moy, asked him the way to Riggs Bank—not to make too fine a point, it seems an odd question to ask a young man who'd just gotten off the train.

Wan listened to his brother with his "hands clasped" and, as a reporter noted, he "swayed frequently." He had reason to. If he repeated his alleged confession, which put the blame on Wu, he would still be incriminating himself as an accessory to the planned forgery and as the killer of Wu. So he denied everything and said that he couldn't remember what had happened that awful Wednesday. He said he'd made the confession because the police had "cursed, pushed, and struck" him and that its details followed "police suggestions.' When the prosecutor chided him for having a convenient memory, he said, "What hurt my feelings I remember well, other things not so well."

The jury went out for a half hour and returned, finding Van not guilty, Wan guilty. Wan collapsed. When he recovered he was sentenced to be hanged by the neck until dead.

"I am innocent and I do not understand American law," he said. "I do not see why they want to kill me."

The hanging was set for December 1, 1920, but Wan's lawyers filed an appeal and it was postponed. By 1923 the sentence had been confirmed by the Court of Appeals. The lawyers carried on to the Supreme Court. On October 10, 1924, Justice Brandeis, speaking for the court, noted that Wan's confession had been obviously obtained by duress. He ordered a new trial.

That took time.

On January 18, 1926, the new trial began. This time the confession was excluded and the prosecutor was unable to produce many of the old witnesses. Police Chief Pullman and four others were dead. Seven had returned to China. The jury went out on February 9 and it was still out on February 10. After 22½ hours the jury foreman, W. W. Upchurch, a timekeeper at the Washington Terminal Company, his eyes bloodshot and his face drawn and haggard, announced that the jury couldn't agree. The judge ruled a mistrial. It was reliably reported that the count had stood ten to two for acquittal. Wan greeted the newsmen with a broad smile and a hearty handshake. "Please excuse me," he said. "I have some reading to do."

U.S. Attorney Peyton Gordon said he'd arrange a new trial as soon as possible.

It took place in the first sweet days of June. This time the jury stayed out for 25 hours before deciding that they couldn't agree. The final count was eight for acquittal, four for conviction.

Peyton Gordon said that was that— "no jury can be obtained which would render a verdict of either guilty or not guilty."

Wan, who'd spent seven years in jail, not counting the time at the Dewey Hotel, took it calmly. He nodded and smiled and accompanied by a friend, the Reverend Peter J. O'Callaghan, left the court. That night he slept in a feather bed and the next day he returned to the D.C. jail to get his hat. He was full of good cheer, and seizing the iron bars of his cell he rattled them loudly and shouted out, "Joe, let me in." Wan had supported himself in jail by selling his favorite food, apple pies, and one prisoner called out: "So long Wan old boy, you won't be selling any pies today."

Then Wan talked to the press. The question of his innocence was, at best, moot. The "confession," which almost got him hanged, seems as likely a version of what really happened as any other that could be offered.

Wan wisely offered none this time around. "The rules of evidence in your law courts seems designed to cover up instead of uncovering actual facts, and so it has happened that many facts if fully understood would, I believe, have exonerated me completely."

He was asked how he'd stood the long ordeal, waiting for the hangman's noose.

"I don't see how I stood it," he said. "I have seen others pass my cell on their last journey through life and I have heard them singing. It was awful.

"But then I learned to laugh. I deliberately practiced laughing, and as the days grew shorter and shorter they passed like minutes. I laughed every time I thought of what they were doing to me. Or I prayed. I always said my prayers at night, but I did not dare spend my days praying. I had to spend them laughing or I would have collapsed."

He nodded, shook hands all around, and smiled a thin, solemn smile. His laughing days, thank God, were over. 45

A Visiting General Quaffs A Fatal Glass Of Lemonade

MRS. ELIZABETH WHARTON, who was inordinately fond of clothes, looked best in black. A raven-haired matron in her fifties but a stunner still, she moved between Washington and Baltimore in the early 1870's with the cool grace of a WASP Lucrezia Borgia.

No one has written doggerel to celebrate her, which hardly seems fair. She seems three times as deadly as Lizzie Borden.

> Lizzie Wharton poured a cup
> And Major Wharton's jig was up,
> When she saw what she had done
> She poured another for her son.

But such doggerel is best with only four lines, and to do Mrs. Wharton justice there would have to be verses to account for two cousins, a visiting general, and the family banker.

Elizabeth was born in Philadelphia, the daughter of a wealthy and indulgent merchant named Nugent. She attended Bishop Doanes' Seminary for Young Ladies in Burlington, New Jersey, was "slender, graceful, of queenly beauty, with jet-black hair, dark eyes, and fair complexion." She also had "an engaging manner, winning ways, and a dashing disposition." She was, as mentioned, unfortunately fond of clothes.

After graduating from the seminary she returned to Philly and began buying sumptuous dresses as if the silkworms were about to go on strike. Mr. Nugent was alarmed. Then Elizabeth announced her engagement to a wealthy Mr. Williamson and father relaxed.

The wedding day arrived, and the church was decked with lilies and the bride with lace. Everybody came but the groom. Mr. Nugent had him hunted down. The explanation was simple. Mr. Williamson had not known that he was engaged. Father Nugent was upset and he decided to put Liz away for a bit in a nice rest home. Before he could she eloped with Lieutenant Harry W. Wharton, of the U.S. Army, a dashing fellow, the son of a Philadelphia judge, though not strong-minded. The young couple moved to Washington and enjoyed Army life. Lieutenant Wharton was no fool. He fought his way into the administrative end

and he was soon supervising warehouses, first in Washington, then in Baltimore. Time went by pleasantly. A son was born, then a daughter. The children grew up. The war came and went, leaving them unscathed. They had a big house, lots of servants and other luxuries, such as a big insurance policy for the Major. The Major died in 1867, which made the insurance worthwhile. The son, now an Army major too, was insured likewise shortly before he passed on, in 1870. Liz bore up. She had her daughter, her looks, her house, the insurance, and she looked magnificent in black.

She kept in touch with friends and relatives in the District and Philadelphia, borrowing $6,000 without security from her father, and $2,500 from her cousin-in-law, Edward Wharton, of 4½ Street, Southwest, Washington, D.C.

She, as always, mixed such business with pleasure; for example, she invited Edward and his wife and teenage daughter over to Baltimore for a pleasant weekend. Edward died rather promptly after arrival, followed almost immediately by the daughter. The wife, or rather widow, bolted back to Washington where she started writing letters to Philadelphia, accusing Elizabeth of double murder.

Elizabeth, realizing that the woman was under a certain strain, refused to get excited, though she pointed out that the daughter had been sickly anyway. She also indicated that she wasn't going to be able to pay back that $2,500 any time soon, but the widow threatened to sue and Elizabeth reluctantly paid up.

Elizabeth borrowed $2,600 from General W. S. Ketchum, of Georgetown. General Ketchum was in many ways the perfect example of a victorious Civil War general. First of all, he had married shrewdly; his wife's brother was General Brice, the Paymaster General. Second, he was a soldier who could, under the pressures of the field, make swift and decisive judgments. In his early career he was posted to Kansas and there he was thrown from a horse, landing, painfully, on his head. From that moment on he had declined to ride horses, traveling when his troops moved as a passenger in the ambulance. He also arranged to be transferred, as soon as possible, to the War Department in Washington. In Washington he continued to show an ability to see and seize an opportunity, particularly in real estate. He was in regular attendance

Baltimore in the 1870's was a fresh and fragrant place, at least when viewed from Druid Hill Park.

General Ketchum.

at the Episcopal Church, he greatly enjoyed the singing of hymns, he brought flowers to neighbors, and, a robust widower, he paid constant attention to Mrs. Eliza C. W. Chubb, a widow and a clerk in the Treasury Department.

In June 1871, Mrs. Wharton invited the General and his playmate to her Baltimore house for the weekend. They went, leaving the Washington depot at 10:40 AM, Saturday, June 24, on the B&O, arriving in Baltimore between 6 and 7 PM, in time for tea. It was a slow train and they arrived hungry.

Mrs. Wharton met them at the door and led them immediately to the groaning board.

As Mrs. Chubb said subsequently: "Mrs. Wharton presided only a few minutes when she was called away. She did nothing at the table except give each of us a cup of tea. When supper was over General Ketchum and I went to the third story, as Mrs. Wharton's house was crowded. We sat together in his room and talked until nearly eleven o'clock, when I bade him good night. While we were there Mrs. Wharton came in and asked if we were comfortable. In the night General Ketchum was taken sick."

He was not the only sick man on the premises.

Eugene Van Ness, Mrs. Wharton's banker, was present and, at the moment, even sicker. Which was unfortunate since he was a man that the General had been particularly anxious to meet.

Mrs. Wharton, after all, owed the General $2,600, she had missed her last interest payment, and she had announced that she intended to go to Europe. The General confided to Mrs. Chubb, coming over on the train, that Mrs. Wharton had excused herself by saying that her man of business, Mr. Van Ness, had confused her about the arrival of some money she had coming. The General, who didn't have to fall twice on his head to get a point, was not about to let her go abroad owing him the principal.

He intended to confer with Van Ness and then confront Mrs. Wharton.

The next day, Sunday, the General came down to breakfast but told Mrs. Chubb that he was not well enough to go to church. She went without him and then went sightseeing around town, returning to the Wharton house at about 8:30 PM.

"The General seemed brighter and better and was sitting in the dining room talking. We sat and talked and retired about eleven o'clock. Some lemonade was offered by Mrs. Wharton to us and he and I partook of it.

The lemonade was prepared by Mrs. Wharton in the dining room. She handed it around on a small plate. Both glasses were together. Mrs. Chubb took the one nearest to her.

The General took the other and poured brandy into his glass. Mrs. Chubb and the General retired, to their separate rooms. "I heard that General Ketchum had been taken sick during the night," Mrs. Chubb recalled, "but I had no conversation with

49

The Evening Star.

№. 38—№. 5,449.   WASHINGTON, D. C., THURSDAY, DECEMBER 14, 1871.   **TWO CENTS.**

EVENING STAR.

Washington News and Gossip.

INTERNAL REVENUE.—The receipts from this source to-day were $300,728.73.

FORTY-SECOND CONGRESS.

This Afternoon's Proceedings.

SENATE.—December 14, 1871.

HOUSE OF REPRESENTATIVES.—Mr. Burchard (Ill.) introduced a resolution calling upon the Secretary of the Treasury for information as to the number of persons employed in the collection of customs.

TELEGRAMS TO THE STAR.

This Afternoon's Dispatches.

ASSOCIATED PRESS REPORT.

FROM EUROPE TO-DAY.

THE SICK PRINCE.
He is Getting Better.

Parliament.

The Poisoning of Gen. Ketcham.

Shooting Affray Between Sporting Men.

him nor did I see him after I bade him good night. I heard him coming downstairs in the night, but I have no idea of the hour. I next saw him on Monday morning, just before breakfast, and he complained of a sick stomach and giddiness." Mrs. Chubb fetched Dr. P. C. Williams. "On Tuesday morning I left the house at twenty minutes of seven, to return to Washington. I first went to General Ketchum's room and talked with him through the keyhole. He told me he was better and would come over on the eleven o'clock train and take dinner with me."

Murders were often more sensational than headlines in 1871. Here, buried among bulletins on the health of the Prince of Wales and on the Forty-Second Congress, is a report on the Annapolis trial of Mrs. Wharton.

The General lasted until Wednesday, June 28. Dr. Williams said that when he saw him "shortly after one PM on that day I regarded him as hopelessly ill." He also suspected poisoning.

Mr. Van Ness, who had been closely attended by his loving wife and family, recovered enough to be sent home. Once home he recovered very rapidly indeed. Meanwhile, Liz got on with business. General Ketchum's body had been scarcely sent home before she arranged to meet the General's two sons at Mrs. Chubb's Washington residence.

One son, Charles, said later, "She commenced to sympathize with us at the death of our father and said she too had lost a true friend; while talking with us and expressing her sympathy, her eyes filled with tears. She said she regretted very much to be compelled to talk about business so soon after my father's death, but that necessity compelled her to do so."

The sons had been under the very distinct impression that Mrs. Wharton owed their father $2,600 plus lapsed interest. She now said that, on the contrary, she had paid the General and had, indeed, entrusted him with $4,000 of her own in Government bonds. She said she wanted the bonds back as she needed the money to go to Europe.

"I asked if my father had given her any receipt for them and she said he had not. She also said when I asked her that she had no witnesses to the transaction. I told her I could not do anything then for her. . . . She replied that she would leave Baltimore on the following Saturday and must have the bonds to make her letter of credit good before leaving." Charles was suspicious. He turned the body over to Professor William E. A. Aikin of the University of Maryland.

On the 4th of July Charles visited Mrs. Wharton, carrying with him his father's pocket diary. It was a meticulous record. It noted, for example, that he had given a penny to a blind colored man. It noted that Mrs. Wharton had failed to pay the interest on her loan. It said not a word about her paying the principal or about her entrusting the General with $4,000. He asked her if her own records showed such. She replied that she kept none. She added that she had noticed during conversations with the General shortly before his death that his mind was growing blurred.

The situation left Charles in a quandry. It was the 19th century and he was a 19th century gentleman. One didn't just call a gentlewoman a liar—even one that was trying to do you out of some $6,600.

Charles was, it turned out, every bit as sound a commercial tactician as his late dad. Since he couldn't challenge Mrs. Wharton directly, he hit her, so to speak, on the flank.

First he tried to trace down the promissory note, which he knew Mrs. Wharton had signed and which he was certain his father had carried with him to Baltimore.

"I went to Mrs. Wharton's residence and she took me up to the room in which my father died. She showed me his valise, hat, linen duster, and umbrella. She brought me the key of the valise, my father's watch, fob, pocketbook, pocketknife, and a small pocket match safe. I opened the valise in her presence, and taking out the different articles of clothing I found there, put my hand in every pocket to see what it contained. I was looking for the note and found nothing. There was a vest also containing three pockets, one inside. My father always had

The Evening Star.

Vol. 38—No. 5,841. WASHINGTON, D. C., TUESDAY, DECEMBER 5, 1871. TWO CENTS.

EVENING STAR.

Washington News and Gossip.

INTERNAL REVENUE.—The receipts from this source to-day were $368,441.51.

THE CABINET met at noon to-day, all the members present, and adjourned about 2 p. m.

MR. J. D. CONNELL, of the Bureau of Statistics, has been promoted to chief of a division.

DURING the session of Congress the President will receive Senators and members of Congress from 10 to 12 o'clock in the forenoon, and other callers during the afternoon.

THE SUPREME COURT, preceded by Marshal Parsons and Clerk Middleton, and accompanied by Attorney General Akerman and Solicitor General Bristow, called in a body to pay their respects to the President at 12 o'clock yesterday, according to immemorial usage.

OF THE FIVE COLORED MEMBERS of the House of Representatives three are upon committees appointed yesterday—De Large, of S. C., on the Committee on Manufactures; Elliott, of the same state, on the Committee on Education and Labor; and Rainey, of the same state, on the Committee on Freedmen's Affairs. Turner, of Ala., and Walls, of Fla., are not members of any committee.

AN IMPORTANT OPINION.—In reply to a letter of the Secretary of War, asking to what extent a railroad which has been aided in its construction by donations of the public lands can be considered a public highway for the free use of the government in the transportation of its troops and property, the Attorney General replies that such a road is, in his opinion, a public highway for its whole length for the use of the government of the United States, and that the latter are not subject to charge for the transportation of its property on such road.

PERSONAL.—Whitelaw Reid, managing editor of the New York *Tribune*, is at the Arlington. .... James N. Ashley, editor of the *Telegrapher*, is in town. .... George Wilkes, who is understood to be here aiding in the efforts to organize an anti-Grant party, was upon the floor of the Senate to-day. .... Gov. Noyes, of Ohio, was also in the Senate Chamber, where he received the congratulations of many friends. .... Senators Nye, Kellogg, Patterson, and Clayton, Speaker Blaine and Representatives Banks and Kellogg called at the White House to-day.

MISS LOTTA K. TURNER, whose suit for $200,000 in San Francisco against the wealthy Mexican, Don Caledonia Ortez, on account of seduction and breach of marriage promise resulted in a verdict of only $7,500, was a clerk in the Treasury Department a couple of years ago. The discrepancy between the amount claimed and that awarded by the jury may probably be accounted for by the fact that she lived in the house with the defendant nearly two years after her seduction was accomplished, and suffered an additional two years to go by before commencing suit.

OUR DELEGATE IN CONGRESS.—Our citizens feel interested in everything which concerns the District of Columbia, and as much depends upon the committee in the House as well as the Senate, we give below the proceedings in the House so far as relates to the right of our Delegate to a place on the committee. Both Houses have declared, through an organic act, that the Delegate shall be placed on the House Committee for the District, and we doubt not the rule will be amended so as to relieve the Speaker of his embarrassment. There is no question but that Mr. Chipman will be of great service to the committee, and can do much toward preparing their work. However anomalous it may seem, the manifest propriety and utility of the thing will, we think, settle the question favorably to the District.

The Speaker.—The Chair desires to submit to the House a question which somewhat embarrasses him. The law reorganizing the government of the District of Columbia provided that the Delegate from the District of Columbia should be a member of the Committee for the District of Columbia. The Chair is governed by the rules of the House, which are made under an express provision of the Constitution of the United States giving to each House the right to make its own rules; and the rules of the House provide that the Committee for the District of Columbia shall consist of nine members of the House. Looking at the duties laid on the Chair by the rule he has referred to under the Constitution, he did not feel at liberty to constitute the Committee for the District of Columbia of ten members; and it becomes necessary, as between the law, which seemed to change the rule of the House, and between the rule of the House as it stands, for the House to determine what course shall be taken. If the Delegate from the District of Columbia is to be present with the committee merely in an advisory capacity, the committee, under the law of courtesy, would no doubt like to have him there. But if he is to be a voting member his function would be a much larger one, and larger than ever was accorded before to a Delegate on this floor. Under the circumstances the Chair has not announced the Delegate from the District of Columbia as a member of the committee, and he will wait the instructions of the House as to what should be done in the premises.

Mr. Dawes.—I move that the rules of the House be so suspended as to allow the appointment by the Speaker of the Delegate from the District of Columbia as a member of the Committee for the District.

Mr. Wood.—It appears to me that this is a very similar question to that presented by the Delegate from Colorado, [Mr. Chaffee,] and that it is a proper question to go to the Committee on the Rules. I propose that it shall take that course.

The Speaker.—The gentleman from New York (Mr. Wood) proposes that the question be referred to the Committee on the Rules. If there be no objection, it will be so referred.

There was no objection.

What with Sir Charles Dilke and his anti-monarchical followers in England, the Fenians in Ireland, communists in France, revolutionists in Belgium, republicans in Spain, liberals in Prussia, and Internationals everywhere, they are having lively times in Europe, and the end is not yet. The triumph of the people in Belgium has emboldened the friends of popular government there and elsewhere. The German Parliament, with all their submissiveness, have shown a disposition to resist the inordinate scheme of taxation proposed by the Emperor and Bismarck, and at a late sitting one of the deputies raised the old revolutionary cry of "War to the palace and peace to the cottage," following it up with the ominous words, "and death to all luxurious idleness!" Bismarck did not deem it prudent to notice them or reply, but continued writing at his desk. In England there is no lull in the agitation. Sir Charles Dilke addressed, on November 29, a large and crowded meeting at Bristol on representation and education. Prof. Newman presided, and a strong republican feeling was manifested by those present. The names of the Queen and the Prince of Wales were received with hisses and groans, while hearty cheers were given for a republic. Sir Charles, in the course of his speech, dwelt upon the inequalities of the British representative system, and declared himself to be a republican, remarking that he made no concealment of the fact. As another sign of the times it may be stated that the Dublin *News* represents that at the Communist meeting in London, which was protected by the police, the banners bore such mottoes as these: "Division of Property." "No Religion." "Down with the Queen." "To H—— with Everything." The women, too, are having a hand in the business, and in Liverpool have organized a vigilance committee "to prevent hasty legislation."

DEATH OF A FIFTY-THOUSAND DOLLAR STALLION.—Dorsey's celebrated stallion Golddust died in Louisville, Ky., last Sunday of inflammation of the bowels. Golddust was one of the most famous horses in the country, and the sire of many celebrated animals. A few days ago his owner was offered $50,000 for him.

SMALL CHANGE is so scarce in Paris that the [illegible]

FORTY-SECOND CONGRESS.

This Afternoon's Proceedings.

TUESDAY, December 5, 1871.

SENATE.—Mr. Kellogg introduced bill to authorize mail steamship service in the Gulf of Mexico, between the port of New Orleans and certain ports of the republic of Mexico.

Mr. Corbett introduced bill to restore the office of director of the bureau of statistics.

MARTIAL LAW IN SOUTH CAROLINA.

Mr. Blair moved to take up the resolution offered by him yesterday, calling on the President for his authority to declare martial law in certain counties of South Carolina. Mr. Blair said the resolution contemplates that the President shall lay before the Senate the manner in which he has executed the extraordinary powers conferred upon him by Congress. He had heard that of the many citizens of South Carolina arrested, nine-tenths of them had been arrested charged with crimes committed before the act of April 20, 1871. The facts alleged in connection with these offences he recognized as having been brought to the attention of the ku klux committee anterior to the passage of the ku klux act.

Mr. Edmunds suggested that it was not proper to discuss the merits of the resolution on a motion to take up, and the Vice President so decided.

Mr. Morton said much of the information called for was given in the message of the President, and also he considered that it was best to delay action until the report of the committee in the late insurrectionary States had been submitted.

Mr. Blair said the information called for was not given in the President's message. The President says he had information to justify him in his action, but does not state from whom he received it. He certainly did not get it from the committee, for the committee had authorized no one to give him any information, and as a member of the committee, he (Mr. B.) was of the opinion that no facts had been brought before the committee, which would justify his action.

Mr. Conkling was opposed to taking up the resolution for the reasons stated by Mr. Morton, and further because the resolution was not in the nature of good faith. It was full of assertion and intimations.

The motion to take up was then put and lost—ayes, 11; nays, 45.

Mr. Kellogg introduced bill to reorganize the district courts of the United States in the State of Louisiana.

CATACAZY.

Mr. Cameron opposed a resolution which was adopted, calling on the President for the correspondence in the Catacazy affair.

The Senate at ten minutes of one adjourned.

HOUSE OF REPRESENTATIVES.—After the reading of the journal—

Mr. Wells (Mo.) introduced a bill to make appropriation for a site in St. Louis for a custom house and post office building. Referred to Committee on Public Buildings and Grounds.

Mr. Dawes (Mass.) demanded the regular order, and this cut off further miscellaneous business.

The Speaker proceeded to call the committees, and Mr. Farnsworth (Ill.), from the Committee on Post Offices and Post Roads, reported a bill (House bill No. 1) to revise and consolidate

THE STATUTES OF THE POST OFFICE DEPARTMENT.

He said this was the same bill that was under consideration at the last session of Congress. It had now been examined by two committees of the House, and was approved by both. He asked that the full reading of the bill be dispensed with.

Mr. Wood (N. Y.) objected, and the bill was read.

Pending the reading of the bill the morning hour expired.

Mr. Hill (N. J.) introduced a bill authorizing the Postmaster General to issue one cent "correspondent" and "post" cards. Referred to Committee on Post Offices.

On motion of Mr. Dawes (Mass.) the House went into Committee of the Whole on the

PRESIDENT'S MESSAGE,

with Mr. Wheeler (N. Y.) in the chair.

Mr. Dawes offered a resolution to refer the several parts of the President's message to the appropriate committees.

Mr. Wood (N. Y.) objected to the proposed reference of certain matters to the select committee on the insurrectionary states. There was no such a standing committee of this House. He denied that there were any such things in this country as insurrectionary states. A committee was appointed at last session to investigate certain matters in the South, and its functions ceased when that duty had been performed. It was improper to refer anything to the committee, as it would continue it, and that was not intended.

Mr. Dawes said he could not enter upon a discussion of a question of fact with Mr. Wood, and that gentleman must know that there is such a committee of the House as that on insurrectionary States.

Mr. Wood denied that the committee was intended to be continued in existence beyond the present session of Congress. Last Congress we had a committee called the Committee on Reconstruction, and the gentleman's colleague from Massachusetts, (Mr. Butler,) made numerous efforts to have it continued. The Committee on Insurrectionary States will cease after it shall have reported to the House. A reference of business to it was a recognition of the committee, and the effect of the reference would be to continue it. He was opposed to making committees in this manner.

Mr. Dawes said that if a simple reference would continue a committee, then this committee would already be continued, because matters had been referred to it yesterday. The committee has not reported yet, and until it does report, certainly all matters pertinent may be referred to it. The committee was made to inquire into disorders in the South, and no one could say whether its continuance would be necessary until after the report had been submitted.

Mr. Wood said that instead of leading to order, the committee was one which was calculated to promote disorder. He (Mr. W) would go as far as any gentleman in the House, or as far as the administration, to promote peace and order in the South, but this was not the way to do it, and he protested against continuing committees as agencies to promote disorder in the South.

Mr. Dawes hailed with joy the announcement of Mr. Wood that the latter would unite with the republicans and the administration for peace and order at the South, and if that was done he thought peace and order would be soon at hand.

Mr. Maynard (Tenn.) said the committee referred to was started for a special purpose, and he thought the report would demonstrate not only the necessity of its original organization, but the necessity of continuing it. He did not want it to be thought that this proposition of reference was a mere side-winder to continue the committee.

After further discussion, the subject was referred to the Committee on Appropriations by a vote of 100 to 86.

A FIENDISH CRIME AND SWIFT PUNISHMENT.—On Sunday last, on Mulberry creek, Franklin county, Arkansas, two young men, named Joseph Forbish and Wm. Chenoweth, aged 16 and 18 respectively, outraged and afterwards murdered a four-year old daughter of Richard Hill. After committing the deed they threw the body into the creek, where it was found, the neck being broken and the body horribly mutilated. Forbish and Chenoweth were arrested, and confessed their guilt. In their confession they stated that they expected the search of the Hills for the missing child would cause the family to leave their house, which they proposed to plunder. While being taken to jail they attempted to escape, and both were killed by the guard.

IMPORTANT DECISION AGAINST MRS. MYRA CLARK GAINES.—In the second district court in New Orleans yesterday Judge T. Wharton Collins decided the case of Joseph Fuentes et al. vs. Myra Clark Gaines in a lengthy opinion. He declares Mrs. Gaines is not the legitimate child of Daniel Clark nor his universal legatee, and therefore orders that the will of 1813 purporting to be the will of Daniel Clark, probated 1855, be revoked and declared invalid, and that the probate thereof be annulled.

Mrs. Gaines relied mainly upon this will in her claims.

AN AMERICAN RUN OUT OF CUBA.—Mr. Revos, a resident of Flushing, who arrived in New York Saturday from Havana, states that he went to Cuba on business. While there he was arrested by Spanish agents, and was given three days to quit the island on pain of death. He showed papers proving himself an American citizen, and appealed to the American Consul for protection, but the latter advised him to leave as soon as possible. Revos departed by the next steamer without transacting his business.

ASSASSINATION IN THE MINING REGIONS.—Morgan Powell, general foreman of the Lehigh Coal and Navigation Company, [illegible]

TELEGRAMS TO THE STAR.

This Afternoon's Dispatches.

ASSOCIATED PRESS REPORTS.

FROM EUROPE TO-DAY.

Telegraphed Exclusively to The Evening Star.

The Prince of Wales Better.

LONDON, Dec. 5, 11 a. m.—The morning bulletin from Sandringham says the Prince of Wales passed a comfortable night. The progress of his case is satisfactory. The symptoms continue to indicate slow but steady improvement. It is understood that the fever, though severe, has at no time been beyond the control of the medical attendants as to the result has measurably subsided.

Gen Sickles and Bride in London.

LONDON, Dec. 5.—General D. E. Sickles and his bride have arrived here on their way to Liverpool to take the steamer for New York.

French Finances.

PARIS, Dec. 5.—A bill authorizing an increase of the circulation of the Bank of France will be introduced in the Assembly, probably this week.

Aumale and Joinville.

PARIS, Dec. 5.—The rumor is generally current and credited that the Duke d'Aumale and Prince Joinville have officially intimated to President Theirs their intention to occupy the seats in the Chamber of Deputies to which they were elected.

The African Diamond Fields.

LONDON, Dec. 5.—The annexation of the diamond fields of the English dominions of South Africa has been completed, in fulfilment of the recent contract sale. It is understood the tender of arbitration, wherein the governments of Germany, Holland and the United States were to act as umpires, arrived too late to suspend the negotiations. News from the diamond fields confirm the report of splendid successes in finding precious stones, but violent storms have visited the district, causing great damage to property and serious loss of life.

After Sir Charles Dilke.

LONDON, Dec. 5.—Right Honorable Robert Lowe, ex-Chancellor of the Exchequer, delivered a lecture at Halifax last night on primary education. He took occasion to make an appeal in favor of monarchy, in the course of which he warmly defended the Queen from the ungracious charges made against her Majesty by Sir Charles Dilke, and censured, in terms of characteristic bitterness, that gentleman's conduct and public utterances.

The Trial of Mrs. Wharton.

ANNAPOLIS, MD., Dec. 5.—The court for the trial of Mrs. E. G. Wharton met at 10 o'clock, Associate Judges Hammond, of Howard county, and Hayden, of Carroll county, taking their seats on the bench with Chief Judge Miller. Attorney General Syester was also present to assist in the prosecution.

The court-room, as yesterday, was crowded to its full capacity, including several scores of ladies, a dozen or more negroes filling up the back ground. Chief Justice Bartol, of the State court of appeals, occupied a seat adjoining the bar. Officers from the naval school and professors of St. John's College were among the audience, apparently taking deep interest in the proceedings.

The prisoner, with her faithful daughter by her side, both heavily veiled, attended by Mrs. Nelson and daughter, sat immediately in the rear of her counsel.

After the formal opening of the court the clerk proceeded to call the names of the talesmen summoned yesterday, from which four jurymen were to be selected to complete the jury, and before exhausting the list John H. Sellman, a farmer; R. W. Sheckles, a farmer; George W. Watkins, a merchant; and Robert H. Welch, a farmer, were declared competent jurors, accepted and sworn in.

The New York Press on the Message.

NEW YORK, Dec. 5.—The *Times* commends the President's message, but considers Boutwell's report a most disappointing one.

The *Herald* commends the message, saying whether considered as embodying statesmanlike views for the prosperity of the country, or as a campaign document from a Presidential candidate, it is well calculated to strengthen General Grant and weaken his adversaries. The *Herald* does not commend Boutwell's report, and says his suggestions as to the reduction of taxes are of a small, peddling nature.

The *Tribune* strenuously opposes the President's recommendation to buy the telegraphs, but finds more to commend than to condemn in the message.

The *World* criticises the message, viewing it in the light of an electioneering document.

The *Sun* thinks the message bungling and boggling, and no message so little worthy of respect was ever sent out by any former President.

The Kuklux Trials in South Carolina.

MOTION TO QUASH THE INDICTMENTS.

CHARLESTON, S. C., Dec. 4.—In the kuklux trial at Columbia to-day Mr. Stansberry, for the defence, moved to quash the indictment against Crosby and others, upon these among other grounds, that the name of the persons injured are not mentioned in the indictment; that the grand jury had decided as to the law instead of the facts; that the indictment was defective in stating the deprivation of the right to vote as taking place at a future date as the United States' constitution and law does not secure to any citizens the right to vote, and that the state and not the federal courts must redress such personal grievances as those complained of. Mr. Stansberry argued two hours in support of his objections. Corbin, for the government, asked for time and replies to-morrow.

"Boss" Tweed, "Slippery Dick," and the Law's Delay.

NEW YORK, Dec. 4.—Charles O'Conor has gone to Albany to oppose the motion for a reduction of Tweed's bail.

The *Tribune* says the application for a reduction of Connolly's bail to half a million will probably be granted to-morrow by Judge Brady.

Testimony connecting Tweed with the Harlem Court-house swindle is said to have been given before the grand jury. Five thousand six hundred dollars, it is stated, have been traced to his hands, while it is also proved to have been paid him by Senator Gennet.

The President's Indian Policy Endorsed.

NEW YORK, Dec. 5.—At a meeting of the Indian Aid Society last night Aaron A. Powell, who lately made a tour among the Indian reservations, endorsed the Quaker policy, and stated that the removal of the Indians from their reservations to one great reservation in the Indian Territory was in the interest of railroad schemes and speculators.

Snow Bound Trains on the Union Pacific Railroad.

OMAHA, Dec. 4.—The Union Pacific train eastward bound reported yesterday as snow-bound at Elm Creek, could make no further progress. Two engines were sent to its assistance, and have either run off the track or been disabled. The storm has been severe along the whole length of the road. The mercury is 16 degrees below zero this morning.

The Ice Embargo on the Hudson.

NEW YORK, Dec. 5.—A heavy gale prevailed all night, and it is still blowing from the northwest and freezing very hard. The prospects of raising the ice embargo on the Hudson river are very slim. The Albany and other interior papers consider the canal closed for the winter. The three hundred boats frozen in will have to lay embedded in the ice and their cargoes be forwarded by rail.

Success of the Revolutionists in Venezuela.

NEW YORK, Dec. 5.—Venezuelan dates of the 15th of November state that the revolutionists succeeded in taking the town of Zaili, after a battle, in which they captured some four hundred prisoners. Pulgar leads the revolution, which has extended around Maracaibo.

Financial Measures in South Carolina.

CHARLESTON, S. C., Dec. 4.—In the legislature to-day a number of financial bills were introduced, among which were bills for the cancellation of all unsigned state bonds, for obtaining possession of sterling bonds now in New York and for obtaining a full exhibit of all expenditures since September.

Alexis Gone Back to New York.

PHILADELPHIA, Dec. 5.—The Grand Duke delayed his departure from this city and visited the Methodist fair at Horticultural Hall, where an afghan was presented by the ladies. He made various purchases and started for New York by the noon train.

Anxious for a Trial.

NEW YORK, Dec. 5.—The quasi Cuban Generals, Ryan and Jordan, are pressing the government for trial or [illegible]

LOCAL NEWS.

THE NORTHERN MARKET QUESTION.

MEETING OF CITIZENS IN FAVOR OF THE CORCORAN SITE.

Their Proceedings Interrupted by the "Savage" Men.

The Disturbers are Ejected and Organize a Separate Meeting.

"A meeting of citizens, (ladies included,)" was called, by an advertisement in yesterday's STAR, to assemble in Liberty Hall, corner of 7th and L streets, last evening, "to take into consideration the procurement of the Corcoran lot for a Northern market site." The hall was crowded to its utmost capacity, and it was soon apparent that a number of persons hostile to the object for which it was called were present and determined to prevent the transaction of business by improper interference with the proceedings.

There was a large delegation from Swampoodle present, as also residents of the extreme northeastern section of the city. John C. McKelden, W. H. Clagett, Joseph L. Savage, Theodore Sheckells, Maurice Murphy, and other friends of the Savage square and of the Columbia one-horse railroad were on hand, backed by "Reddy" Thomas, "Marse" West, "Citizen" Hatton, "Old Man" Pat Foley, and others who have made themselves notorious in local politics. It was apparent from the first that these men were determined to carry things their own way at all hazards, but, as the following report shows, they were unsuccessful. The disturbing elements were mostly on the south side of the room, while the friends of the Corcoran square were on the north side. Shortly after seven o'clock General John S. Crocker was called to the chair, and the call having been read, he stated that if there were any persons present unfavorable to the object of the meeting, (the selection of the Corcoran square, 7th street, between O and P, for a site for the Northern Market,) they could retire. While Gen. Crocker was speaking, there were cries of derision from the disturbers, and shouts of

"HURRAH FOR SWAMPOODLE!"

"Three cheers for Crow Hill!" interspersed with calls for "Clapp," "Clagett," and others. Finally, something like order was restored, and Mr. W. H. Clagett read another call, stating that he was deeply interested, and had come under that call. He was familiar with the subject from the beginning. Before he could proceed further, there were cries of "order," and shouts of "Dry up,"

"YOU'VE LOTS TO SELL!"

The Chair requested Mr. Clagett to withhold his remarks for the present.

Mr. Clagett pressed forward with a paper in his hand, and sawing the air, he shouted something which could not be heard, amid cries of "Complete the organization!" "How many lots do you own?" Jerry Robinson said he "wanted a decision on a p'int."

COMPLETING THE ORGANIZATION.

The following list of vice presidents and secretaries was submitted by Rev. J. G. Henning:

Vice Presidents—Hon. D. L. Eaton, Hon. Wm. Helmick, Gen. O. O. Howard, Gen. J. S. Crocker, S. R. Bond, A. S. Pratt, Zeph. Jones, Thos. E. Green, Joseph Brooks, Hon. J. C. Harkness, W. H. Gaines, W. H. Chase, T. L. Tullock, Hon. Peter Campbell, Hon. Horatio King, Judge Moore, R. B. Clarke, Fred. Smith and J. E. Thompson.

Secretaries—Arthur Shepherd, A. C. Spalding, S. H. Kauffmann, (not present,) N. Sardo and R. J. Beall.

The hostile party still shouting themselves hoarse, the Chair said: "This meeting was called in the interest of the Corcoran square."

Cries of "Take a vote," &c.

Mr. Maurice Murphy, (who lives near the Savage site.)—"I understand that the whole question is to be discussed."

Voices.—"Read the call," &c.

The Chair.—"I will appoint as tellers Messrs. R. J. Beall and John F. Beitz."

Great confusion here ensued, amid which the question of appointing tellers was put and declared lost.

The question was put on the election of the officers, and it was declared adopted; Paddy Foley, "Marse" West, "Reddy" Thomas, Jerry Robinson and others in the meantime trying to stop the proceedings by cheering for

"SWAMPOODLE" AND "CROW HILL."

General Crocker declared if there was not better order preserved he would call in the police, and Mr. Chase, police commissioner, went amongst the rioters and attempted to expostulate with them. Thomas and West defied him or the police to put them out. Lieutenant Eckloff, with six or seven officers, at this time came up, after which better order was preserved for a while.

A motion was made and adopted to appoint

A COMMITTEE ON RESOLUTIONS,

and the following were appointed:—S. R. Bond, J. C. Parker, W. W. Burdette, R. J. Beall, and G. W. Stickney.

The disorder was here renewed, Marcellus West's voice being heard above the others, and as some of the police went towards him there were loud cries of "Put him out."

General Eaton was introduced, and, after considerable disorder on the part of the Savage men, who sang out "sit down" and "we want Clapp," &c., he succeeded in making himself heard. He said he presumed they would like to hear

THE TRUTH.

He had as much right to speak as others, and if they would hear him he would willingly listen to some one on the other side. [Voices.—"That's the talk;" and at the request of the chair, most of the participants sat down.] He had voted in the Council to refer the selection of the site to the committee on markets, and he thought that that committee had erred in judgement in selecting the Savage square. Now look at it—the district to be benefitted is bounded, perhaps, as follows: I or K street on the south, 11th on the west, Boundary, or the ridge beyond, on the north, and 1st or North Capitol on the east, and about the center of this district you will find the corner of 7th and P streets, and for this reason he believed the Corcoran square was the proper site. [Voices.—"Bound it by Bladensburg," "What will Swampoodie do?"] He did not own an inch of property near the square, and personally it made no difference to him, but he was

LOOKING TO THE FUTURE.

[Voices, "What will Swampoodle do?" and commotion, in which Pat. Foley became quite obstreperous and was remonstrated with by the police.] The ground at the Corcoran square is well drained, lays well, and cellars can be made there; but on the other square the ground was low, and it would be impossible to have dry cellars. Why not put the market where the city is growing. [Another question on behalf of Swampoodle was asked, and amid some confusion Mr. Foley was escorted to the door.] Is the drainage as perfect as the Savage square? [West—"Yes, perfect drainage." A voice—"By two sewers on a dead level," and laughter.] He then referred to the terms, saying that Mr. Corcoran would give the ground to the city. [Mr. Murphy—"What will it cost the people?"] The city would pay one hundred thousand dollars and the interest, but it would go to the Art Gallery, which had already cost Mr. C. $300,000, which would benefit the whole people. The people should be proud of such a benefaction. [A voice—"How much did he give to suppress the rebellion?" Reddy Thomas—"Was it like the Smithsonian, for the benefit of the rich?"] Mr. Eaton answered by saying it mattered not how Mr. Corcoran stood politically, this money would not go to his family, but would be used for the public good, and that as soon as the gallery was endowed it would be opened. He had nothing to say against the Savage square except that it was not so desirable as the other. [Voices—"Why not?" &c.] The truth must be heard. If any pledge had been given in regard to this matter it was given in September last to Mr. Corcoran, and he had made arrangements to deed the ground then. [Mr. Clagett asked what authority he had for the statement. A voice—"Who wants authority for a gift?"] In the Corcoran square there were 106,000 feet, for which $100,000 is asked, and in the other square about the same quantity, for which $130,000 is asked. The Corcoran square is assessed at $45,000, and the Savage at $[illegible].

Mr. Burgess asked to correct the statement, as the books now show Savage square $[illegible], and the other $[illegible].

Mr. Eaton explained that his figures were those of the old assessment. The value of the Corcoran square was less than $1 per foot and that in a neighborhood where ground has been selling at from 75 cents to $1.25 [A voice—To $1.50] while in the neighborhood of the Savage square corner lots have sold within a year at 60 cents.

The disorder here became very great, and the police led several to the door.

Mr. Bond, from the committee on [illegible]

an inside pocket made in his vests in which to carry money or valuable papers. He instructed my brother and myself to do the same."

He found no note. So he checked back with Professor Aikin. Professor Aikin had summoned Professor F. T. Miles, professor of anatomy and clinical professor of nervous diseases at the University of Maryland, Dr. Samuel Chew, professor of materia medica at the University of Maryland, and Dr. Williams, the attending physician for the General in his final hours. They gathered at Weaver's Funeral Home. In Dr. Chew's words, they examined "the abdominal viscera, liver,

On the left, in column five, is an account of the opening day of the Wharton trial. The first four jurors picked were three farmers and a merchant.

spleen, and kidneys. Then we examined the alimentary canal." They found a whitish substance. They sent it off for chemical analysis. It turned out to be tartar emetic.

Tartar emetic is a poison. The doctors agreed that the General had not died a natural death. But they also agreed that there wasn't enough tartar emetic in the stomach to kill. However, as Professor Miles pointed out, it would not be the poison in the stomach that would kill— it would be the poison absorbed in the tissues of the liver and the kidneys. But no examination was made of the tissues of the liver and the kidneys.

At any rate it was all decidedly suspicious since Mrs. Wharton had sent Mrs. Chubb to the drugstore for some tartar emetic just a day or two before the General died.

Word was sent to the Baltimore police. Deputy Marshal Jacob Frey came to call on July 7. He asked Mrs. Wharton what, if anything, she thought had happened to General Ketchum. Mrs. Wharton said the poor man had come for a visit and gotten dreadfully sick.

Marshal Frey asked if there was any tartar emetic around the house and she said there was, she used it herself. He asked what for, and she lowered her glance and said as a cosmetic for her chest.

He asked how many servants she had and indicated he'd like to talk to them. She named them off and said that she was planning to leave for Europe the next day, but she certainly wouldn't want to do that if any of her servants were under suspicion.

He told her he thought she probably had better not leave until the whole matter was cleared up.

She said he had been very kind to drop in and keep her informed and she would like to make him a little present of money. He said he couldn't take presents. She said she'd like to give him one anyway.

"I told her we would talk that over after the case was cleared up. I called again on Saturday . . . about 10 AM. Her daughter came to the door and told me her mother was not at home but wished to see me. I named the hour in the afternoon at which I would meet her and at that hour met her . . . She again insisted upon my taking some money and that time she spread the note out and it was $20. She told me to take it and buy myself a present."

Once more he declined. On Monday he returned and announced that "circumstances had come to our knowledge which made it necessary for us to place a guard over her house to prevent any person connected with her house leaving it."

On July 10 Marshal Frey made his final call, with one warrant charging Mrs. Wharton with "feloniously, willfully, and of her malice aforethought, poisoning, killing, and murdering General Ketchum," and a second charging her with attempting to do the same to Eugene Van Ness.

Mrs. Wharton went to jail and her daughter was allowed to share her room. They fixed it up with curtains and pictures. They spent the summer and fall there. On December 3 Mrs. Wharton was transported to Annapolis for trial, her lawyer having asked for a change of venue. Mother and daughter, dressed in mourning and wearing heavy veils, went by hack to the steamer *Sam'l J. Pentz.* On

53

The Evening Star.

VOL. 38—N°. 5,855. WASHINGTON, D. C., THURSDAY, DECEMBER 21, 1871. TWO CENTS.

EVENING STAR.

Washington News and Gossip.

INTERNAL REVENUE.—The receipts from this source to-day were $906,845.

INTERNAL REVENUE OFFICERS NOMINATED. Wm. S. Davis has been nominated for assessor of Mississippi; John A. Place for assessor of the twenty-second New York district, and Clark Center for collector at the sixth ohio district.

POSTAL MATTERS.—The Postal Committee of the House will report bill directing the Postmaster General to issue cards on stamp paper, about the size of an ordinary envelope, one side for the address and the other for written or printed matter, at one cent postage.

NOMINATIONS.—The President sent the following nominations to the Senate to-day: John A. Place, assessor internal revenue 2d district, New York.

FORTY-SECOND CONGRESS.

This Afternoon's Proceedings.

THURSDAY, December 21.

SENATE.—The Secretary laid before the Senate a message from the Vice President that he would be absent from the Senate chamber to-day.

the voyage to Annapolis, Mrs. Wharton expressed delight at the view and scenery of the bay and discussed the day's news, making no reference whatsoever to the occasion of her journey.

The steamer docked at 9 AM and she was received by her associate counsel, Alexander B. Hagner, Esq., Dr. Stewart, an old friend, and some 50 or 60 curious bystanders. She "appeared considerably annoyed by the attention she attracted," but quietly got into a waiting carriage and left for the Anne Arundel County jail.

The trial began December 4; the courtroom was crowded with a large number of ladies in attendance as well as the most prominent male citizens of Annapolis.

Mrs. Wharton entered on the arm of J. Crawford Neilson, a friend, and shortly thereafter took her place in the prisoner's box, having first removed her veil. Her daughter, veiled still, took a seat a foot away. The mother seemed calm and resigned, even when some citizens stood upon the benches to get a better view.

It took two days to pick a jury and the State then made its opening statement, charging her with murder. Mrs. Chubb was called and she told of the fatal trip to Baltimore. The press noticed that Mrs. Chubb's testimony had not been as telling against Mrs. Wharton as anticipated.

And then the trial settled down to an interminable display of legal and scientific arguments.

By December 7 reporters were already observing that the trial was "fully as tedious as was anticipated." Each side summoned dozens of doctors and chemists. Forensic medicine was still in its infancy. The possibility of proving by chemical tests that a person had been poisoned had just occurred to the courts a relatively few years before.

The experts did establish a few things. The General had been found bung full of tartar emetic.

The trial neared its end on January 22, 40 days after it had begun. The courtroom was as crowded as ever, a trainload of the Washington *haute monde* having arrived especially for the occasion. Men were observed clinging to the tops of the doors as they swung open and shut. Mrs. Wharton's daughter had succumbed to the strain and stayed away. Among those present, however, were Commodore Decatur, the Honorable John Thompson Mason, Secretary of State, and a large number of Army and Navy officers.

The lawyers made their final arguments.

The defense argued, in effect, that since the symptoms of poisoning displayed by General Ketchum were approximately also the symptoms of cerebrospinal meningitis, he had, obviously, died of spinal meningitis.

The science of the time was not quite adequate to prove a cause-and-effect relationship between the tartar emetic in the tummy and the painful death of General Ketchum.

It was easy, then as now, to find expert witnesses on either side of the question. But the main force at work at the trial was not the new one of forensic medicine but the sacred American, nineteenth-century tradition that there were only two kinds of ladies, virtuous ladies and whore-ladies. The former did not murder anybody.

The latter probably didn't either, but at least they conceivably might.

Mrs. Wharton was obviously not a whore-lady; she was the personification of the upper-class matron of the Gilded Age. One could as easily believe her a murderer as believe Henry Ward Beecher an adulterer.

The all-male jury returned a gallant verdict: not guilty.

Mrs. Wharton returned to her proper place in the social world of Washington and Baltimore. As far as the old records show, there were no further sudden, mysterious deaths on her premises.

Still one wonders. Did she continue to have weekend house parties? If she did, were there unusual numbers of regrets from those invited? And did those who came develop a habit of passing up the lemonade or, perhaps, switching drinks with the hostess when she wasn't looking.

The Shoot Out At Generation Gap

"If I can succeed . . . I have done something for the tens of thousands of other boys . . . who must tread the same road in blind childhood. . . ." Clarence Darrow pleading for the lives of Leopold and Loeb.

IN MOST RESPECTS MICHAEL BURTlett and Allen Johnson had little in common with Nathan Leopold and Dickie Loeb. The thrill killers of 1924 were the overindulged sons of millionaires and strikingly homosexual. They were also students of conspicuous achievement—Loeb was the youngest graduate of the University of Michigan and Leopold was a university lecturer in ornithology at age 18.

By contrast, Burtlett and Johnson lived standard lives among middle-class suburban houses, curving streets, and mass-designed shopping centers of the early 1960's. Their parents were not overindulgent (indeed Mike's were old-fashioned disciplinarians), their school grades were undistinguished, and, as was said of the man who fell in love with a lady horse, there was nothing queer about Mike or Allen.

Still there was a link across the years; they were two of Darrow's ten thousand, the emotional descendants of the original alienated kids. Mike and Allen grew up in the era of the mindless, motiveless murder. They would kill in that peculiarly 20th-century fashion. For half a century, from Leopold and Loeb to Charlie Manson, young Americans shot and stabbed the innocent, almost casually. Mike's stepfather, James Hoover, would speak for scores of bewildered victims when, staggering from his living room, he cried out, "What have I done?"

To understand (or to attempt to understand) it is necessary to know the way it was in the early sixties. Mike Burtlett and Allen Johnson were growing up in a ghetto—in a closed community, surrounded by look-alike young people who spoke the same inarticulate language, had the same rock star heroes, and who were ignoring, suspicious, and fearful of the world outside. They were teenagers in the suburbs.

The suburbs had begun with the automobile; people no longer needed to live

57

next to their places of occupation so they drove to the outskirts of town and divided into homogeneous subdivisions. Mike Burtlett reached the dangerous age of puberty in the outskirts of Washington, D.C. He and his neighbors lived in small, neat houses on quarter-acre lots and met in drive-ins and shopping centers. There wasn't much for the young to do out there, but whatever it was, they needed a car to do it.

They lived in a dream world, changing into a nightmare—Kennedy was in Camelot a few miles away and suburban households were almost suddenly on the edge of affluence. Mike's parents, James and Susan Hoover, were teachers at the high school where Mike was a pupil. To these Depression survivors, their combined salaries seemed almost indecent. They could afford small, even medium-sized luxuries, but they were cautious—having a little extra was no reason to rush out and spend it. Waste not, want not. Their lives were as neatly arranged as their one-story brick rambler. They had lived day in, day out in a world of properly behaved teenagers—he taught mechanical drawing, she biology. He was coach of the tennis team, she was the class advisor. They were serious and industrious, and they spent their lives among the young, confident that they understood them.

They did not understand Mike. Mike was 16, a good long-distance runner, tall for his age and thin. He blushed easily. His parents were demanding—a neighbor would later recall that Mike always had his nose in a book. It was not his choice. His parents intended that he should go to medical school. They pushed. Mike resented.

In the early sixties many young men and women were resenting; a creeping estrangement, soon to be known as the Generation Gap, was splitting the three-bedroom homes of the great middle class. It was fashionable to philosophize about the proper place for adolescents. The *Washington Daily News* excerpted *Teen Age Tyranny,* a pretentious book by Fred and Grace Hechinger. It told parents to stop "abdicating the rights and privileges of adults for the convenience of the immature."

Washington School Superintendent Carl

Teenage suburban social life depended, rain or shine, on the automobile and the shopping center.

F. Hansen was locked in a debate with the School Board on the handling of fractious pupils. He recommended the use of "nothing heavier than the open hand, a foot-long ruler, or a light-weight paddle."

The Hechingers and the Superintendent had missed some major factors. They and all the other grownups were outnumbered. There had been a teenage population explosion—the babies of the post World War II were now old enough to drive cars. The world had changed—a suburban wall was wrapped around the young and they had acquired the new, basic, homogeneous right of affluence—spending money, a car, days by the side of the pool. Marshall McLuhan would announce that the TV medium was the message, that egocentric individualism and linear thought were out. (At first Mr. McLuhan saw the change as an improvement but later he would change his mind.) Isolation, alienation, ennui, loss of identity, and distrust of authority were in.

Mike's high school principal would

In the summer he met Allen Johnson at a dance. Allen was 19, Mike was 16. They became friends. Mike told Allen of his troubles at home. Mike set off a fire-extinguisher on the last day of school. His stepfather restricted him to the house and yard.

Allen called and asked him out, and was told he was confined. Mike would say later that Allen then advised him that Mr. Hoover, as a stepfather, had no right to restrict him and that Mike should kill him.

Mike got off restriction and he and Allen went into Washington. This time, Mike would say, Allen offered an elaborate plan: Mike should put out the stove's pilot light and go out for the evening. The gas would kill his parents in their sleep. Mike should return late, go to bed, and find them dead in the morning. It was, of course, a harebrained scheme—the tiny bit of gas that would escape from a pilot would have little effect on those sleeping in another room. The assumption seemed to be that it would kill the parents, but not affect Mike at all.

The next day—according to Mike—a new plan was born: Mike would stab his stepfather. Allen would shoot Mrs. Hoover. The dead parents would be stashed in the trunk of the family car and driven 50 miles away and dumped in the woods. A friend of Allen's would pose as Mike's parents and order train tickets by phone. When people asked where his parents were, Mike would say they were on a trip.

Was Mike serious? Could a fairly bright young man believe that he could get away with such a mindless plan?

Yes indeed, he was and he could.

Mike went to Allen's house on Sunday. He said he was going to buy an ice pick.

On August 3, 1960, Allen came to Mike's house. Mrs. Hoover said she was going out, and that Allen could not visit while she was gone. Allen left. She left. Allen came back. Mike said he was going to get the ice pick that very day. At 10 AM Allen phoned Ann, his girl. He told her that Mike had just killed his parents. Then he said he was kidding. Ann said "Mike is just dumb enough." Allen went home and then to Ann's house on Pineywood Lane. He told her that Mike was really going to do it at 3 PM and that he,

later say that Mr. Hoover, Mike's stepfather, had "won the friendship of just about all the youngsters he came in contact with."

But friendship between teacher and pupils can be no more than a cordial exchange of hellos in the halls.

Mr. Hoover was demanding. Mike could not avoid his demands. A very bright boy might have met them and have had time for lighter things, but Mike was not that bright. They became grim opponents, engaged in constant struggle, which Mike never won.

At Easter in 1960 Mr. Hoover announced his vacation plan. Mike would study. They would then take a holiday trip to West Virginia.

Mike composed a plan of his own.

Driving the family's four-year-old Chevy back, he would deliberately wreck it, killing his father. Before he did, he saw the flaw. He could not control the smash-up—he might be killed and his stepfather might escape. He brooded on.

He could put Drano in his father's whiskey. He did, or at any rate he later told his friends he did, but his stepfather merely got sick.

Mike, would then come and pick him up. Allen and Ann went swimming. Allen phoned Mike to see if he'd killed them yet. He hadn't, it was too risky in the daylight. He'd do it that night. Mike's stepfather drove Mike to a hardware store and sent him in to buy paint. Mike bought an ice pick too. Allen went home from the pool. Ann went to the home of Mrs. Peter F. Brown to set her hair. She told Mrs. Brown that a boy she knew named Mike Burtlett said he was going to kill his parents that night and then drive to Maryland and dump their bodies in the Patuxent.

"Did you ever hear anything so ridiculous?" Ann asked. "You know a person wouldn't do anything to their parents like that."

Mrs. Brown was alarmed. She and Ann started searching the phone books. They looked for Burtlett and found none. They called the operator. She had no Burtletts on her lists. They looked again and grew more upset.

Allen arrived home at 5:30 PM. Mike came over at 7:45. He told Allen he'd bought the ice pick. Mike would later testify that Allen told him that he shouldn't use it—that he shouldn't kill an animal like that, that it would be better to use a gun. Mike said he had a .22 rifle but no bullets. They went to a friend's house and said that Allen was going hunting and needed bullets. The friend gave them seven or eight. They arrived at Mike's house shortly after 8 PM.

They went to the front of the house and set off firecrackers; Mike said later it was so the neighbors wouldn't suspect anything when they heard the rifle.

They went to Mike's room. Mike said the plan was for Allen to kneel behind Mike's bed with the rifle pointed. Mrs. Hoover was ironing in the living room. Mr. Hoover was snoozing in a chair. Mike would sit behind Mr. Hoover. When he coughed Allen was to shoot Mrs. Hoover while he stabbed his stepfather. Mike said he lost his nerve. Allen came into the living room and asked Mrs. Hoover if he could borrow the rifle. She said yes. Allen sat down with it in his lap and watched TV. Mike sat behind his stepfather. Firecrackers exploded outside. Mrs. Hoover went out to see who was making the

Because he was restricted from using the family's '56 Chevy, Mike Burtlett decided to kill his stepfather.

racket. Mike stabbed his stepfather in the chest and when he rose from the chair he stabbed him again and again.

Allen had gone through the kitchen and into a small utility room on the way to the back door. Mike came into the kitchen and called to his mother. "Come quickly, Daddy's real sick." His stepfather staggered in after him, covered with blood, saying "what have I done?"

Ann and Mrs. Brown were still trying frantically to find Mike's parents. They had called Allen's house but Allen wasn't there. Ann remembered that Mike's parents were teachers. Mrs. Brown knew the principal. She called him. He said he thought she was upset over nothing. "I know that boy well. He's one of the nicest boys we have and his parents are very nice. You don't have a thing to worry about." But he gave her the parents name —Mr. and Mrs. James Hoover—and their phone number. She called the number. The line was busy. She called the police.

As Mr. Hoover staggered toward Allen, the .22 in Allen's hand went off. The bullet hit Mr. Hoover's right thumb and then, deflected, lodged in his stomach, a couple of inches above his navel. Mrs. Hoover came in from the yard. Mike didn't notice. Her husband was covered with blood and she tried to help him toward the bathroom. Mike stabbed her again and again. The handle came off the ice pick. The steel point was buried in her back, four inches deep. The boys went out the back door.

Mrs. Brown said to Ann, "I bet it has just happened." She asked the police if there had been a murder. The desk man turned her over to a lieutenant. She asked if he'd heard anything about a Mr. Hoover. He asked her what she knew. She told him. "You're just a few minutes too late," he said. Ann screamed and screamed.

Mike and Allen ran across the yard to the Hoover car. Mike got behind the wheel. They drove to a nearby shopping center. Mike called home to see if his parents were dead. The line was busy. Mike said he was leaving. Allen said he wasn't, he hadn't done anything wrong, and he was going home. Mike left, driving north. Allen asked Frances, a friend of Mike's, to drive him to the Big Pin Bowling Alley. They passed Mike Burtlett's house and the lawn was filled with cops. Allen ducked below the dashboard. At the bowling alley, he tried to call Ann but she wasn't home. He went home. His parents and Police Sergeant Harry Kelly were waiting. It was only a few minutes after 9 PM. He looked at his parents and Kelly and said, "I've just seen a horrible tragedy."

Officer Kelly asked what happened. Allen's parents said he shouldn't talk until he had a lawyer. Mr. Johnson tried to get one by phone. Kelly took Allen into the bedroom. Mr. and Mrs. Johnson protested. Kelly said that if they didn't leave him alone he was going to put them under arrest. Kelly asked Allen to go outside. Allen said he would if Kelly promised not to arrest him. They got in the police car and drove to the bowling alley. Two detectives met them there and took Allen to headquarters.

The next morning a policeman in Bucks County, Pennsylvania, found Mike sleeping in the family Chevy.

A lot of things were over now, forever, including the friendship of Mike and Allen.

Mike's case would swiftly be resolved. The Juvenile Court waived jurisdiction. At the hearing his grandmother embraced him and broke into tears. He said he was sorry. His mother had been released from the hospital a week earlier. She sat behind him in the courtroom, crying quietly. His lawyer said Mike had already been "well tried in the newspapers." Mike told police that he expected to be sent to a detention home and released in a few years.

His mother said, "I want to help him,

do all I can for him. I feel so utterly helpless, so at a loss for any explanation. I have been hurt deeply."

She looked back, not in anger but in bewilderment.

She was learning of resentments she'd never suspected—of fury engendered by a refusal to let a teenage boy use a car. She was trying, but baffled. Should her husband have simply let Mike drive when and where he wished?

"An automobile is not something to be played with. James and I both felt that a car is not a toy, that a child ought not to have a car to ride around aimlessly."

In Washington the Deputy Police Chief, head of the Youth Division, said a "get-tough" policing on teenagers was needed.

Mike said he was sorry. He said that his mother would be taken care of by his late stepfather's insurance.

The high-school principal gave his considered views on teenage compulsions: "They can't seem to stand being denied the auto. That will make them meaner and uglier than anything I know. Parents are almost helpless. They either have to let the boys have the car or they have an attitude to fight. They say money is the root of all evil. I say cars are the root of all evil around the high school."

Allen Johnson went before the judge and said that the gun had gone off accidentally—that he had been trying to open the jammed back door when it did.

Mike Burtlett pleaded guilty. He was tried, to determine the weight of evidence against him. He was sentenced to 48 years.

Allen's trial was set. Mike would be the principal witness against him.

Allen and his brother testified that Mike had been talking about killing his stepfather for a long time. Allen said he'd thought Mike was kidding.

Mike took the stand and said he'd gotten the idea for the killing from Allen. He admitted he'd considered killing his stepfather by auto crash or poison in the spring, but that the idea had "left my head" until Allen suggested it again.

In Mike's version of the final, fatal ten minutes, Allen had told him, "Now is the time."

Allen's version was radically different. 61

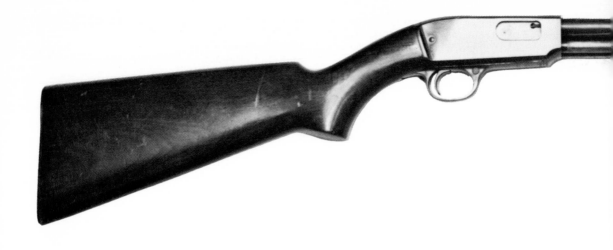

He'd been sitting, rifle on lap, watching TV. Mike's mother went out to the yard to see who was exploding firecrackers. He started to leave too. As he passed Mike and his sleeping stepfather, he said he was going to the bowling alley to see Ann. When he got to the kitchen, he looked back to see if Mike was coming with him and saw Mike "acting like a cat," stabbing his stepfather. He tried to get out the back door but the door was stuck on a scatter rug. He forced it with his shoulder while holding the gun at knee level. The rifle, jarred, went off and the bullet hit Mr. Hoover.

The Commonwealth Attorney asked the jury to give Allen life.

The jury went out for four hours and twenty minutes, returned, and said it couldn't agree.

The judge declared a mistrial. Allen's mother collapsed in the arms of a friend. Allen's bond was reduced to $10,000.

He was tried again a few months later.

This time the Commonwealth Attorney reminded the jury that Mike Burtlett had been convicted of murder in the first degree and asked, "Are you going to let Mike bear the whole burden?"

Allen waited in the courthouse corridor

with his family and four teenage girl friends, cheerful and relaxed.

The jury was out six hours. It returned and the court clerk read the verdict—guilty.

Allen stared. The jury gave Allen forty years.

The judge said, "Sergeant I remand this boy to your custody."

Allen banged his fist on the railing, then walked away, flinging open the door. The jailer hurried after. Allen's mother, who'd been waiting in the next courtroom, fell to the floor, saying "Oh my God, oh my God."

Allen's capable attorney believed the severe sentence reflected a widespread sentiment. Which boy had been the prime mover? Mike had begun the deadly sequence but Mike had testified that he had been persuaded by Allen. Allen's lawyer would say later that the "sympathy in the town was with Mike."

Allen's lawyer appealed. His appeal, crisp and lucid, covered, as appeals do, a variety of points. But the key one was on the prosecutor's harsh suggestion to the jury; Mike had gotten 48 years, shouldn't Allen get as much? The Appeals Court agreed that the prosecutor's suggestion

Mike's parents had a .22 rifle, but Mike and Allen had to borrow the bullets from a friend.

had been too strong. It ordered a new trial. Allen got it. This time his sentence was five years.

Looking back it seems a proper reduction.

Allen said he thought Mike was kidding.

The words of the young are seldom precise, but it does seem probable that when Allen and Mike talked of killing it was unreal, like violence on TV. Death on TV has no unpleasant aftermath, even when it is rerun in the summer. In real life violent death is horrible. Mike's stepfather did not cough politely, turn gracefully, and fall. He staggered grotesquely across his suburban living room, blood spurting from his wounds, gasping out the teacher's last pitiful question to the class. "What have I done?"

Allen would insist that the gun went off on its own while he banged his shoulder against the door in panic, trying to get out. It is possible.

Mike's behavior is harder to fathom. He had told his plans, all too freely, to his friends.

He had recounted them again in court:

". . . My father came in to take a shower. I was going to hit him over the top of the head with a fireplace poker but I lost my nerve then. I then planned to stab him with the ice pick . . . but I also lost my nerve here too . . ."

People hadn't really believed.

His older brother would try to decipher Mike's hate.

"Our parents weren't strict. Of course it depends on what you mean by strict, but Mike had a driver's license at 16 for example. I didn't have one until I was a senior in high school. I don't think that Mike felt under any great pressure to get good grades just because the folks were teachers. I would have said we were a close family. We used to play golf together."

Mike and Allen are both out of prison now.

And Mr. Hoover is long dead.

He died without being able to understand, even a little, what he'd done to deserve such an end.

63

Is Laughing Anne A Husband Killer?

IN THE SPRING OF 1935 A GOOD many middle Americans were tipsy. Prohibition was gone but its drinking habits lingered on.

The newly legal boozing centers were called "taverns," an improvement on the evil saloon. Taverns were everywhere, speakeasies with the shades up, pool halls with the lights on, or picturesque new efforts to recapture the village good fellowship of an imaginary golden age.

Frank Abbo's Lincoln Way Tavern in Rockville was, loosely speaking, respectable. It had checkered table cloths and no sawdust on the floor. The customers were solid citizens, each a vertebra from the backbone of the community. Still it was possible to rent a room at the Tavern just for the afternoon and the bartender, John "Googy" Carnell, was a popeyed man with a past—he'd been a cop once but he'd become, by his own modest account, a "petty racketeer."

Francis "Slom" Lyddane, a mild, stocky employee of the State of Maryland, came often to lunch. His wife, Anne, private secretary to the president of the Farmers Bank and Trust Company,

popped in every day, though seldom with Slom.

Arthur Beall was the possessor of one of Maryland's finest old names, pronounced "Bell," and the proprietor of the prosperous garage in Darnestown. He was also the sparkplug of the Gaithersburg baseball team.

Mrs. Beall—Josephine—may have dropped in too, though certainly not often. In the opinion of even her dearest friends, Josephine was not the life of the party. Anne was. She was blond and beautiful. Slim and sort of aristocratic. She had tapered fingers and a finely modeled, slightly longish nose. She had a tinkling laugh—clear as a bell. She wore clothes well. She liked a drink and she liked, in her own words, "to run around." She was given to moments of impatience. But she was always a lady. Well, almost always.

Back in 1932 there had been rumors that she was running around with Arthur Beall. When Arthur came trotting in from the ballfield, triumphant, Anne was always on hand to give him a squeeze. In the thirties that wasn't exactly a sin. Booze was as much of a national pastime as base-

The Lyddanes, the woman charged and the alleged victim, remained close and calm throughout the trial.

ball, and there was a certain amount of sipping going on in the bleachers. And after a nip a lady sometimes felt expansive. Still there was talk and that June it took on an edge.

Josephine Beall was approximately nine months pregnant and nervous. One evening she looked out the window and saw a car parked in the driveway. She went out and found Arthur and Anne sitting in it. Arthur jumped out of Anne's car as if he were going after a high fly, grabbed Josephine, and shouted, "Don't make a fuss." Anne started the motor and backed up, right into a ditch. It took her a while to get out and as she drove off Josephine, still held by Arthur, heard her laugh, loud and clear. Tinkle, tinkle. Josephine had her baby the very next day, and then she filed for a divorce naming Anne as corespondent. There was hell to pay at the bank. Banks may foreclose mortgages on old ladies living alone in family homesteads, but they can't stand unbalanced sexual bookkeeping.

The bank president called Anne in and told her that if the divorce caused a scandal she would have to leave. Anne laughed. She told him there was no danger; she was discreet. She was, too. When she wanted to get hold of Arthur she had her pal, Townsend Howes, the editor of the *Montgomery County Sun,* call on the phone. If Josephine answered he said to tell Arthur that the Gaithersburg Athletic Association was having a meeting.

Calm returned to Darnestown. Mr. and Mrs. Beall negotiated, and Arthur turned over $12,000 worth of property to Josephine. Josephine withdrew her suit.

Slom Lyddane, one of the world's mildest tempered men, had stopped sleeping with his wife, Anne, during the period when "Take Me Out To The Ball Game" was her theme, but after the Bealls made up he and Anne made up too.

Life went on and Anne became immersed in the small but fascinating routines that make the years slip by. When the State of Maryland was about to fire Slom from his job at the Montgomery County Liquor Dispensary, Anne went to Annapolis and lobbied successfully with the state legislature. She and Slom went out four or five times a week, but her work at the bank did not suffer. Indeed, as a token of appreciation, the bank bought her one of the new noiseless typewriters. She still dropped in at the Tavern everyday, and on at least one or two afternoons she and Arthur slipped into a Tavern bedroom. Going out to parties four or five nights a week can be exhausting and she probably needed a nap. Slom grew more contented every day. Anne insured his life for $10,000. Arthur had added a few inches around the middle, but he was still hot stuff on the ballfield.

All seemed well but Anne was restless.

The nature of her restlessness was never fully explained—at least not by Anne.

Googy, the bartender, later would recall

one particular afternoon when she came by and asked him casually if he could arrange to have someone shoot Slom. Also Mrs. Beall. Googy, who had some disreputable friends, went to the District and looked up Harry "Rags" Thomas. Rags and Googy had met in Lorton when Rags was doing time for bootlegging.

Rags came to Rockville, and he and Anne met in a room at the Tavern.

Anne gave him a few bills. Rags left. Anne came back to the bar. Googy said later that she took a seat and announced, "We've got Slom all tied up." Actually, Slom was still loose as a goose. Time went by. No word from Rags. Googy brought in a new killer named John Martin Boland. Mr. Boland, pudgy and respectable looking, really seemed more like a bookkeeper. Like a bookkeeper, he was precise about money. He wanted $200 in tens and twenties. Anne went home to Slom and told

him that some fellows were planning to kidnap him and that she needed $200 to buy them off. Slom gave her the dough. Boland then enlisted the help of one Edwin J. Davis, another Lorton alumnus. There were further conferences with Anne. Googy said the boys now wanted something more than the money; they wanted the key to the bank.

Winter became spring.

Slom still wasn't tied up.

Someone wrote a letter to Googy. Anne always insisted that it wasn't she, but it was written on her new, noiseless typewriter. It said:

"Googy,

"I most certainly do not intend to let you or that other party get away with this last transaction. That other so-called friend of yours did me dirty and you know it. Now if you and this other friend of yours are trying to do the same thing you are going to be badly mistaken as I am not going to let you get away with it. I mean this and unless I hear from him by tomorrow night I am going to start checking on him and before I do this naturally, of course, I will have to get you to give us the lead-way. I am as much implicated if not more so than either of you but I don't care what happens to me. If you do not go through with this deal, I mean every word of this and will give until tomorrow night to get in touch with me. I have plenty of friends that will help me as I have done plenty of favors for some of them. It will be to your friend's advantage to get in touch with me and either go through with the deal or return my money. I can make it plenty tough for all of us and I don't give a damn what happens to me if the deal doesn't go through. I mean this— either get in touch with that friend and give me my money or get him to get in touch with me."

Googy was a feckless fellow. He put the note in his pocket and forgot about it. Then one fateful Friday night he was strolling around downtown Washington drunk. It started to rain, a cold March rain, and Googy had sense enough to get out of it. He did not, however, have any sense left over. He chose as a refuge the Eighth Police Precinct. The cops booked him automatically for being drunk. While searching him they found the note. My 67 my. The precinct men called in the best minds of the entire Metropolitan Police. They questioned Googy for seven-and-a-half hours. Googy found the whole experience trying. He was particularly unhappy because the place was so cold. In the end he confessed all and agreed to go out to Rockville just to warm up. The Montgomery County authorities turned the matter over to the Grand Jury and once more Googy told all.

The Grand Jury indicted everyone on a splendid variety of charges.

Anne denied everything.

Well, almost everything.

Josephine Beall got mad all over again.

Arthur went into a slump.

Slom smiled vaguely and had his picture taken for the newspapers, beaming at his wife over the morning coffee cups.

The bank announced that it had changed its locks. It said it had done it some time earlier when it heard rumors that a robbery was planned.

The Washington *Herald,* under the feverish direction of Cissy Patterson, assigned a dashing young reporter named Pat Frank to investigate the case from all angles. Pat, who would eventually write the book, *Mr. Adam,* viewed life as a daily potential for disaster, chicanery, and headlines.

Slom and Anne attended Sunday mass at St. Patrick's, then went riding in Rock Creek Park. Googy, who was scheduled to be the prize prosecution witness, was reported missing. He turned up at the last minute and the trial began. Three judges were sitting—Chief Judge Hammond Urner and Associate Judges Arthur Willard and Charles W. Woodward.

Everything had a slightly bizarre air.

In retrospect, it is difficult to decide who was tipsy when. State's Attorney James Pugh opened with a slashing attack, implying that Anne was a wicked woman. Anne's attorney, State Senator Stedman Prescott, promptly challenged Pugh to a duel on the courthouse lawn. The courtroom cheered. Rockville Mayor Douglas M. Bland huffed and puffed and asked the judges to slap both attorneys under peace bonds. The judges threatened to clear the court but ignored the lawn. Pugh and Prescott, after due consideration, ignored it too. Anne sat demurely in a

black silk dress with a deep white collar. She looked like a pretty Puritan. Senator Prescott regained his composure sufficiently to demand that Anne be tried separately. The judges thought that over and said yes.

Poor pudgy Jack Boland went on trial alone.

Googy had been granted immunity. He talked endlessly and in rich detail. He was afflicted either with imagination or total

Mrs. Lyddane had a capable attorney named Stedman Prescott, an odd story, and a buoyant nature. Here, leaving the courthouse, from left to right, are Francis "Slom" Lyddane, Anne Lyddane, Stedman Prescott, and Kenneth Lyddane, who was also a member of Mrs. Lyddane's legal staff.

recall. As he pictured it, Anne Lyddane was not the type of casual employer who hires a workman and then leaves him to his task.

In Googy's version she was in there day after day full of helpful suggestions. They might, for example, arrange to hold up Slom on payday and then polish him off so it would look like the unfortunate results of a routine robbery. Googy said she suggested March 25 as the payday she had in mind.

Googy, despite his immunity, also tried to persuade the judges and the rest of the folks listening in that he had never intended to arrange any real killing, no matter what he'd told the boys at the Eighth Precinct. He had, he said, been "rum dumb" when he unfolded the plot, and, furthermore, the Eighth Precinct had been as cold as ice that damp March night. "I was suffering unbearable tortures," he said.

After he had arranged for Anne to meet Rags Thomas and Jack Boland, however, he said he began to realize that Anne was a demanding woman. "I told Jack if you fool around with that woman, you will wind up in the electric chair."

Jack Boland took the stand finally in his own behalf but he was laboring under obvious difficulties. In some states, New York for example, no one can be convicted on the unsupported testimony of a supposed accomplice. Maryland has always enjoyed a more rudimentary system of justice than that. Furthermore, Jack, or "Bobo" as he was sometimes known, was not a prepossessing character. He had chosen to be tried by a panel of judges rather than by a jury on the theory that a jury would have difficulty believing anything he said. A sound point, but one that overlooks the fact that judges are human too. Boland, who had run a floating dice game in happier days, pronounced "first" as "foist" and implied that any incriminating things he might have said earlier about his activities had been the result of the thoid degree, and that in truth his intentions in the Lyddane case had been toward nothing more evil than accepting money under false pretenses. As Googy had more or less admitted, he was no killer.

The judges heard Boland out and then retired to their chambers to think the 69

Arthur W. Beall was Anne's dear friend.

gloves. He wore a sheepish grin. Getting a jury turned out to be difficult. State Senator Prescott fought hard to keep married ladies who were past their first youth out of the jury box. With one thing and another, the court soon ran out of prospective jurors. The judges sent out the county police five different times to round up possible jurors from the streets of Rockville. As word got around, the courthouse neighborhood was deserted by everyone over 21. A jury was finally collected, and it was one tailored to Senator Prescott's design—twelve middle-class, middle-aged men. Anne Lyddane smiled demurely. The State began to produce its evidence once more.

Googy, who must have been getting hoarse at this point, went over the details he'd supplied at Boland's trial. He had seen Anne and Arthur in the bedroom at the Lincoln Way Tavern "at least twice." He had been standing at the bar polishing his glassware and minding his own business when Mrs. Lyddane had asked him "casually" to have someone shoot Slom. She had given him $200 for Boland, he said, and he had kept $50 for himself and forwarded the rest as directed. With Googy supplying most of the details, Prosecutor Pugh built his case with the care of a good bartender making a pousse-café. Evidence was introduced to show that Anne had not only insured Slom for $10,000, she had hiked the amount to $15,000 that very spring. Furthermore the policy provided for double indemnity—a $30,000 payoff—in case Slom's departure was sudden and violent, like being shot in a holdup on payday.

Josephine Beall, Arthur's once-trusting wife, took the stand, wearing a red jacket and a permanently disillusioned expression. She recalled in detail the painful past, including the laughing incident in the driveway and the phony phone calls from Anne's pal, the editor of the *Montgomery County Sun*. She had called Anne on the phone, she said, and once visited her, trying to persuade her to leave Arthur alone. But Anne had kept right on. The prosecution rested. Googy rested. Prosecutor Pugh told friends he felt the second presentation—against Anne—was even stronger than the first.

Meanwhile the three judges got to un-

whole thing through. A few hours later they announced that they had reached a unanimous decision in the case, but they declined to say what it was. They would keep it a secret, they said, until after Anne Lyddane was tried, so that the decision on Boland could not influence the jury that would hear the evidence against Mrs. Lyddane. But the *Washington Herald's* Pat Frank was too good a reporter. Just before the trial ended, Frank had another reporter, Dave Lee, boost him up through the second-story window of the judges' chambers. Frank hid in the judges' bathroom shower during the deliberations, and the next morning his front page banner story anounced the verdict. Chief Judge Urner got really mad. The *Herald's* action was "wholly unjustified" he said, and he indicated that he was inclined to hold everyone from Cissy Patterson on down in contempt of court.

Anne Lyddane, who had more confidence in her charms than Bobo had in his, decided on trial by jury. She arrived at the courthouse with Slom at her side. She wore a light blue silk dress and white finished business. They took time out to order the three crusading journalists of the Washington *Herald*—managing editor Mike Flynn, city editor Ray Helgenson, and demon reporter Pat Frank—to show cause why they should not be cited for contempt.

Anne Lyddane's lawyers began her defense and her chief counsel, Senator Prescott, said that he would admit that his fair client had not been without flaw. She had, he said, committed "indiscretions."

Slom took the stand, natty in gray. He said that Anne was a fun-loving girl and that he knew she'd been running around with Arthur back there at the time the divorce suit was filed. He said, on cross examination, that Anne hadn't slept with him then. Now, he said, everything was going smoothly. They were sleeping jointly and soundly, and he didn't for one moment believe that Anne had ever tried to get him shot.

Finally, with the preliminaries taken care of, State Senator Prescott put Anne herself on the stand, a dazzling picture of innocence, dressed entirely in white.

She, like Prescott, admitted her indiscretions but she had an explanation, of sorts, for everything. Those evil fellows, Boland and the rest, had a "terrible" picture of Arthur and herself. They had decided to blackmail her by threatening to show it all over Rockville. You could imagine what they'd have said at the bank. Not to mention at the meetings of the Gaithersburg Athletic Association. Anne said she had not told Slom because Slom, though understanding, might have been embarrassed by that picture. So she told Slom instead that she needed $200 to buy off some fellows who were planning to kidnap him. Anne was on the stand three hours. There were those who were unkind enough to say that a jury that would believe her story would believe anything.

Senator Prescott wound up the defense with a parade of character witnesses—all prominent, mostly men, including Maryland's Secretary of State, Thomas L. Dawson. They all said that Anne was a lovely girl and, to the best of their knowledge, as truthful as an assembly of bishops. Prescott made an impassioned plea. How could they convict this lovely

Arthur's wife, Josephine, who was not Anne's dear friend, named Anne as co-respondent in a divorce action that was filed but later withdrawn.

young woman on the basis of her supposed accomplices, low-lives like Googy, Bobo, and Rags?

Prosecutor Pugh argued with some logic that if anyone, Anne included, set out to hire killers they'd naturally go to low-lives, not to Sunday School teachers.

The 12 middle-aged men went out and stayed out for nine hours and then they came back in and said they couldn't make up their minds. Some saw it one way, some saw it the other.

The judges ruled a mistrial. Anne left the courtroom, free, accompanied not by Slom but by her two sisters. They chatted happily as they skipped down the courthouse steps. Prosecutor Pugh was so annoyed he refused to see anyone.

With Anne Lyddane past the danger point, the judges felt free to announce the verdict in the Boland case. It was the same verdict that Pat Frank had announced a couple of weeks before—Bobo was guilty as charged. Guilty of conspiring with Anne Lyddane to kill her husband and, sort of incidentally, to kill Mrs. Beall.

Poor Bobo.

There was, he'd found, a double standard in Rockville.

General Sickles Cuts A Swath In Lafayette Park

O**N A COOL SUNDAY AFTERNOON** in February 1859, Philip Barton Key, son of the author of the Star Spangled Banner and the handsomest man in Washington, strolled up Jackson Place, on the edge of Lafayette Park, paused, drew a handkerchief from his broadcloth coat pocket, and waved it gently in the air.

He was, though he knew it not, waving a final farewell to Washington and the world and setting the stage for the most capital capital crime in the history of the Capital.

By the next dawn's early light, Philip would be dead. Congressman Dan Sickles of New York would be lodged in the lice-infested District jail at 4th and G streets, Northwest. And President James Buchanan, "Old Buck," would have successfully tampered with a potential witness for the prosecution.

It was a crime of passion, which was at every turn excessive.

The lady in the case, Teresa Bagiolo Sickles, was excessively beautiful, excessively indiscreet, and was to suffer exces-

sively as a result.

Mr. Key was not only the handsomest man in Washington and the son of Francis Scott Key, he was also the nephew of Chief Justice Taney, of the celebrated Dred Scott decision, and bizarrely, was the District Attorney of the District of Columbia. He would have been the prosecutor if anyone had been murdered other than himself.

Everybody who was anybody in Washington was involved in a greater or lesser degree, a circumstance explained in part, perhaps, by the fact that in 1859 Washington was a smaller, simpler place and most everybody was somebody or at least thought they were.

The first somebody was, of course, the benign bachelor President, who loved peace and friendship and hated strife—domestic, national, sexual, or sectional. Among those most blessed by his friendship was dashing Daniel Sickles, Congressman from Tammany Hall. Whoever named him named him well, for Sickles cut a wide swath, galloping from White House to whore house and a popular favorite at both.

He was a small, slim man, marvelously erect, his eye as stern as his morals were lax, and his face adorned by a combined goatee and mustache, shaped like the front half of a black mushroom. He had married the lovely Teresa when she was 16 and he 32, both alumni of an extra-

Philip Barton Key and Teresa Sickles.

ordinary boarding house operated by Lorenzo Da Ponte, a bohemian in his 90's and—hold your hat—a former librettist for Mozart, a Catholic priest, a friend of Casanova, a grocery store keeper, and a libertine, though not, naturally, all at the same time.

When Sickles moved into his menage as a young man, Da Ponte was a retired professor from Columbia College and the adoptive grandfather of Teresa Bagioli, age one. As Teresa ripened into very young girlhood, Sickles, who had ripened into a lawyer and a politician with an unbelievable (bad) reputation, took her here and there, seducing her, it was said, in French and Italian—two of the Romantic languages they'd both learned at Professor Da Ponte's knee.

On September 27, 1852, they were married by Mayor Kingsland of New York, and in 1853 the rising young Tammanyite was appointed secretary of legation under James Buchanan, Ambassador to the Court of St. James.

He went to London without Teresa, who was pregnant, but he didn't go alone. He was accompanied by Fanny White, a rising young prostitute, whom, it is said, he escorted to a reception at Buckingham Palace, where he introduced her to Queen Victoria as Miss Bennett, the daughter of

Daniel Sickles had a fine, distinctive hand. He became a Major General in the Civil War and played a conspicuous, if confusing, role at Gettysburg.

James Gordon Bennett, publisher of the New York *Herald.* Mr. Bennett, an old enemy, never really recovered from the insult.

When Buchanan returned to the United States and was elected President in 1856, Sickles went to Congress and beautiful Teresa took her place in Washington society. The Sickleses met Philip Barton Key, and Sickles, the pal of the President, made sure Key was reappointed as District Attorney. During the winter and spring Sickles kept himself busy with political chores, and Mr. Key escorted Mrs. Sickles around to hops and balls and racing meets. Such was the custom of the time and place.

In the fall of 1857 Dan took over the Stockton home on Jackson Place, a three-story, flatfront painted white, just to the south of the venerable Decatur House overlooking Lafayette Park. He bought a handsome coach and a spirited pair of horses, and he hired a half dozen household servants. As a Congressman he made a cool $3,000 a year.

The Sickleses entertained extravagantly and were invited to extravagant entertainments in turn—though Dan, politicking in Washington and womanizing in New York, often left the actual attendance to Teresa and her willing friend, Philip Barton Key. Soon, it developed, Teresa and Philip were intimate in every sense of the word. They didn't always go to balls and public gatherings. Rather often Teresa had her coachman drive way out in the country to the Congressional Cemetery, which lies quiet and lonely-still on the banks of the Anacostia. She would get out and Mr. Key would be waiting, his horse's bridle in hand. And then while the coachman was left holding the bridle and Dan Sickles was left holding the bag, Teresa and Philip would disappear among the trees where only the dead were witnesses. Dead men tell no tales and, surprisingly, neither did the coachman.

But there was a young clerk named

Photo by Brady.

Eng d by J C Buttre.

MAJ: GEN. DANIEL E. SICKLES.

BACK VIEW OF THE HOUSE HIRED BY PHILIP BARTON KEY, WHERE HE WAS IN THE HABIT OF SEEING MRS. SICKLES—VIEW OF THE NEGRO NEIGHBORHOOD.—FROM A SKETCH BY OUR SPECIAL ARTIST.

THE SICKLES TRAGEDY.

THE late tragedy at Washington still occupies a large share of the public mind. The excitement caused by it has somewhat abated, but the tragedy is of too recent a date not to have a strong interest for the community.

We abstain from giving an opinion upon the affair, preferring to deal with the facts alone, but as many different opinions are entertained, we condense the following from the information contained in the Washington correspondence of some of our most prominent and influential journals, without pledging ourselves to their opinions.

It is placed beyond a doubt that whatever may have been Mr. Sickles' failing at one period of his life, however wanting in morality, since his marriage he has been a changed man, attentive and kind, even to a fault, to his wife ; never seen in any of those questionable places of resort with which Washington abounds, and by his deportment generally showing that he had thrown off the vices of his early manhood. Political ambition seems to have taken a hold on Mr. Sickles' mind, and both at his wife's receptions and his own more peculiar meetings, all that Washington boasted of talent and probity were to be seen. It is impossible that a man who had labored hard and unceasingly to obtain his late position should forfeit all the fruits of that perseverance by one rash act, unless under the influence of a sudden and uncontrollable passion.

Mr. Sickles' love for his wife was not alone founded on admiration of her personal charms, but on certain traits congenial to his habits and temperament.

Mrs. Sickles was in her manner more like a school-girl than a polished woman of the world, joyous in her disposition, with a fearlessness of character that seemed almost unfeminine, and with a hoydenish love of sport that made her ready at all times for any kind of amusement.

Another most striking point in her character was the seeming absence of feeling or sentiment. She seemed to have an utter dis

THE OPERA-GLASS THROWN BY KEY AT SICKLES AFTER RECEIVING THE FIRST SHOT.

regard for admiration, and flattery, though administered in its most seductive forms, was thrown away upon her.

There has been a current report that Mr. Sickles had for some time past manifested great jealousy, and that Mrs. Sickles had complained of the strict surveillance under which she was placed. No

(Continued on page 264.)

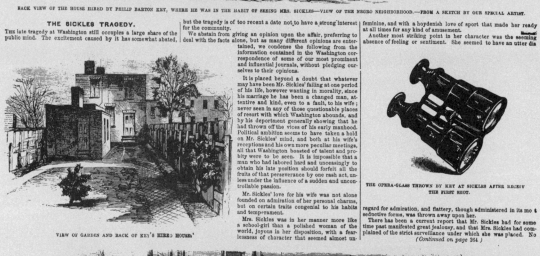

VIEW OF GARDEN AND BACK OF KEY'S HIRED HOUSE.

MRS. SICKLES LEAVING THE HOME OF HER HUSBAND, ON THURSDAY, THE 10TH OF MARCH—CARRIAGE WAITING TO CONVEY HER TO THE RAILROAD—GRIEF OF THE HOUSEHOLD.

The illustrated newspapers had achieved a peak of graphic excellence by 1859. At the top is a rear view of the humble house where Mrs. Sickles and Philip Barton Key met on the sly. Mrs. Sickles went into domestic exile after the slaying. In the bottom engraving the gifted artist depicts the scene not, perhaps, as it was but as it should have been.

Samuel B. Beekman who had worked in Sickles' campaign and who had, since getting his post in Washington, become a family friend. He had, as is the custom of awkward young men under such circumstances, fallen deeply and silently in love with Teresa, who was about his own age though a great deal more poised. He took to trailing Key and Mrs. Sickles, and one windy evening in March, after a half dozen drinks at Willard's famous bar on Pennsylvania Avenue, he told all to Marshall J. Bacon, who worked with him in the Interior Department. Bacon told George Wooldridge, a clerk in the House of Representatives and a sort of unofficial secretary to Congressman Sickles. And Wooldridge, after brooding about the matter, called Sickles aside in the House chamber.

Sickles summoned Beekman who denied everything.

Sickles then told Key of the nasty rumors going about.

Key—acting absolutely outraged—sent a note to Wooldridge demanding an explanation of the gossip. Wooldridge replied that Marshall Bacon had told him that Key and Teresa had been out horseback riding and that on one occasion, at least, "they stopped at a house on the road toward Bladensburg and that Mrs. Sickles had a room there and remained one hour and a half; also, she took off her habit, and that he had no doubt there was an intimacy between Mr. Key and Mrs. Sickles."

Mr. Wooldridge added, with perhaps a touch of malice since the communication was after all addressed to Key: "Mr. Bacon told me also in a manner that assured me it was so, that Mr. Key boasted that he only asked 36 hours with any woman to make her do what he pleased." Key then sent a note to Bacon, who told him, truthfully, that Beekman had been the originator of the story. Beekman, who was just an innocent young coward, more jealous of Key's success than of Sickles' honor, lied flatly and totally and said he'd never told any such story to anybody.

Key bundled off the whole correspondence to Sickles, pointing out that no one would admit to having originated the awful rumor.

Sickles was satisfied.

So all should have been saved for Teresa and Philip B. But Philip was as bold as he was bad and Teresa as foolish as she was unfaithful. In October 1858, Key galloped up 15th Street, near Vermont Avenue, and stopped before a small, shabby brick house.

"Is this house for rent, Madam?" he asked, pointing. "I don't know," the woman replied, "you'll have to ask the colored man."

The woman was the humble wife of a White House gardener—Washington was a small place then and even the humble were likely to have some connection with the exalted. It was such a small place that only a man naturally foolish or foolishly in love would think that he could conduct an affair in the heart of the city, two blocks away from the stately home of his well-known mistress. Philip Barton Key was just that sort of man.

He rented the house from its owner, John Gray, "the colored man," and some two months later he arrived, first with an armload of wood and shortly thereafter with a shy young lady who kept her face hidden by her black velvet shawl.

The first to notice, perhaps, was Nancy Brown, the gardener's wife. The visits continued, at least one a week, with the handsome Key arriving first, lighting a fire and hanging a red ribbon from the upstairs window. Then came the shy girl, cloaked in the shadow of her shawl.

The affair was the worst kept secret since the British slipped up on Washington in 1812. Soon the residents of the shabby neighborhood, two blocks from the splendor of Lafayette Park, looked forward with unabated interest to the weekly visit of the romantic pair of society folk. Mrs. Brown and her friends had little difficulty identifying Mrs. Sickles. Another resident, Sarah Ann Seeley, who had lived in Georgetown once when Mr. Key also resided there, knew him right off. When the pair slipped in on a winter afternoon, a score of eyes were usually watching from behind upstairs curtains, from the street corners, maybe from the tree branches.

Somebody dropped Dan Sickles a friendly note.

It was obviously either someone who lived on 15th Street and had studied the situation at close hand or an outlander who had done a lot of detective work. The note, if mildly illiterate, was nevertheless an arresting document and Dan Sickles found it so.

It got quickly to the point: ". . . There is a fellow I may say, for he is not a gentleman, by any means by the name of Philip Barton Key & I believe the district attorney who rents a house of a negro man by the name of Jn. A. Gray situated on 15th street b'twn K & L streets, for no other purpose than to meet your wife Mrs. Sickles. He hangs a string out of the window as a signal to her that he is in and leaves the door unfastened and she walks in. With these few hints I leave the rest for you to imagine." It was signed R. P. G.

Sickles was a public man. He functioned best, as at least most easily, when his affairs were in public print and he himself was surrounded by well wishers.

He reacted characteristically to the note from the mysterious Mr. (or Mrs.) G. He ran up to the Capitol, sought out a reporter with whom he occasionally played whist, and asked him to put an ad for him in the *States* and the *Star*: "R. P. G., who recently addressed a letter to a gentleman in this city, will confer a great favor upon the gentleman to whom the letter was addressed by granting him an early, immediate, and confidential interview."

R. P. G. never replied and Sickles didn't wait. He ordered George ·Wooldridge to begin an investigation and George did a thorough and conclusive job. He rented a room across from the 15th Street house and toured that sordid neighborhood asking sordid questions. He also asked questions of Sickles' household servants.

There really was no room for doubt. The neighbors described Mrs. Sickles down to the fringe of bugles on her velvet shawl. The servants said they'd often seen Philip Barton Key stand in Lafayette Park and signal Mrs. Sickles with a wave of his handkerchief.

Sickles called Teresa to his bedroom and Teresa confessed. At Sickles' insistence she wrote out a detailed confession full of such specific spicy details as "There was a bed in the second story. I did what is usual for a wicked woman to do. . . . I met him in 15th Street. Went in by the back gate. Went in the same bedroom and there an improper interview was had. I undressed myself. Mr. Key undressed also. . . . I do not deny that we have had connection in this house, last spring, a year ago, in the parlor, on the sofa."

Sickles summoned his closest friends to his side by telegrams and they came, among them Samuel Butterworth, a fellow Tammanyite. Through the day Sickles paced his drawing room floor, his eyes streaming, his voice declaiming, his friends advising.

Should he challenge Key to a duel? Perhaps that was the only course.

He paced and paused and stared out his window.

And whom did he see strolling across the way but Philip Barton Key.

Philip came abreast of the Sickles' townhouse and Dandy the Sickles' greyhound, went loping across the street to lick his hand. Sickles stared. Betrayed, as it were, by his dog.

Key ignored the hound and looked at the house. At the upper windows. He drew his handerchief from his pocket and waved it solemnly.

"That villain," Sickles shouted, "he is out there now, *making signals.*

Sickles spoke further to Butterworth and then dashed upstairs to fetch his pistol. Butterworth put on his coat and went outside. He overtook Key on Pennsylvania, just opposite the White House, and hailed him in a casual way. He did not shout "all is discovered" or anything like that. He merely said "Good afternoon" and such, and Key suspecting nothing, stopped and answered inconsequentially, in kind.

They chatted as Sickles came tearing out of his house and went around the man, and can not look you in the face!" Butter-worth says he counseled moderation, and at least a delay; that he left the house for a few minutes, and on his return was informed by Mr. Wooldridge, who was in the library, that during B.'s absence Key had twice passed the house, waving his hand-kerchief three times as a signal. What followed is best stated in Mr. Butterworth's own language; and the annexed diagram will help the reader to an idea of the localities.

While conversing with him Mr. Sickles came into the library and said that he had "seen the scoundrel mak-ing signals;" and he added, "My God! this is horri-ble!" I said, "Mr. Sickles, you must be calm, and look this matter square in the face. If there be a possibility of keeping the *certain knowledge* of this crime from the public you must do nothing to destroy that possibility. You may be mistaken in your belief that it is known to the whole city."

He instantly replied, "No, no, my friend, I am not; it is already the town talk." I then said, "If that be so there is but one course left for you, as a man of honor—you need no advice." After a few moments' silence Mr. S. said that he "was satisfied that Mr. Key had been in the habit of making his signals from a window of the Club-house opposite; and what surprised him very much was that his wife strenuously denied this, though freely confessing her guilt." He then walked into the hall, and said to me, "Come, go over with me to Stewart's room in the Club-house, and he may be able to inform me whether Key has a room there, and for what purpose

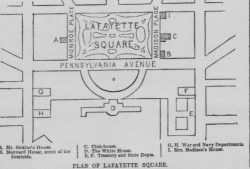

PLAN OF LAFAYETTE SQUARE.

A. Mr. Sickles's House.
B. Maynard House, scene of the homicide.

C. Club-house.
D. The White House.
E, F. Treasury and State Depts.

G, H. War and Navy Departments.
I. Mrs. Madison's House.

he uses it." I assented, and walked out into the street, supposing that Mr. Sickles was following me. I left the house for this sole purpose.

When I left Mr. S. in the hall I am satisfied he had no weapons on his person. He was without his overcoat. He said nothing to me about weapons, or the probability of encountering Mr. Key. I walked slowly down the Av-enue, on the south side, to the corner, and as I was cross-ing the street I saw Mr. Key advance a few steps toward me. He saluted me, saying, "Good-morning, Mr. But-terworth. What a fine day we have!" I responded, and said, "Have you come from the Club?" He said, "I have." I asked, "Is Mr. Stewart in his room?" He an-swered, "Yes; and he is quite unwell." I then said, "I am going to see him. Good-morning," and turned to leave him. As I did so I saw Mr. Sickles, for the first time after leaving his house, coming rapidly down Six-teenth Street, on the side next the square, and then near the corner. I had walked about thirty feet on my way to the Club when I heard Mr. S. exclaim, in a loud voice, "Key, you scoundrel, you have dishonored my house—you must die!"

I turned immediately, and saw Mr. K. thrust his hand in his vest or side coat-pocket, take a step in the direc-tion of Mr. Sickles, and simultaneously I heard the dis-charge of a pistol. Mr. Key then rapidly advanced on Mr. Sickles, seized him with his left hand by the collar of the coat, and seemed to make an effort to strike with something in his right hand, which I then supposed to be a weapon. Mr. Sickles backed into the middle of the street, when he succeeded in extricating himself from Mr. Key's grasp, drew a pistol from his overcoat-pocket, presented it at Mr. Key, who retreated backward up Six-

HOMICIDE OF P. BARTON KEY BY HON. DANIEL E. SICKLES, AT WASHINGTON, ON SUNDAY, FEBRUARY 27, 1859.

Park on the opposite side. Key left But-terworth and turned left, from Pennsyl-vania Avenue to Madison Place. He was heading toward the National Club, an upper class gentleman's sanctum on the corner of the square.

Sickles met him head on: "Key, you scoundrel, you have dishonored my bed —you must die."

Key, who had cut a gallant figure up till then, if nothing else, dodged behind a tree and shouted, "Don't shoot."

Sickles, a slow man to take advice, shot and missed, and shot again. Key fell and Sickles shot and shot, excessively. Finally he pointed the pistol point blank at the head of his fallen rival. This time the gun misfired and the frozen specta-tors—there were dozens—took the oppor-tunity to grab the gunman.

If Sickles was shocked by Key's actions, Key was certainly surprised by Sickles'. On the fatal day, the gay seducer stood in Lafayette Park, waving his handkerchief as a signal to Mrs. Sickles. Sickles saw him, and a short time later, when Key sauntered by once more, he came hurtling from the house, pistol in pocket, his stovepipe hat fixed firmly on his head. Key threw his opera glasses at Sickles (they are lying near Sickles' left foot), but to no avail.

Key went to the National Club, but not as he'd planned. He was still breathing when they carried him in, but by the time a doctor arrived he was dead.

J. H. W. Bonitz, a callow White House page, who'd seen the massacre, galloped across to the Executive Mansion to tell Old Buck. The President–Dan's old mentor and still his loyal friend–advised Bonitz, a potential witness, to get out of town at once, before he could be cast into jail as a material witness. He gave him traveling money and a razor as a farewell gift and sped him on his way, but Buchanan proved as inept in quashing the case as he was in quashing the approaching civil war. Lafayette Park had been simply loaded with witnesses.

Sickles handled the chore himself. He didn't succeed in stopping the whole thing, but he did manage to totally mess up the prosecution. Key, of course, had been District Attorney, so his former assistant, Robert Ould, took over. Key's pals, dubious of Ould's ability, hired John Carlisle, an experienced advocate, to assist in the prosecution.

Sickles hired James Topham Brady, Thomas Francis Meagher, and John Graham, three of the most dazzling lights of the New York bar, and all old pals, for the defense. Then to make double sure, he also hired Edwin Stanton, Lincoln's future cabinet member, and Philip Phillips of the Washington bar. Then to make three times sure, he hired three other high ranking counselors named Chilton, Ratcliffe, and Magruder.

The defense rapidly became the prosecution. The trial began and Sickles' eight great attorneys set about prosecuting the late Mr. Key as a libertine and a disgrace to the Star Spangled Banner and Mrs. Sickles as a round-heeled lady who leaned over backwards to please her casual acquaintances.

The jury reached its verdict and convicted . . . Teresa and Philip Barton Key. Sickles got off, but not lightly.

Up until the moment when Philip Barton Key had waved his handkerchief in the park, Dan Sickles had nourished a not-too-wild hope that some day he would follow his old pal Buchanan to the White House.

He had a lot going his way–talent, friendships in high places, a great willingness to spend money, the shrewd knowledge of practical politics, a running start, and relative youth.

He also had had a most dubious reputation, both as lawyer and lover, but it was a giddy age with still giddier days approaching.

But even the most sophisticated electorate would not send a gunman to the White House–for one thing, in this case it would have been in obvious bad taste to play the National Anthem at his inauguration.

Teresa remained Sickles' wife–he supported her but seldom visited either her bed or board. Society was even sterner; she was cut dead forevermore by all respectable matrons.

Sickles' career was wrecked–or to be more precise, one of his dozen careers was wrecked.

He would go on to be a Civil War general who almost gallantly managed to turn victory into defeat at Gettysburg; Ambassador to Spain and the illicit boyfriend of Spain's exiled Queen; military governor of North Carolina; and a resounding combatant in the post-war struggle of the robber barons who were building America's railways and watering its stock.

He left Washington, more or less permanently, after his explosive day on Lafayette Square, but he left mementos behind him.

The Park, thanks to the twentieth century's craze for preservation, is still recognizable as the sedate promenade it was in 1859.

Congressional Cemetery, where Teresa and Philip met among the gravestones, is still there beside the river, with the same rows and rows of unbelievably ugly tombs. And part of Dan Sickles himself is firmly lodged in our midst.

At Gettysburg he had a leg shattered by a shell and amputated by a surgeon. And when he was up and hobbling around he found the bones and brought them to Washington where he presented them to the Army's medical museum. The Institute of Pathology has them still, and anyone wishing to see Sickles' shin may search it out.

President James Buchanan, familiarly known as Old Buck.

Seducer Dies By Brother's Gun

I N 1870 A LADY WAS NEVER A SEN-
suous woman.

Married ladies were presumed to
be frigid.

Unmarried women were (1) vir-
gins; (2) harlots; or (3) unfortunate maidens who had been seduced. In Washington
and the surrounding green countryside
there was a strict romantic tradition govern-
ing seduction and its consequences. When
a seduction was discovered everyone had
a fixed role to play.

The seduction of Myra Black, of Cumberland, Maryland, was discovered in the
latter part of 1869.

Myra was a beautiful country girl with
big, brown eyes. Everyone had assumed
that she belonged to Category Number
One.

Colonel William W. McKaig was, first,
a sprig of the gentry, then a tall, handsome, gallant soldier, then a foul seducer,
and finally, a bloody corpse.

Harrison D. Black, Myra's father, was
poor but proud and often drunk.

H. Crawford Black, Myra's brother, was
quiet, slight, and noble. He was penniless
but with prospects, and firmly in the

clutch of the romantic tradition.

Everyone played his role to perfection
except Myra. Myra was trying to enjoy
life and running head-on into stuffy con-
ventions every time she winked her eye.

In the early 1860's the stretch of Maryland west of the District—Montgomery,
Frederick, and Allegany counties—had
been a hotbed of rebellion—"Maryland,
My Maryland" was sung as a seditious bal-
lad from Rockville on out.

Crawford Black, 17, and Bill McKaig,
23, left Cumberland in 1863 to join the
Confederate Army. Both, in the phrase
used later by the *Evening Star,* were
"members of respected families." The Mc-
Kaigs, however, were notably better off—
Bill's father owned the town foundry.
Crawford's father owned nothing much
but a sensitive soul and what he considered
a proud name.

Some young men start out as winners
and some as losers. Young McKaig was
commissioned in Jefferson Davis' service.
Young Black was a private and soon a
prisoner of war—he had two years of
privacy in the Union prison camp at Fort
Delaware.

The Evening Star *reported that the Black
murder trial had "excited intense
interest" in Frederick, Maryland, where
the trial was being held.*

84

After the war they came home—Mc-
Kaig to become a Lieutenant Colonel in
the Maryland National Guard, the guiding
light of the family foundry, and the leader
of a robust double life. He drank, he
played cards, and he fooled around with
women. In Washington, as he frequently
was, he roistered up and down Pennsylvania Avenue, from Cobb's saloon to the
Willard.

Young Black found life less fun and
more challenging. Commerce in Cumberland was turgid, so he went to the Nation's Capital looking for employment. In
official Washington there was a certain
antipathy toward Confederate soldiers. He
made some impressive friends here but the
time was not ripe for him to become a
government clerk. So he went south—way
south. He joined the Army of the Emperor
Maximilian of Mexico, an ill-fated mon-
arch, seduced, in a manner of speaking, by
Napoleon III, who had given him the
throne and all sorts of fancy promises.
Black stayed until the end, which came
suddenly for Maximilian, before a firing
squad in 1866.

Meanwhile, back in Cumberland, the
dashing Colonel McKaig had been doing
his thing. He was 30 years old, unmarried,
and in the words of a local observer, "remarkably fine-looking, large in stature but
well proportioned, and possessed of all
those attractions of mind and heart that
make a man a genial companion." He had
black, rather curly hair and bushy sideburns, and in the rococo opinion of another observer, was a "man of powerful
person, uncommon appearance, and elegant accomplishments."

He had known Myra all her life. His
appearance at her humble home became
anything but uncommon. He had left her
a mere schoolgirl and returned to find her
on the verge of ripe womanhood, a remarkable beauty. He escorted her here and
there, to church socials and lawn fetes,
and as they strolled along Cumberland's
main thoroughfare, Baltimore Street, his
hand gallantly at her elbow as she stepped
delicately over the curb, the Blacks,
mother and father, suspected nothing but
the best. They cherished the not too faint
hope that their daughter was about to
marry into the foundry.

Colonel McKaig, however, was thinking of other things. In a matter of months —possibly weeks—after his return, he and Myra were bedding down whenever the opportunity presented. It presented itself most conveniently when they could arrange to be out of Cumberland at the same time, meeting in Washington or Baltimore for a stolen night or two of dalliance.

On June 20, 1866, the Colonel, somewhat tipsy, wrote Myra a letter: "My own Dearest," it said, "I will make an attempt to answer your note just received but I fear I shall fail before I get through. Even if I do, I shall consider the time well spent. I unfortunately took a drink the other day and you know how I am when I once get a taste. I cannot stop until I get too much, and that is the reason I did not see you when you were out this morning. I was up street playing cards and drinking and I did not come out until 3 o'clock in the evening. I had a very good time but ten to one would sooner have been with my little pet. Oh! you hard hearted little thing! How dare you tell me that I am losing all love for you?"

It meandered on for a few paragraphs and got to the point. "I swear (no I won't swear either because you say that is not proper and you know I try to do everything you like) but I will be dogged if you let this opportunity slip and don't spend the night with me while you are up town. I shall never speak to you again, because it will be your fault alone, as there is nothing in this world to prevent your coming. All you will have to do is to bring a couple of thick veils and not loop up your dress and you can go away the back way in the morning, and nobody will be the wiser. Now my dear I should like to see you before the place is closed, so that we can understand each other, and I will have to leave that for you to arrange. And so, good-bye, my dear, and think of me as none other than yours. Forever."

It is an interesting note, and it tells us at least as much about Myra as about Bill. She was not a shy ninnie cunningly led astray, and the Colonel was not much of a man of the world. For one thing he couldn't hold his liquor. He was at least as young as his years, rather spoiled, greedy in all directions at once, but handsome and well made. Myra, to be blunt, liked to go to bed. She was more interested in his physique than in his foundry.

He was a cad, but to Myra an attractive one.

If she had wanted to make a rich marriage, she had had her chance. In the spring of 1869, shortly before Bill wrote the drunken note, she had become engaged to a "man of high character and position" who shall be nameless because no one now knows his name. He wanted to take her west. Myra resisted. Bill McKaig, the cad, helped her. He called on the gentleman and announced that Myra had, to his personal knowledge, lost her membership in Category Number One. The man left town never to return.

Myra was so little infuriated that she didn't even mention it when she next wrote Bill. He remained her lover. In October he married a Miss Hughes, of nearby Virginia. Miss Hughes, like a proper lady of the time, remains a dim figure. We do not know her first name. She was even dim at her own reception. When the bride and groom returned from their honeymoon, the McKaigs held a magnificent reception. Their rambling, wooden mansion was ablaze with gas light, and several hundred of the most acceptable members of Cumberland, Hagerstown, Baltimore, and Washington society attended. Colonel McKaig led laughing Myra up to his shy bride, and Myra toasted the former Miss Hughes with bubbling champagne. If Myra's heart was breaking, it was as well hidden as her past. Then the Colonel took Myra by the arm and together they led the procession to the refreshment table.

Myra's brother, Crawford, meanwhile had been working hard, far from home. After his service with the late Mexican Emperor he had gone to the western frontier, clerking in an Iowa store. In September 1869 he came home and took a job with the Franklin Coal Company. Myra and Bill celebrated his return by popping into bed. It was, in a way, a first for both. Previously they had coupled in Washington and Baltimore and Cumberland, but never before in the McKaig's master bedroom. Now Mrs. McKaig the younger, the former Miss Hughes, was having Colonel Bill's baby and the household, including Bill's parents, was standing by. Bill and Myra slipped upstairs.

It was a fateful roll in the hay. Myra became pregnant. She kept her cool and her own counsel. Brother Crawford, the anchor man of the family, was now supervising the Franklin Coal Company's operation in Piedmont, West Virginia and returning home a couple times a month for fresh linen and a few words with his mother. Crawford, in an age that believed totally in Horatio Alger, was Horatio Alger's little hero come to life. He believed in the great American myths, and since he believed in them they worked. He believed that a poor but honest boy could start at the bottom and work to the top. He was only 24 but he had a full and humble life behind—he had been a POW, a foreign mercenary, a frontiersman, and a dutiful son. And with the Franklin Coal Company he was about to be a success. He was in almost every way the opposite of Colonel McKaig, the dasher, drinker, and despoiler. He was slight, still boyish, clean-shaven, thin-faced, blue-eyed, quiet-spoken, fair-minded. He was totally trusted by the mine owners and, more remarkably, he had the affection and respect of the rough and ready men who dug the coal from the West Virginia hills.

In the spring of 1870 Myra confessed to her parents what she could no longer conceal. Her mother and father, distraught, shipped her off to have the child. She had a fine boy, and only then did she announce that Colonel Bill McKaig was the father.

Mr. Black got the official word on a Sunday afternoon and went to the Fair Grounds racetrack outside Cumberland, shotgun in hand. When Colonel McKaig came up he took hazy aim and blazed away. The shot hit the Colonel in the upper left arm—a severe but not a permanently disabling wound. Colonel McKaig reacted as readers who have been studying his character must know he would. He denied he was the father of Myra's child. He said that Myra was a bad woman who had gone to bed with lots of men. He said he had seen her behavior in the big city. Disgusting. And he filed charges of aggravated assault against her father. He was behaving in the only way a late 19th-century scoundrel could be expected to behave.

During the hot summer, his arm restored, he carried two and sometimes three pistols wherever he went, denounced Myra to one and all, and said that he was determined to send her father to the penitentiary. Myra, out of town nursing the boy, was unable to defend herself, and the elder Blacks were ill-equipped to carry on a feud.

Crawford was busy superintending the mines at Piedmont.

There are strong indications that no one had gotten around to telling Crawford that he was an illegitimate uncle. He did know apparently that his father had winged the Colonel, but it is possible that he considered it a drunken assault on a respectable citizen.

His Piedmont landlord, a busybody named William Henshaw, hid the Cumberland papers recounting the shooting so Crawford wouldn't see them. Ignorance is bliss, and there was sort of a conspiracy to keep Crawford happy. But on Friday, October 14, 1870, a Cumberland Grand Jury met and indicted the senior Mr. Black for assault with intent to murder.

The next evening at supper at the Piedmont boarding house, Landlord Henshaw brought the matter up. He said that one A. Beall McKaig, a relative of the Colonel's, had told him that Black senior was sure to go to prison. Crawford replied, painfully, that he had not been able to "learn the truth of the Fair Ground," that his father had been in "no condition of mind" to tell him what it was all about.

Landlord Henshaw promptly filled him in. He said that Colonel McKaig had, on that occasion, publicly denounced Myra as a "strumpet."

Crawford turned pale and said, "My God, is it possible?"

He caught the nine o'clock train to Cumberland, arriving home at 11 PM. There was obviously something wrong. Myra was absent. Father Black was "lying stupid from the effects of strong drink." Mother Black was sobbing and unable or unwilling to talk. Crawford went to bed, still in the dark.

The next morning, Sunday, he went to town to see a lawyer cousin, Lloyd Lowndes. Lowndes was defending the indicted father, and he told Crawford that Myra was vitally necessary as a witness. He said the key to the defense was the fact that Colonel Bill had been playing around with Myra and had written her a very spicy letter that proved the point. The letter, he said, had been thoughtfully preserved by a friend of the family's named Roman. Crawford went to Mr. Roman's house and read the letter. It was the drunken missive the Colonel had sent Myra asking her not to loop up her skirts and to drop by for an evening of hanky panky. Crawford went home, dazed, still followed by Lowndes.

Crawford paced his room all night, falling on his bed exhausted at dawn. He woke at 7, missing the train back to Piedmont. He put on a slouch hat and, at his mother's insistence, drank a cup of coffee. Then he put on an overcoat he'd borrowed from Henshaw, though it was a warm day.

He told his mother that he had some mining company bills to pay and he went to town, his hat over his eyes, his right hand plunged deep in his pocket. It was 7:20 AM. At the western end of Baltimore Street a wooden bridge crossed Will's Creek. Ryan's Liquor Store was on the creek bank. On that October morning a goodly crowd was already at Ryan's, and Dr. L. K. Hummerlshine; George Garner, a dentist, who had come up from Washington to look for work; and Enos Davis, a dray man, were standing by the door.

Colonel McKaig crossed the bridge, walking from his home to his foundry, swinging a cane in his right hand. Davis said "Good morning" and the Colonel said "Good morning" back. Thirty yards up Baltimore Street, on the opposite side, Crawford Black was approaching.

In ensuing months there would be differences of opinion about what happened next, but the essential elements were confirmed by all.

Colonel McKaig spotted Black. He switched his cane from his right to his left hand and reached for something on his hip. John Long, a bartender at Furguson's Saloon, would insist that he saw something metallic in McKaig's hand that reflected the morning light.

McKaig began to cross the street diagonally, heading straight for Black. They met in front of Medore's cobbler shop. Black pulled a pistol and fired. McKaig

THE DISTRICT IN CONGRESS.—The House to-day adopted the Senate amendment to the deficiency appropriation bill, transferring all the powers now held by the commissioners for the improvement of M street northwest and for the improvement of the Washington city canal to the Board of Public Works of the District of Columbia, and the commissioners by the amendment are directed to transfer to the Board of Public Works all books, papers, and other property in their possession pertaining to the works under their charge; and private property shall be assessed for the improvement of M street, and 7th street southwest, from B street to the river, heretofore authorized by law, as provided in the act of February 21st, 1871. An amendment offered by Mr. Cook, authorizing the Board of Public Works to connect the Washington city canal with the government canal running into the United State arsenal, was adopted. Another amendment offered by Mr. Cook, allowing the Baltimore and Potomac Railroad Company to run their track up 6th street from Virginia avenue, was ruled out under the point of order that it was not germane to the subject.

THE BLACK-McKAIG CASE.
Murder Trial at Frederick.

The trial of H. C. Black for the murder of W. W. McKaig, Jr., at Cumberland, in October last, commenced yesterday at Frederick City. Nine jurors were obtained from the regular panel; and pending the selection of three more from the regular panel, the court adjourned until to-day. The social standing of the parties concerned, the eminent legal talent which is arrayed on each side, and the character of the alleged provocation for the murder, combine to create an intense interest in the case. There was during the proceedings to obtain a jury some skirmishes between the opposing counsel, which indicated how close is to be the interest.

The correspondent of the Baltimore American gives the following particulars of the first day's proceedings:

"At 10 o'clock the Crier announced the sitting of the Court, and at once the crowd began wending their way thither, all anxious to get a glimpse of Black, the prisoner, and the celebrated counsel engaged in the case, until every available space in the large chamber was filled. The Court, Judges Maulsby and Lynch, promptly called the bar to order, and announced its readiness to proceed in the case of the State of Maryland vs. H. Crawford Black, indicted at the October term of the Circuit Court of Alleghany County for the killing of W. W. McKaig, jr., on the 11th of October last, in the city of Cumberland. The sheriff, Hiram Bartgee, Esq., produced the prisoner in court, who took a seat with his counsel, D. W. Voorhees, of Ind.; A. K. Syester, of Hagerstown. Col. Downey, of Wyoming Territory; F. J. Nelson, of Frederick; Lloyd Lowndes and W. Price, of Cumberland, at a table fronting the jury box; whilst Isaac D. Jones, Attorney General of the State of Maryland; Milton Whitney, of Baltimore; Francis Brengle, State's Attorney for Frederick county, and the father and brother of W. W. McKaig, Jr., sat at another quite near. The able array of counsel have contributed no little to the presence of the vast crowd, as all seem anxious to witness the struggle between these great minds over the life of the prisoner. Mr. Whitney was appointed by the court of Alleghany county to assist in the prosecution, and Attorney General Jones by the Governor of the State, both of which appointments were made at the earnest request of McKaig's friends.

THE ACCUSED.
The prisoner, Black, is about twenty-four years old, quite handsome, with brown hair and blue eyes, and of rather delicate frame, and does not have the appearance of one that would commit the crime of which he stands indicted. He has a very intelligent face, is dressed par excellence, and seems quite confident of the result, although at times he seems rather nervous, and especially is it apparent when he casts his eye toward the gentlemen who are here assisting in

Public feeling, The Evening Star *said, was "decidedly in favor of Black" as the Black-McKaig murder trial got underway.*

87

threw up his hands. Black fired again. McKaig "trotted" toward a lamp post on the sidewalk, then fell to the pavement on all fours. Black fired a third time. McKaig staggered to his feet and retreated to the middle of the street. Black followed and fired again.

McKaig fell and lay still.

"This is what you get for ruining my sister and trying to put my father in the penitentiary," Black said to the corpse. Then he turned and addressed the crowd. "I have still got a shot for any damned scoundrel who says I did wrong."

He walked down the street, met a deputy sheriff, and gave him his gun.

Frightened spectators carried the dead man a few steps to the office of one Dr. Smith. Colonel Bill's brother, Mervin McKaig, arrived and opened Bill's vest, disclosing three wounds—in the ribs, the neck, and the shoulder—and two holsters and two guns. One gun was in a holster and the other in a special pocket in the dead man's pants. A third gun was outside lying in the street.

The reaction to the Colonel's murder and Crawford's arrest was notable if confused. In the words of the *Evening Star* the funeral was attended "en masse by the people of Cumberland" and the town's business places were closed from 4 to 6 PM in honor of the occasion.

But everybody liked Crawford Black too. And the proper attitude toward seduction had been firmly established for years—when a rascal impregnated a young lady and failed to make it right it was the duty of the young lady's closest male relative to shoot the rascal down.

The case was called rapidly, but before a jury could be picked the State's Attorney announced that it would be impossible, in his opinion, to find 12 fair and impartial jurors in Cumberland, so the case was switched to Frederick. The trial opened on April 11, 1871.

It was impressive. Three judges sat, William Pinckney Maulsby as Chief Judge, with Judge John A. Lynch of Frederick, and Judge William Veirs Bowic of Rockville, at his sides. The judges all had good connections—Maulsby had run for Congress and lost, but his father-in-law was Congressman John Ritchie. Bowic had been a "leading politician" and

Lynch's daddy had been one of "Maryland's most prominent Democrats."

The Honorable Isaac D. Jones, Maryland's Attorney General, led the prosecution, and Congressman D. W. Voorhees of Indiana, the defense.

Crawford Black was lodged in the Frederick County jail though the officer in charge offered to find him "quarters in one of the hotels." Crawford was thrifty.

The *Baltimore American* reported breathlessly that Myra had not entered a nunnery as previously announced but was in Frederick at the City Hotel and eating "at the public table with child in arms."

The reporter promised that "the babe or its photograph will be here in court, and then I will tell you whether it resembles William W. McKaig, the dead man."

The courtroom was jammed. There was a large delegation from Washington, including "many whose names are familiar words in current political history," and witnesses ranged from "the exquisite gent to the low black-guard who is drunk on his arrival, drunk whilst here and will be drunk when he leaves."

"Demi-mondes from Washington and Baltimore" were on hand, apparently as prosecution witnesses who would testify "in reference to Miss Black's behavior when visiting those cities."

Crawford's mother, Mrs. Black, was there in deepest mourning. Myra stayed in her hotel.

The prosecution opened with the Honorable Milton Whitney, a special assistant, addressing the jury. "Mr. Whitney led off and his bright eye flashed as his powerful brain sent its logical scintillation to illuminate the mind of the court."

The flash of Mr. Whitney's eye did not disturb the defendant. The "grateful ladies of Frederick County" had sent Crawford two bouquets of flowers and "during the entire session of the Court he was constantly smelling them in an appreciative manner."

The testimony revealed that the encounter on Baltimore Street had not been the first between Crawford and Colonel Bill.

After the Fair Grounds incident, the Colonel had taken to skulking around

Trial lawyers looked like, and frequently were, statesmen in the nineteenth century. Myra Black's brother had the good fortune to be defended by the Hon. Daniel W. Voorhees, the well-haired Congressman from Indiana.

with a pair of loaded pistols.

John Long, a bartender, had seen Mc-Kaig at the Baltimore and Ohio depot a couple of weeks before his sudden death. "Just as he got to Shaw's corner he stepped behind the depot and peeped out down Baltimore Street. This excited my curiosity, and I looked down the street in that direction and I saw Mr. Black coming up. When Black was nearly up to us McKaig drew behind the building, and he had a revolver in his hand, down by his side. Black hesitated at the door of the barber shop and then turned and went down the street. McKaig followed him down to Furguson's Saloon, and I saw them no more."

Among the facts of the final fatal shooting, there was one point of confusion. Did McKaig have his pistol in hand when he crossed the street toward Black? Two witnesses said he did not, 11 said he did. When his body was picked up and carried to the doctor's office a gun fell to the ground; but no one noticed if it fell from his hand or his holster.

The defense had two prongs—pointing in opposite directions but equally logical in the eyes of the law. First, his lawyers argued, Crawford's behavior on the 17th of October had been compelled by his sudden awful knowledge that the Colonel had betrayed his sister.

Second, the lawyers said, Crawford hadn't misbehaved in any significant way until the Colonel had come at him gun in hand, and he had then merely defended himself.

The panel of three judges decided that the fact of Myra's seduction was beside the point. It ruled that the fact that Crawford *believed* the Colonel had seduced her was enough to establish a motive. The ruling gave the defense the best of it both ways. The letter written by the Colonel was admitted in evidence, and it established that the Colonel had gone to bed with Myra rather often. But when the State tried to call witnesses to show that Myra had gone to bed with lots of people, the judges said no.

The final arguments took days. The trial was the high point not only of the legal session but also of the Frederick social season.

Attorney General Jones said the letter allegedly from Colonel McKaig could not have been written by him, since the Colonel was an educated man and the letter bore the "impress of ignorance and vulgarity." A pretty conceit but not persuasive. Gentlemen like the Colonel have often been vulgar, and when tipsy they might well garble their syntax. Jones made a somewhat stronger point by saying that the letter "affords not the slightest indication of a case of seduction." True. It established hanky-panky but not seduction.

Congressman D. W. Voorhees, the defense's biggest gun, made the final argument on behalf of the prisoner on the 21st of April, a cool, clear day. A large number of Senators and Congressmen had come over from Washington to see their colleague in action. Voorhees poured it on for three-and-a-half hours, moving the ladies in the audience to tears.

Milton Whitney Esq. had the last word for the prosecution. He knew he was battling against the tradition that had freed Representative Sickles when he had gunned down his wife's lover in front of the White House. The Sickles case had been cited by both sides to prove, apparently, opposite points. But Whitney tried to bring the jury back to Frederick and down to earth.

'Strip it of all its theatrical surroundings and let us lay it bare and naked before you as an American jury," he cried. "Let us see where the truth and where the error is."

Mr. Whitney had a fine legal mind. Carefully and with flair, he went over the bloody sequence—stressing that under the law there was no provocation for murder. Crawford's plea of self-defense was dismissed curtly: "I say again this question of self-defense was an afterthought, not dreamed of till the commencement of this trial."

He put some basic questions to the jury:

"Do we live in a land of law and order? Is human life of any value? Has it any security? Have our homes any protection? Will the government under which we live discharge its obligations? Shall we continue to pay taxes to support our courts of justice? Is a premium to be paid for lawless violence? Is this fearful tragedy committed in Cumberland to be ended in a disgraceful farce in Frederick?"

The jurors retired to consider a verdict a few minutes before three o'clock.

They then went to dinner.

And they returned with a verdict at five minutes after four.

When they were seated the clerk directed the prisoner to stand. He stood erect, with his clear blue eyes looking full into the faces of the jurors. The audience scarcely seemed to breathe. The play was nearing its end and the entire company was performing to perfection. The chief judge asked the foreman if the jury had reached a verdict. William Feaga, the foreman, said it had.

"Gentlemen of the jury, look upon the prisoner at the bar," said the chief judge. "Is he guilty or not guilty?"

"Not guilty," Foreman Feaga replied loud and clear.

A deafening yell came as from one mighty throat and the entire assembly rushed forward to touch, if possible, the flesh or at least the clothing of the delivered young man.

Sheriff Lamon embraced Crawford with tearful affection.

Crawford rejoined his mother, who stood, still in deep mourning, weeping within the bar. Together, escorted by the exultant crowd, they walked back to the City Hotel.

It had all gone according to tradition.

But wait—who was that peeking through the upstairs window at the hotel? Myra, to be sure. And why was she not shouting and laughing?

Well, for one thing it had all been so unnecessary. Young Bill McKaig hadn't deserved to die. Poor Billy. Poor Myra. Born a hundred years before the pill.

Darling Girl Guns Bureaucrat

I N 1865 LOVELY MARY HARRIS, charged with the murder of Adoniram Judson Burroughs, pleaded insanity and virginity.

Or to put it another way, she said she was just a poor maiden who had only figuratively lost her head.

She was poor, the 19-year-old daughter of an Irish immigrant, and though she may have stretched the truth in both her pleas, she was at least a nice girl who had gotten justifiably upset.

Adoniram, on the other hand, was the least appealing of figures, a stuffy bureaucrat, the GS 15 of his day.

Mary shot him down, smack in the middle of Washington, outside his Treasury Building office, within earshot of Lincoln's White House.

Their story was all that was dear to a Victorian novelist, the poor and beautiful girl, the rich and cowardly seducer, the broken promise, the broken heart, the apparent triumph of evil, and then the swift and awful revenge. Actually there was a thing or two to interest a latter-day novelist; Adoniram J. Burroughs was the Humbert Humbert of his time. He met his

Lolita in Burlington, Iowa, in 1858, when she was but a 12-year-old shopgirl and he was an overripe 26. He had pursued her into her simple home, posing as a friend of the family, bouncing her prettily on his knee while breathing heavily through his nose and pretending to peer through the stereopticon, she wiggling half knowingly, he giving her a prankish squeeze above the knee.

As Mary bloomed, Adoniram threw caution to the winds, and in time the sprig of the gentry and the little shopgirl had the attention of everyone in Burlington including, rather belatedly, William Harris, Mary's papa. Mr. Harris said that Mr. Burroughs' attentions had become those of a suitor, and since nothing good was likely to come of that he specifically forbade Mary to see Adoniram any more. When the crisis came, Mary was an advanced 14, Adoniram a juvenile 28, and the century a tumultuous 60. Fort Sumter had not yet been fired upon, but the country was astir with rumors of war and profits, and Burroughs decided to leave town. Mary insisted that she did not ask him to write, but he wrote and kept

writing even when she was lackadaisical about answering. On September 23, 1860, he dropped a line from Eddysville, Iowa: "My dear, dear Mollie, I hope to meet and clasp you to my bosom. Sometimes I think you don't love me, but I can not wholly doubt the constancy of your affections." On October 5 he announced his plans—he was going to make a fortune in Pike's Peak, Chicago, or New York, the three spots that he felt offered the best

opportunities—and he added that he was "tired of single blessedness, or rather single cussedness," and he dreamed of life with a "certain little black-eyed, curly-haired, mischief-loving girl." He added a P.S., saying he would like to be with her right then, but not in Eddysville.

On October 12, he wrote "O come, do come, won't you, dearest?"

By February he was in Chicago—Pike's Peak and New York having lost

The Treasury Department, an odd place to cash in one's chips.

out—and he was writing that he had "not yet found a way to make $10,000 a year but I hope to soon." He signed this, rather coolly, "My love to many friends in Burlington and to yourself the same, yours truly, A. J. Burroughs." One can't make too much of that signature, though, since very few young men would want to sign their letters "Adoniram." The pursuit of the elusive $10,000 per annum (the equivalent in the 1860's of maybe $50,000 to-

Evening Star.

Vᵒ. XXV. — WASHINGTON, D. C., TUESDAY, JANUARY 31, 1865. — Nᵒ. 3,719.

WASHINGTON EVENING STAR.
PUBLISHED DAILY, (EXCEPT SUNDAY,)
AT THE STAR BUILDINGS,
Southwest corner of Pennsylvania av. and 11th street,
BY W. D. WALLACH.

The STAR is served by the carriers to their subscribers in the City and District for TWELVE AND A HALF CENTS PER WEEK.

Price for mailing—Single copy, three cents; one month, seventy-five cents; three months, one dollar and fifty cents; six months, three dollars; one year, five dollars. No papers are sent from the office longer than paid for.

The WEEKLY STAR—one dollar and a half a year.

AMUSEMENTS.

CANTERBURY HALL.

FORD'S NEW THEATER.

LAST NIGHT BUT TWO
of the engagement of the Eminent Tragedian

EDWIN FORREST

GROVER'S THEATER.

AMUSEMENTS.

OFFICIAL.

The First Corps—Notice to Veterans.
HEADQUARTERS FIRST CORPS,
Washington, D. C., Dec. 27, 1864.

TELEGRAPHIC NEWS.

The Steamer Eclipse Explosion.

New York Gold and Stock Market.

From Arkansas—Election of Senator.

Death of the Treasurer of New Jersey.

Overland Mail Facilities.

LOCAL NEWS.

THE TRAGEDY IN THE TREASURY BUILDING.

CORPORATION AFFAIRS.

day) continued through 1861, and he kept Mary informed, regularly, by mail. By November Mary wrote that she believed the correspondence had attracted the attention of both the parish priest and the Burlington postmaster and that the word was getting around that she intended to marry "outside the church with an anti-Catholic."

Burroughs wrote in December that he was going to Washington to get a major's commission, Fort Sumter having been fired on some months earlier. Mary replied that she was calling the correspondence off and asked that he be kind enough to send her a picture to remember him by. "I will send you a picture if you wish," he answered on January 19, 1862, "and must this be the finale? O my God, how bitter." He was actually over-dramatizing. He kept on writing and she kept on answering. Eighteen sixty-two went by with Burroughs practically commuting to Washington in pursuit of a majority, with the priest, if not the postmaster, taking an intense interest in Mary's mail, and with Mary's father ordering her once and for all to give up her highborn boyfriend.

Then in early 1863 Mary got a fateful letter from one Miss Louisa Devlin, who kept a millinery shop on Clark Street in Chicago. Miss Devlin said that she was a friend of Burroughs' and she said that if Mary ever came to Chicago she could meet him at her shop. Mary came, arriving in March, and settled down with a job at the shop and a home with Miss Devlin and her sister Jane. Burroughs came to call at once. He had finally gotten his commission, a captaincy not a majority, and he arrived in uniform and sat on the Devlin parlor sofa with Mary on his lap, twisting her black curls with his fingers, just like old times. (One is faintly suspicious of Miss Devlin. It was apparently at Burroughs' instigation that she invited Mary, a stranger, into her

home. There is another strange aspect of what might be termed the Devlin factor, which will be noted in time.) Burroughs' repeated promise that he would marry Mary as soon as he got his commission collapsed in some confusion almost at once. He got on a horse, in line with his military responsibilities, and fell off. He realized that war was hell and promptly resigned. At the end of 1863 he got his civil service job in Washington, and Mary once more found herself waiting for the postman. In August 1864 a very odd letter arrived, signed J. B. Greenwood.

It suggested that Mary meet the undersigned at a well-known house of assignation on Quincy Street in Chicago. Mary asked, "Who can write such a letter?" and, after studying the handwriting, she and Miss Louisa Devlin decided that the answer was nobody but that former soldier boy, Adoniram Judson, himself. Miss Devlin now revealed herself as a mistress of intrigue. On her instructions Mary wrote an answer to general delivery, apparently accepting J. B. Greenwood's strange proposal. A friend of Miss Devlin's then watched the post office until "J. B. Greenwood" came to pick up his mail. J. B., according to the friend, answered the description of A. J. Burroughs all but perfectly. Mary herself took a picture of A. J. to the postal clerk and the clerk said it sure looked like J. B. Greenwood, except Mr. Greenwood had a heavier, more concealing beard. Mary and Miss Devlin then went to the house of assignation on Quincy Street, where the proprietor said that a gentleman answering Burroughs' description had waited for hours, nervously, peering out the front window. Mary decided to go to Washington and confront Burroughs in the flesh, but when she arrived at his office in the Treasury Building she was told that he was back in Chicago. She returned and in a few days got another letter from J. B. Greenwood, regretting the missed appointment on Quincy Street and asking for another.

On September 15, Mary, in a huff, went to see Burroughs' brother, the Reverend John C. Burroughs, an august figure, who was not only a clergyman but the president of the University of Chicago. Mary asked the Reverend Burroughs where A. J. was and what he was up to. The reverend replied untruthfully that A. J. was in Washington bureaucrating away. Actually, the reverend was scheduled to join A. J. and another young lady in matrimony that very day, right there in Chicago.

Mary went home despondent, and then the next day she read about the nuptials. The news had a remarkable effect on her and to a considerable degree set the stage for her future plea of temporary insanity. From being the pink picture of good health, she became a distraught young lady with a lackluster complexion and a wild eye. Once, the Miss Devlins found her fully dressed at dawn about to leave the house for a walk along the lake front. Another time, she asked Jane Devlin if she'd like to read "a fine letter" from the hand of A. J. Burroughs, and when Jane replied that she wanted to read nothing from such a contemptible cur, Mary attacked her with a carving knife. She tore a handsome patchwork quilt to pieces, and one morning she announced that she wished to "spread all the preserves in the house over the carpet." In time, she somewhat recovered her self-possession, and in January 1865, on the advice of the Devlins, she decided to come to Washington, D.C., and file a breach of promise suit against her faithless friend. She arrived January 30, filed her suit, and was suddenly seized with a desire to see old A. J. in the flesh. Walking through the winter mud, she caught a horse car on Pennsylvania Avenue and rode a mile to the magnificently simple Treasury Building. Inside, she peeked through Burroughs' door, saw him at his desk, and waited. When quitting time came, out popped Burroughs, and Mary drew a pistol and the gun went rooty-toot-toot.

It was the beginning of Washington's most event-packed winter. The war was drawing to a close and the Union had been preserved. There would be a surrender, an assassination, a wild man-hunt, a swift military trial, and a mass hanging. Mary's case was destined to be slightly lost in the rush. Only slightly, though, since it did have all the elements needed to fascinate the Victorian mind, and Mary was more than a mere beauty—she was apparently feminine allure incarnate. Almost all the men involved seem to have been smitten.

The jailer, Herbert Beale, was at pains to fix up her cell "as comfortable as possible."

The reporter from the *Evening Star* noted that "none can see her without sympathizing." When the time came to pick a jury, Judge Andrew Wylie refused to dismiss a juror simply because he admitted a predisposition in favor of the defendant. "If we do that we'll never get a jury," the judge said. And it was not simple stark sex appeal either. Two respectable ladies, who'd never met Mary before, volunteered their services as her constant companions and moral supporters and ran errands for her all winter long.

The trial began on July 3 in the old courthouse on Judiciary Square, but it went unreported the first few days since the local press was preoccupied with the sentencing and then the hanging of four persons convicted of assassinating Lincoln, including the somewhat innocent Mrs. Surratt. The fact that Mrs. Surratt was the first woman ever so treated in the District of Columbia must have been cold comfort to Mary Harris, who was about to go on trial for her life. On July 9 the jury was finally seated and the trial began. Mary arrived in black silk dress, silk coat, black bonnet trimmed with straw, and black lace veil, carrying a brown silk parasol. She was flanked by her three attorneys, former Congressman from Indiana, the Honorable D. W. Voorhees; former Commissioner of Patents, Judge Hughes; and J. D. Bradley, chief defense attorney, who turned out to be her main champion. The two local volunteer ladies and Miss Louisa Devlin stayed sturdily at her side throughout the proceedings.

The first witness, Policeman George H. Walker, said he'd been sent to the Treasury after the shooting and he'd found Mary alone in a room. It suggests something of her charm that his first question was not on the slaying but on her welfare. "I asked her if she had any friends," he testified, "and she replied, 'none at all.' " Walker was a singular cop, and if later policemen had proved as reserved as he, there would never have been a Mallory Rule. As they were going to the jail, the hack turned from F Street into 5th, and Mary said, "I will tell you all about it."

Walker replied that he did not wish to hear about it. Mary said that in that case would he send a telegram to Miss Louisa A. Devlin in Janesville, Wisconsin (Miss Devlin had moved), saying: "I have arrived in Washington, shot Burroughs, come on or telegraph." Walker said he'd be glad to. Mary then went on to tell him all about everything, whether he wanted to hear it or not. She did not, she said, ask for sympathy for herself but for her family. The late Burroughs had caused her to be driven from home and friends and had seduced her and taken her to a bad house in Chicago, and she had told him that if he didn't keep his promises, she would have revenge at the risk of her life. She added that she'd bought the pistol a year earlier in Chicago. It was a story that she would not so much change in substance as in meaning. She seemed to be saying that Burroughs had deflowered her and introduced her into prostitution. But the next witness cleared it all up. He, the Secretary of the Treasury, the Honorable Hugh McCullough, Burroughs' former boss, had talked to Mary after Walker. He had found her asking aloud, "Why did I do it? Why did I do it?" Having asked the question, she gave the answer. Burroughs and she had been engaged, and he had jilted her and married another. The Honorable Hugh asked if he had done her other injury and she had replied certainly not, "with a great deal of energy." To make it clear that he was dealing with the essential sexual point, he asked her again if she was "a virtuous girl." She replied, "Yes, as God is my witness." McCullough said that he had asked the questions "delicately," because he'd been impressed by the girl's tragic manner. "I told my wife that I realized for the first time the difference between real grief and horror."

Mary's strong implication of virginity was backed up by the introduction of a formal statement, which she'd made later. She denied that Burroughs had seduced her, but said that it wasn't his fault that he hadn't since he'd tried to get her to meet him at a house of assignation in Chicago. When she realized his intent of "causing her to enter a disrespectable house for the purpose of casting her off, she was driven almost to distraction."

Mary by this time had clearly made a strong and favorable impression up and down the line. The *Star* reporter was moved to describe her as "19 years of age, evidencing much intelligence and no little refinement of manner, extremely attractive in personal appearance, having a fair skin with very dark brown hair which hangs in ringlets over her shoulders and jet black eyes which now however are somewhat sunken and bloodshot. She is rather below the medium height, of graceful figure, and neatly attired."

A series of witnesses unfolded the story, almost day by day, and almost all of them, prosecution or defense, seemed pro-Mary. The most pro-Mary was Miss Louisa Devlin, and when District Attorney Carrington objected to one of the defense questions asked her, Judge Wylie told him he was wasting his time and ordered him to sit down.

The witnesses took Mary from Chicago to Baltimore, where she spent the night, and on to the Treasury Building. One witness, a Mr. Brown, said that he saw Mary draw her pistol but had assumed that it was some kind of a joke. He had immediately headed for the exit, moving, as he said when asked, "not very slowly." At the bottom of the stair he had heard the pistol shot and had asked a bystander what he thought it was. The bystander said it didn't sound like anything much to him, and Brown, relieved, had gone on home without poking any further into the affair.

With the proper foundation laid, Mary herself took the stand. She emphasized her virginity, again. She was aware that people had reported that there had been improper relations between her and Burroughs in both Burlington and Chicago, but this she denied. "If these stories had been true I would never have had the heart to come to Washington to seek redress."

Then she got down to facts. A few days before leaving Chicago she was walking along the street when she saw a display of pistols in a shop window. Many of the ladies of Chicago carried pistols, she said, especially when traveling. She bought one. The morning of the day she left town, she read the printed directions and loaded the gun, just for practice. She was called to breakfast and forgot to unload it. (No one pointed out that this contradicted her earlier statement to Policeman Walker that 99 she'd bought the gun a year before.) After arriving in Washington and filing her suit, she had felt a frantic desire to see the unworthy Burroughs. She had put on a "hubin," a sort of hood, though she did not ordinarily wear one, and a veil, and so disguised had gone to the Treasury, found Burroughs' office, and peeked in.

"The moment I looked at him sitting there so comfortably, the thought of all I had suffered and his being the cause enraged me and my hand involuntarily pulled back the trigger of the pistol in my pocket." The gun now cocked, she'd roved about, "not knowing how or where except that I kept my eye on his room until men began to come out." Burroughs appeared and "I felt suddenly lifted up, my arm was extended to so stiff as iron, and I saw him fall. I knew nothing more until I was called back as I was leaving the building." The facts and her virginity were hardly in dispute. The cross-examination of the defense witnesses had been mild indeed, particularly after the judge made the District Attorney sit down. (At one point the D.A. had asked Louisa Devlin how many young ladies she employed in her millinery shop and she had declined to answer. The question suggests the millinery shop may have sold something more personal than hats. But the D.A., perhaps discouraged, did not pursue it.)

The prosecution's principal witness was A. J.'s reverend brother, John, and he proved no tower of strength. Mary had said he had told her A. J. was in Washington just a few hours before he, the reverend, had married him in Chicago on September 15.

Now Reverend Burroughs said that Mary had come to see him "on the 16th of September, or one or two days either way." Which put him in the position of practically admitting he had lied to her about his brother's whereabouts.

The trial now focused on the one unsolved question, Mary's temporary insanity. The most remarkable witness on this was Mary's own attorney, J. E. Bradley. By today's rules the whole thing seems improbable, but Mr. Bradley took the stand to testify that in his considered opinion Mary had been temporarily insane when she shot Adoniram down. After noting that Mary, when he first interviewed

By the time Mary Harris went to trial, most of Adoniram's guilty secrets had become public property. The trial was covered in great detail, but the account was discreetly tucked away on an inside page.

her, had a pulse of 110, he abandoned the medical for the rhapsodic. He had rarely, if ever, met a more intellectual human being. He had never heard her use a harsh word against anyone except the Reverend J. C. Burroughs. She was full of virtues, practical as well as spiritual. She wrote a beautiful rapid hand and did bookkeeping. She had asked him, "Mr. Bradley, do you think I am a very bad girl?" She had spoken, like a child, of the pranks she had played with Adoniram when "I was a great fat girl weighing a 110 pounds." She had expressed a desire to see Burroughs' child (born after his death) and—here even Mary seems to have gone too far—she had hoped the widow Burroughs did not think hard of her. Throughout she had exhibited two remarkable traits—amiability and truthfulness.

After a while Bradley got a grip on himself and got back to the subject at hand. He said he had, as a lawyer, studied hysteria and insanity for 20 years. He said that it was clear to him that Mary, though ordinarily as stable as a judge, had been driven to distraction by the emotional pressure of Burroughs' betrayal.

The defense also produced Dr. C. H. Nichols, superintendent of the General Hospital for the Insane. He said that Mary's "brain and nervous system are large and active," and that she suffered from dysmenorrhea (painful menstruation) from 1863 on, and that she was having a period the day of the shooting. (He had written the question on a card, and she had replied, in writing, that she had been unwell for three days.) Dr. Nichols said a disappointment in love can trigger insanity. And then, abandoning his role as pure scientist, he, like the lawyer and the jailer, spoke out for Mary as a man. "She is an uncommonly sprightly and engaging girl," and she impressed him with her "virtue, truthfulness, and uncommon candor."

NEW YORK, July 5.—Chief Justice Chase
and his daughter arrived at the Saint Nicholas
Hotel last evening, and will leave this evening
for Providence, R. I.

LOCAL NEWS.

THE TRIAL OF MISS HARRIS.
The Jury Made.

In the Criminal Court, Judge Wylie presid-
ing, this morning there was a large attendance
of spectators, the bar being fully represented—
the interest being in the case of Miss Mary Harris, who is charged under an indictment for the
murder of Adoniram Judson Burroughs, in the
hall of the Treasury Department, on the 30th of
January last.

District Attorney Carrington and Assistant
District Attorney Wilson, who are to conduct
the prosecution, were present, and Messrs.
Bradley, Fendall and Mason, of the counsel for
the accused—Mr. Voorhees and Judge Hughes
not having arrived yet.

On the opening of the Court, Mr. Bradley
stated that when the empanelling of the jury
was commenced on Monday it was without
certain depositions being at hand which were
necessary for the defense. The depositions
from Burlington, Iowa, had arrived, but those
from Chicago have not, from what cause he
could not imagine, unless it was owing to the
illness of one of the witnesses. Messrs. Voorhees and Hughes had neither arrived yet—the
former having missed connection with the cars
at Cincinnati. He would therefore ask that the
case be postponed until to-morrow.

Judge Wylie remarked that he was adverse
to postponing the case, and would prefer that
the case be proceeded with.

Mr. Bradley said that on Monday the jurors
were chosen with the express understanding
that the counsel of the defense should stand to-
day as they did then, having the right to move
a continuance or postponement.

Mr. Carrington regretted the application for
a postponement. It had already been continued from the March term to the present, and
had been once postponed. He would ask the
court to confine counsel to the rules of practice
and require an affidavit showing that the
counsel had used due diligence, stating what is
intended to be proved and that he may know
so as to be able to say whether or not he will
admit what is alleged.

Mr. Bradley said he needed no instructions
from the District Attorney. He had not asked
for a continuance, and wanted no indulgence.
When the case was called at the last term he
stated to the Court that a witness whose evidence was important was absent, who was in
the service of the Government, and who had
been ordered by the Secretary of War to report
here; when it was agreed to set the case for the
first Monday in July. As for the District Attorney being informed of the nature of the evidence
from Chicago and Burlington, he placed in his
(the District Attorney's) hands, on the day the
commissions were issued, copies of the inter-

payable to the court, an
lan, Esq.,) was directed
come up.

Resolutions were adopt
to have on their wagons
number of license, unde
from $2 to $5, and auth
tendent of Roads under
mittee on Improvements
work on the roads as the
ble.

On motion of Mr. Plan
directed to call upon May
of him what arrangement
the debt now due to the C
tion, and inquire what
pay the amount of the cit
judgment affirmed for the

Mr. Plant reported that
Mayor, who informed hir
the city for advances in 1
county roads would be
September, and that he
tion of the Councils to th
of the coroner.

The President was dire
revenue by borrowing an
wants of the court.

A license was granted
to keep an ordinary on A
vote of 4 to 2, this being
kind granted by the pres

LARCENY CASES Mo
was arrested by officer
Ward, on a charge of gr
tried and dismissed. Jol
by officer R. Johnson, an
grand larceny by T. J.
sent to jail for court.
charged by George Phil
ceny. The accused ha
ployed in Phillips' resta
by Mr. Phillips interferi
on Monday. He was pu
race was captured by of
was sent to jail for court
were all arrested in the 7
posed of by Justice Tho

In the Fourth Ward of
two young men, John W
phy, who were charged
by Matthias Konig. The
court by Justice Walter.

In the 6th precinct Ch
11 years, was arrested by
charge of grand larceny
was delivered to the Dis
ence to a bench warrant

In the Seventh Ward,
vester Branigan were a
ton, charged by Felix G
larceny. They were h
Jas. English was charg
by John D. Godfrey.
cer Walsh, and after
jail for court. Thomas
Dr. Bliss with grand lar
by officer Cullem, and v
military. These cases
Handy and Boswell.

It really wasn't fair to poor Carrington, the D. A.

Lawyer Hughes summed up for the defense. Mary was "that slender girl with the little hand and toyish pistol." And, "no greater master of ineffable cruelty, no greater seducer of female virtue" had ever appeared than Adoniram J. Burroughs.

Carrington was reduced in reply to say that every woman in the country knew how to cure painful menstruation, "by going to bed with hot bricks and hot tea." It didn't do him any good.

The jury, including that gentleman who'd been inclined toward Mary when Judge Wylie had waved him into the box, found Mary not guilty.

"The words were scarcely uttered," wrote the enamoured reporter from the *Star*, "when a tremendous shout went up. Some ladies waved their handkerchiefs, others cried for joy, many crowded around Mary Harris and kissed her. Many gentlemen came pell-mell over the benches to greet her. Mr. Bradley took her in his arms and carried her to an adjoining room. . . ."

She went out to the Hospital for the Insane under the admiring eye of Dr. Nichols, to have her sanity confirmed and then, naturally, she did what a proper Victorian heroine should do. She married the hero, J. D. Bradley, the gallant man of law and sentiment, and lived, one sincerely hopes, happily ever after.

This is an example of the kind of pistol popular with ladies in the 1860's. Mary Harris told two different stories about when she bought hers.

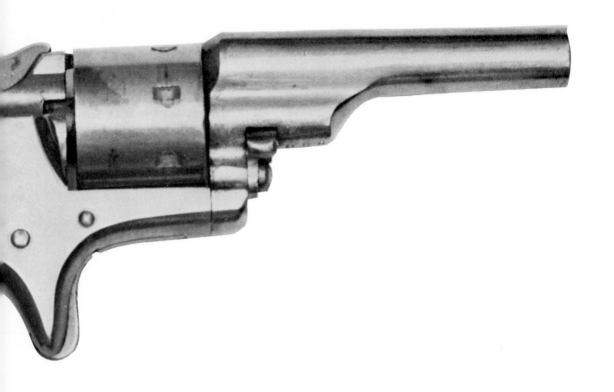

Lola Drills The Dentist

JAMES SEYMOUR AYRES, A DASHING young dental student, found early one spring morning in 1901 that Hell hath no fury like a scorned woman, especially one who is a bit long in the tooth.

It was a lesson learned too late, because, as subscribers to the *Evening Star* learned by mid-afternoon, James had been riddled to death by bullets.

"One . . . missile had entered the unfortunate man's left leg, another the left arm, and the third one penetrated his breast in the region of the heart."

The *Star* and, most notably, the residents of the Kenmore Hotel seemed to find the event more mystifying than is altogether understandable. "Murder or Suicide?" the headline asked, although a reflective reader might wonder how many young men commit suicide in installments. Further, the story went on to say, several persons had heard someone call, "Help," and a neighbor who heard the shots had seen a lady in a night robe leave Ayres's room by the fire escape.

Mrs. Warfield, the fat wife of the hotel proprietor, offered the theory that Ayres was cleaning his revolver when he accidentally shot himself once and was then in such pain that he committed suicide by shooting himself two more times. Another theory was that the mysterious woman had struggled with Ayres to keep him from committing suicide and that the gun kept going off during the wrestling match.

In 1901, perhaps, proper Washingtonians were slow to think the worst of any lady, even one who skipped down fire escapes in her nightgown. But it did strike everyone that it would be a good idea to find out who the lady was.

It was a difficult question, for the late Mr. Ayres, though only 21, was a man of parts. He was a clerk in the Census Office as well as a prize pupil at the Columbian University School of Dentistry. (Columbian became George Washington three years later, when the Washington Memorial Committee gave them $500,000.) He was the tall and handsome son of one of the Midwest's leading Republicans, the sometimes suitor of a Congressman's daughter, a dancing fool, the beau of the Kenmore Hotel, and the finest example of the gas jet set ever to come out

105

Weather—Fair to-
morrow; light to
winds, mostly northerl

MRS. BONINE'S TRIAL

She Pleads Not Guilty to the Charge of Murder.

APPEARANCE IN COURT

With Her Life in the Balance, She Is Entirely Self-possessed.

Her Husband and Two Little Sons and a Sister from Missouri Watch the Proceedings Within the Railing—Work Begun in Impaneling a Jury to Consider the Famous Kenmore Hotel Tragedy of May Last—Sixty Talesmen Ordered to Appear.

The first day of the trial of Mrs. Lola-Ida Bonine on the charge of murdering James Seymour Ayres was occupied in the unsuccessful attempt to secure a jury. When the court adjourned for the day the veniremen had temporarily qualified: George H. Vermillion, John D. Robinson, Walter J. Fry, George P. Bury, Cornelius Carmody, Henry E. Armstrong, Thomas F. Kane, George W. Thomas, Arthur Moore, William P. Cofer, William L. Koontz, and George L. F. Downey. The majority of these men are certain to be challenged before the trial begins. The defense has sixteen challenges remaining, having used four, while the prosecution's five challenges have not yet been invoked. A list of sixty talesmen was drawn from the jury box last night and the men were summoned to be in court this morning.

Mrs. Bonine answered "not guilty" in a low but distinct voice when arraigned.

District Attorney Gould asked all the would-be jurors if they had any bias or prejudice against circumstantial evidence. The counsel for the defense utilized four of its twenty challenges—excluding negroes from the jury.

HER COLORS FALSE

Seizure of British Vessel in Service of the Boers.

LOOKS LIKE FILIBUSTER

Field Guns and Powder in Hold and Quarters for 500 Men.

Liberal Leader Declares that He Despairs of Overcoming the South African Peril So Long as Chamberlain and Milner Are in Power—Anti-Chamberlain Crusade in Germany Gathering Force and Bitterness—Government Ignores the Agitation.

London, Nov. 19.—The government has caused the detention of a British steamer which was fitting out, ostensibly for a pleasure cruise, at Victoria docks, on the ground that the vessel was laden with contraband of war destined for the Boers.

Ottawa, Ont., Nov. 19.—Hon. Dr. Borden, minister of militia, has arrived home from Boston, where he was on private business, on account of the cables which are passing between the Dominion government and Great Britain in regard to sending more troops to South Africa.

Denounced by German Veterans.

Berlin, Nov. 19.—The anti-Chamberlain movement in Germany is growing, in spite of the remonstrance issued officially by the Deutscher Kriegerbund, the society of veterans of Berlin to-day held a large and enthusiastic meeting of this kind in which the utterance of Mr. Chamberlain at Edinburgh were heartily denounced.

GOVERNMENT WILL WIN OUT.

French Deputies Likely to Authorize Loan Asked by the Cabinet.

Paris, Nov. 19.—The Chamber of Deputies to-day continued the discussion of the bill authorizing a loan of 26,000,000 francs, in 2 per cent. perpetual rentes, to reimburse the treasury for its outlay in connection with the Chinese expedition and the indemnification of French sufferers in China.

AMERICA TO LEAD THE WORLD.

France Advised to Take Advantage of Our Proverbial Friendship.

Paris, Nov. 19.—M. Jules Siegfried lectured to-night at the Musee social on his recent tour in America, repeating as extended from the opinions already expressed in the interview cabled to America last July.

BOSTON GETS FAMOUS WOMAN CROOK.

Tessie Hamilton Was Sought by Detectives from Several Other States.

Toledo, Ohio, Nov. 19.—Anna Evans, alias Tessie Hamilton, Tessie Ellis, and Mary Murray, for whom possession, the officers of three States fought at the Union Station last Saturday, was again turned over to the Boston detectives this afternoon, and he is taking her to Boston to-night.

RANSOM NEGOTIATIONS OFF

Report that Consul General Wants Troops to Deal with Brigands.

Sofia, Nov. 19.—It is reported that Mr. Dickinson, the United States diplomatic agent here, has informed the government of Bulgaria that the abductors of Miss Ellen M. Stone and Mme. Tsilka, with their captives, are concealed in a defile of the Belieritza Mountains, near Samokoff, district of Dubnitza, and has requested that troops be sent to surround the place and liberate the captives.

EVICTED WOMAN SHOOTS TWO MEN.

They Had Taken Possession of House from Which She Had Been Evicted.

Creston, Iowa, Nov. 19.—Mrs. Charles Edwards, a widow, living three miles west of here, early to-day shot Alva Nearly, colored, and Herman James, white, when she claims were attempting to prevent her from occupying a board farm where the shooting occurred. Nearly was shot through the body, and he will die, but James is not seriously hurt.

GOT HIS WISH AS TO DEATH.

Engineer Michael Sprath Stricken Down at the Throttle.

Chicago, Nov. 19.—Michael Sprath for thirty-five years an engineer for the Lake Shore road, dropped dead in the cab of his engine to-day. It was the death he had often told his friends he hoped for coming upon him when his head was still on the throttle.

LEFT A DEAD ROBBER BEHIND THEM.

Police Believe Charles M. Kinney Was Shot by His Companions.

Hutchinson, Kan., Nov. 19.—The safe of the Missouri Pacific Railroad depot here was blown by robbers early to-day. Afterward a man, believed to have been one of the robbers, was found dead with a bullet hole through his heart.

CONTINUED ON SECOND PAGE

Mrs. Bonine went on trial on November 19, 1901, and the Washington Post's *own special artist was there. The defendant, who is shown wearing a hat that resembles a wasp's nest, pleaded "not guilty" in a low but distinct voice. The courtroom was the same one in which President Garfield's assassin, Charles Guiteau, was tried and sentenced.*

of Port Austin, Michigan.

The Kenmore was a six-story, flat-front building painted white, with a fire escape zigzagging down its front. It stood in the 200 block of North Capitol Street, an address that is now buried under the sod of the Capitol Plaza. It was a hotel that seemed somehow full of young ladies, young ladies all ready to have their heads turned by young Mr. Ayres. It was perfectly respectable. But there was more hanky-panky going on in 1901 than members of the present generation might think. And in the spring young Ayres's thoughts turned lightly to the same thing that had been on his mind all winter. He was, to put it delicately, operating on several levels. He was courting the daughter of Congressman Weeks of Michigan. He was tomcatting around the hotel. He was escorting Miss Agnes Marcy to Muellers Dancing School. He had persuaded Miss Marcy that he was a mysterious, romantic figure. "I'm a bad boy," he told her, "but I won't tell you all."

He added that he also drank. "When I feel blue and despondent, I drink," he said. He was perhaps hinting broadly that the naughtiness of which he wouldn't speak was naughtier than the naughtiness of drinking. He was, to the best of his ability, a seducer of ladies.

And, on the fatal night of May 14, he was gliding around the hotel card room as a two-piece orchestra thumped it out behind potted palms. It was, he had announced, his last night on the premises. A pal, J. V. Wiggins, of Texas, recalled later that Ayres had been in a fine state of mind on that fatal evening. "He had everything to live for," Wiggins said later. "He had passed his examinations and had packed his effects to move to a clubhouse on L Street. His trunk and his telescope were partly packed." Ayres, as far as the record shows, was neither a sailor nor a peeping tom. A telescope in 1901 was a sort of expandable suitcase.

After whirling the girls around the floor, Ayres had been called to the hotel lobby, where a bunch of the boys made mock speeches of farewell and had then carried him off to a nearby saloon. Mr. Wiggins had seen him return about midnight and had exchanged a friendly word.

Meanwhile, the young lady who roomed next to Ayres, Miss Mary Minas, of Indiana, pretty but nervous, had been entertaining some lady friends at a game of cards in her room. The ladies left a bit after midnight and one had almost stumbled down the stairs. Somebody had turned down the gas jet in the hall.

Shortly after 2 AM, Miss Minas awoke with a start. Three shots were in the process of ringing out. "I heard him call for help and then he groaned and cried most piteously for five or ten minutes. That somebody had been killed, I felt certain, and I was surprised in the morning when I failed to find the dead body of a burglar in the hall." Concealing her surprise as well as she could, she naturally went down to breakfast. There, breaking bread with her closest friend, Mrs. Lola Bonine, the subject of the sound in the night came up. Miss Minas summoned a waiter, Daniel Woodhouse, and asked him to go up and knock on Mr. Ayres's door and see if he was in good health. Woodhouse went up, knocked, and, when no one answered, peeked through the keyhole. There was Ayres, sprawled in a pool of blood.

As Mrs. Bonine suggested later, it was too bad that Miss Minas, or someone, hadn't sounded the alarm. It was, indeed, a curiously leisurely bit of alarm sounding, because, it developed, dozens of people had heard the shots. When the father of the deceased subsequently arrived from Michigan, he was moved to say: "If this murder had been committed in the village of Port Austin, there's not a man, woman, or child of the 700 citizens but who would have raised an alarm and sought to rescue him." Still, once the cops had been called, there were plenty of men, women, and children who were ready to come forth with a clue or two. The first clues were, of course, right there at the scene of the crime. 107

Lying in the vicinity of the corpse was a Harrison and Richardson .32 revolver with a blood-smeared barrel. "The ownership of which," the *Star* stolidly noted, "is a matter of interest to the detectives."

The next clue was one that was, one might say, a few years ahead of its proper time. On the sill of the room's window was a bloody handprint, a small print, a woman's-size print. Over in France, Alphonse Bertillion was still renowned for his method of identifying criminals by measuring their earlobes, and his incipient interest in measuring fingertip whorls was still unpublicized.

The handprint, it would seem, was almost certainly that of the mysterious lady who had been going down the hotel fire escape. She had been seen by two or three people. The best witness was Thomas A. Baker, a clerk in the office of the Fish Commission, who lodged next to the Kenmore. Lying in bed, he had heard the shots and had gotten up and gone to his window. "While watching I saw a form come from a window on the fourth floor and descend the fire escape leisurely to the second floor. The woman was in her night robe and stocking feet. She used her left hand on the rail of the fire escape and held up her gown with her right hand. When she reached the veranda on the second floor she entered a room."

"Cherchez la femme," as they probably didn't say in Port Austin, but the Kenmore had an overabundance of femmes. There was Miss Minas and her best friend, and Miss Kate Lawless, and a lady cloaked in the magnificent name of Miss Mattie St. Clair Woolum, and a dozen others.

James Seymour Ayres, the gallant lad, had danced attention on them all.

The police—Inspector Boardman and Detectives Williams, Weedon, Parlam, Horne, Flather, Peck, Bauer, and Trumbo —talked to the ladies and searched their rooms. They all denied being the lady descending the fire escape or, for that matter, having any idea who she might be. The police did find one gentleman who, it seemed, had actually spoken to her. R. P. Hopkins had heard three shots and had leaned out his hotel window. He had seen what he first believed to be a man's head but what proved, on second

glance, to be merely a man's skull. It was lying on the fire escape by the window. (Ayres had a spare skull which he used as a sort of paperweight. He had rendered it himself from a fully fleshed specimen.) Hopkins, after identifying the skull as a skull, had cried out, "What is the matter?" A woman's voice had answered, "I don't see anything here." Hopkins, rather oddly satisfied, went back to bed. The identity of the woman remained a mystery. The undertaker, Hines, took charge of the body, and the dead young man's father arrived and spoke highly of his son. "I believe he only yielded to some of the temptations that surround a young, intelligent, and affectionate young man."

The coroner's jury met at the sixth precinct on New Jersey Avenue, a select panel which included two gentlemen whose names have lingered on through their business establishments: George A. Harvey, restaurant proprietor, and J. William Lee, undertaker.

It developed as the mystery began to unfold that at least two anonymous letters had been written, one before the crime, one after. The first had been addressed to Congressman Weeks and had informed him that young Mr. Ayres, who had been courting his daughter, was a libertine. The letter had greatly annoyed Mr. Ayres, though it had not, apparently, succeeded in turning the Congressman against him.

The second letter was signed "Chambermaid" and was sent to the police. It suggested that Miss Minas was the killer.

The coroner worked his way through the witnesses and there gradually emerged a picture of Ayres that clearly established him as a Don Juan and suggested clearly that he had been done in by a bloody-handed lady who had resented either his

On the ninth day of the trial the court bailiff, a stalwart fellow named Joyce, stood before the jury stripped to his waist with three circles of court-plaster fixed to his chest, arm, and thigh, showing where the bullets had hit the late James Seymour Ayres. The Post *did not show a picture of Mr. Joyce's naked torso, although a few days later it did show him well covered in coat, shirt, and tie.*

The Washington Post.

Weather—Fair and continued cold to-day and to-morrow; fresh northerly winds.

THREE CENTS.

K AND FIRE

...s of Life in ...Collision.

NUMBER 150

in Cars and Slowly to Death.

STRANDED AT UNALASKA.

Unenviable Plight of Passengers and Crew of Overdue Vessel.

Seattle, Wash., Nov. 27.—Advices from the North being news that the long overdue schooner, Ralph J. Long, from Nome, lies stranded at Unalaska, with 115 passengers. The vessel is out of food, the passengers have spent all their money to obtain the absolute necessities of life, and they now appeal for help to the War Department. L. Frank Brown, of this city, presented a resolution to the Seattle Chamber of Commerce to-day, reciting the facts in the case and urging the necessity of immediate aid for the passengers and crew.

TO PROVE BRIBERY CHARGE

Big Row Promised in the Ranks of Missouri's Democracy.

Representative Cardwell Is Collecting Evidence to Prove Corruption in Party Machine—Sues the St. Louis Republic for Libel.

AS A HUMAN MODEL

Bailiff Joyce Poses Half Clad in the Courtroom.

WOUNDS LOCATED ON HIM

A Remarkable Scene Yesterday in the Bonine Trial.

Deputy Coroner Glasebrook Testifies that the Bullet Wounds Found in Ayres' Body Could Not, in His Opinion, Have Been Self-Inflicted—Upon Cross-examination He Describes Bruises and Abrasions of the Skin Both Upon Deceased and Mrs. Bonine.

MRS. BONINE IN CHARACTERISTIC ATTITUDE

FOUGHT FOR BRIDGE

Stronghold of the Liberals Weakly Defended.

FALLING BACK ON COLON

Popular Sentiment at Panama Very Bitter Toward Americans.

Colon, Colombia, Nov. 27.—It was learned on the highest authority this afternoon that Gen. Jeffries is with Gen Alban on the Colon side of Barbacoa, and that 300 men from Panama are now marching to join them.

FEATURES OF TO-DAY'S PAPER.

PART ONE.
Pages.
1—Frightful Railroad Catastrophe.
   Human Model in Bonine Trial.
   Suicide Rather than Exposure.
   Rebels Fall Back on Colon.
2—Accused of Theft of State Papers.
   Tobacco Habit in Public Schools.
3—Busy Day at the White House.
   Postmaster General's Report.
4—Scenes of Virginia and Maryland.
   Clash in Pan-American Congress.
6—Editorial Comment.
   Noble Prisoner Set Free.
7—Mine Rules Pay its Way.
   Events in World of Sport.
9—District Revenues Deficient.
10—Municipal Affairs.
PART TWO.
11—To-day's Thanksgiving Services.
13—Financial and Commercial.

HIS CHOICE WAS DEATH.

City Treasurer Young Could Not Face Exposure.

Louisville, Ky., Nov. 27.—After being offered an evening newspaper which and his books were under examination by expert accountants, Stuart R. Young, city treasurer of Louisville, this evening went to the rear of a warehouse at Sixth and Nelson streets and committed suicide by shooting himself behind the right ear with a pistol.

The Washington Post.

Weather — Fair,
warmer; to-morrow fair
east to south winds.

WASHINGTON, SUNDAY, DECEMBER 1, 1901—FORTY PAGES.

Y WIN

the Pres-
eet.

XCITING

stery Wit-
Crowd.

ified Their
the
ntial Part-
and
Excite-
11 to 5.

Probably the
of that eve-
n this com-
tnry crowd
of Franklin
Ahnapolis
to 5. The
Nova
s great am-
e after the
athletic en-
latics three
the chain-
country.
of the Chb-
patch by the
prisoner
t for their
n the watch-
ly used for
len. There
hundred

Luck with West Point

There was an element of luck in the victory of the West Point eleven this afternoon. They were outplayed by the Annapolis team in both halves, but it was a
case of too much Italy. This great little
quarter back ran the Army team with rare
judgment, and besides making the entire
eleven points for his team, prevented at
least two touchdowns by the West Brit-
liant tackling ever seen on Franklin Field.

PISTOL WAS AYRES'

Will Prove Ownership, Says Mrs. Bonine's Counsel.

ACCUSED NOT TO TESTIFY

Father of Dead Youth Last of Government's Witnesses.

**Says He Found Mrs. Bonine Devoid of Sym-
pathy When He Talked to Her About His
Dead Son—Macroscopist Testifies Regard-
ing Absence of Blood Stains on Accused
Woman's Wrapper—Prosecution Rests Its
Case—Opening Statement by Defense**

An old, white-haired man, whose eyes
filled with tears as he talked, was the
last witness against Mrs. Bonine, charged
with the murder of James Seymour Ayres.

CRASH IN THE FOG

Crowded Ferry-boat Sunk in San Francisco Bay.

LOSS OF LIFE UNKNOWN

Early Estimates of Number Drowned Vary from Twenty to Fifty.

**The San Rafael Cut Down in Collision with
the Sausalito—Boat Almost Immediately,
but Many of the Passengers Were Res-
cued—Wild Rush for Life Preservers and
Escape from the Sinking Vessel by Jump-
ing Overboard—A Passenger's Story.**

San Francisco, Nov. 30.—The ferryboats
Sausalito and San Rafael collided to-night
in a dense fog, and the San Rafael sank
in between ten and fifteen minutes.

EXPOSURE CAME AT LAST.

Brokers Fleeced Customers of $300,000 Before Detection.

New York, Nov. 30.—Frank Dillon and
John F. Bennett are under arrest charged
with operating in conjunction with two
other persons, not yet arrested, a bogus
stock brokerage business which promises
that they were members of the Stock Exchange. It is charged that the men received $300,000 from customers.

ANARCHIST IN THE CROWD.

Arrest in Philadelphia of Man Who Talked of Killing President.

Philadelphia, Pa., Nov. 30.—Late to-night
the police officials admitted having arrested a man this afternoon for uttering
anarchistic sentiments concerning President Roosevelt. The arrest was made in
the business section of the city.

OUSTE

Governor

Governor
move

NO MIN

Mr. Roosevel
in Expl

Appointment o
Removed Willi
Governor Is A
dans in Musk
Second—$10,0
Political Enem

The Presiden
Thomas B. Fe

On November 30 a "microscopist" testified that he could not find, through his newfangled instrument, a single spot of blood on Mrs. Bonine's wrapper. The point was against Mrs. Bonine, who had told police that Ayres had fallen on her after shooting himself and had gotten blood on her velvet collar.

display of affection or his lack of affection.

The inquest went on and on for days, with no clue to the lady's identity except the insubstantial one (and as it turned out, the inaccurate one) of the postcard from the "chambermaid."

Then suddenly and dramatically, the name of a certain lady was on every tongue.

Eliza Gardner, of 611 3rd Street, Southwest, a chambermaid at the Kenmore, was being questioned.

"Did you ever see any ladies go to his [Ayres's] room?" the coroner asked.

"No sir, I never saw Mrs. Bonine in his room," the chambermaid replied.

"I didn't ask you that."

"I know you didn't, but I thought you were going to."

And, in a very few minutes, it developed that Eliza had seen Mrs. Bonine in Ayres's room many a time.

"Well, she often came there when I was in there and said she wanted to borrow a book of his and she'd go to the table and pick it up and go out with it."

The coroner, naturally, wanted to know why the maid had said a few minutes before that that she'd never seen Mrs. Bonine in the room. The maid replied that she meant she hadn't seen her in there with Mr. Ayres. It also developed that Eliza was the chambermaid who had sent the note falsely accusing Miss Minas.

Lola Ida Hemri Bonine was immediately the center of attention. She was 34, the mother of two boys and the wife of a traveling salesman who was on the road every day but weekends. Another witness, William W. Pearce, the hotel handyman, was found. He had found her in Ayres's room on two occasions when he went there to fix a broken lock. She had told him she would go into the bathroom and that he should not tell anyone she was there.

Mary Grayson, a maid, said that she was in Ayres's room one day when Mrs. Bonine came in and he told her, Mrs. Bonine, to get out and stay out. Mary said that Mrs. Bonine later called her aside and said, "He's only mad with me because he thinks I told people around the hotel that he drank, and I never did anything of the kind."

Miss Minas was recalled to the stand and she said, when asked, that Mrs. Bonine had gone to Mr. Ayres's room at night. She said she also understood that Mrs. Bonine and Ayres had had a misunderstanding about the Inaugural Ball.

The coroner's jury recessed for the weekend and Mr. Bonine returned from his commercial travels in the Shenandoah Valley. He said he had complete and absolute trust in his wife.

Mrs. Bonine said she realized she was under suspicion by the detectives and she declared her innocence.

Next, the detectives received an emergency call to rush to a downtown theater to interview a man who had important information on the murder. They rushed and were met by a prominent gentleman who suggested that they hold a euchre party and that in the course of the evening that mention be made of Ayres's name. The amateur Sherlock said that when the name was mentioned the guilty party would show undue excitement. The police declined.

On Sunday night Mr. and Mrs. Bonine asked Detective Edward Horne if he'd care to dine out with them. He accepted. They went to a lunch room on C Street, Northwest. Bonine excused himself, Mrs. Bonine and Horne ate steaks. Mrs. Bonine said, casually, that she had "a thought" about the murder but that it might "affect the deceased." Horne replied that nothing she could say would affect the dead. They left the restaurant and she went to the railroad depot to mail a letter. Then they walked back to the hotel. Horne asked her if she'd decided to tell him what she knew. "No," she said, "I'll tell it to you tomorrow. My God the strain is horrible. My innocence is all that keeps me up."

The next morning, as promised, she 111

had something to tell.

She told it to Horne, as a police stenographer took it down.

"I was in the room when the shooting occurred. He came to my room and rapped on the door. I opened the door and saw he had on his pants, vest, shirt, and shoes. He wanted to come in my room but I told him no, that my boys were asleep. He then said he had a chill and asked for some bromo quinine tablets. He asked me if I would not come to his room and talk over the little difficulty we had had, as he was going to leave the hotel in the morning. I told him I would. I put on clean linen and a fancy wrapper, slippers and black stockings, but no corsets, as I never wore corsets with that wrapper. I went to his room and put my hand on the knob when he partly opened the door, and I went in. He had nothing on but an undershirt and he had a pistol, holding it down this way. He said, 'Now will you do what I want you to do?' and I ran toward the window."

She tripped, she said, and fell against Ayres and somehow the gun went off a few times.

At the conclusion of her confession she fell on her knees before her husband, asking his forgiveness and assuring him that she had not been guilty of any improper relations with Ayres.

Nobody, with the possible exception of Mr. Bonine, believed her. Mr. Bonine was, remember, a seller of patent medicines—and a man who believed rhubarb root would cure galloping consumption would probably believe anything.

Various people said that they had not only seen Mrs. Bonine coming out of Ayres's room, they'd seen her coming out of the room of a number of other young men as well.

The hotel janitor told how Ayres had brought home a decapitated head and had put it in a box of lime in the basement, the point being to burn away the fleshy reminders of the previous owner. He said that he had seen Mrs. Bonine pick up the skull while it was still cooking, so to speak, and poke her fingers through its eye sockets while making ribald remarks.

The enterprising *Star* queried a far-flung correspondent and reported that

This dainty pistol was the kind used to kill James Seymour Ayres.

back in Macon, Missouri, her girlhood home, Mrs. Bonine had been considered "very pretty, with a host of admirers. She could have married nearly any of the young men of Macon."

Mrs. Bonine appealed for bail but bail was denied. As summer came and passed, things looked black for Mrs. Bonine.

But for some reason, ladies who shoot gentlemen are never in as much trouble as one might think. By the time her trial began, on November 19, 1901, there had been an obvious, if curious, change of attitude.

She appeared in court, flanked by her husband, two sons, two sisters, and a brother, and the *Star*, recording the shift in the wind as clearly as a weather cock, noted that she was "petite, attractive, and apparently refined."

She wore a dark blue dress, "which

she made herself," a black hat with a black feather, and black kid gloves.

And . . . "she has all the little graces and those indescribable niceties of movement and manner and expression which indicate the possession of refined femininity in generous quantities and is the very person one would expect to give way to nervous hysterics on slight suggestion owing to her evidently high strung organization. . . . She is a perfect Joan of Arc, so far as vitality is concerned, and is altogether a marvelous woman."

It seemed clear that the *Star*, at least, was not in favor of burning this Joan of Arc at any stake.

The defense attorneys, led by Charles A. Douglass, hinted broadly that they intended to put Joan on the stand, but, as a matter of fact, they never did.

The courtroom was jammed with ladies

and the curiosity of the women irritated the more stuffy men, such as the justices of the Supreme Court of Washington. One of these was stopped in the courthouse by a well-dressed lady who asked if he would "kindly tell me where the room is in which Mrs. Bonine is being tried."

The justice, swelling up like a toad, replied, "I will not and I will further say that the place for you is at home with your family, if you have one."

The defense relied on two points. One, that Mrs. Bonine's aged mother lay dying in Missouri. As the *Star* noted, when Mr. Douglass referred to this, "Mrs. Bonine wiped a single tear . . . her sisters and brother sobbed unrestrained, and the eyes of one of the jurors was noted to be suspiciously moist."

The other point of defense was that 113

The Washington Post.

WASHINGTON, SATURDAY, DECEMBER 14, 1901—FOURTEEN PAGES.

Weather — Rain, probably turning into snow at night; clearing and colder to-morrow.

THREE CEN

Hero of Manila Gives Schley the Credit for the Victory at Santiago.

"In the opinion of the undersigned, the passage from Key West to Cienfuegos was made by the Flying Squadron with all possible dispatch, Commodore Schley having in view the importance of arriving off Cienfuegos with as much coal as possible in the ships' bunkers.

"The blockade of Cienfuegos was effective. Commodore Schley, in permitting the Steamer Adula to enter the port of Cienfuegos, expected to obtain information concerning the Spanish squadron from her when she came out.

"The passage from Cienfuegos to a point about twenty-two miles south of Santiago was made with as much dispatch as possible while keeping the squadron a unit.

"The blockade of Santiago was effective.

"Commodore Schley was the senior officer of our squadron off Santiago when the Spanish Squadron attempted to escape on the morning of July 3, 1898. He was in absolute command, and is entitled to the credit due to such commanding officer for the glorious victory which resulted in the total destruction of the Spanish ships.

"GEORGE DEWEY, Admiral United States Navy."

NO OFFER FROM FORAKER.

Secretary Malloy Denies Rumors of Proposed Compromise in Ohio.

Columbus, Ohio, Dec. 13.—John R. Malloy, secretary of the Republican State executive committee, returned to-day from Washington, where he had a conference with Senator Hanna and Congressman Dick, chairman of the Republican State committee, relative to the controversy over the organization of the Ohio legislature. To-night Mr. Malloy gave out the following statement:

"From what I have learned since my return to Columbus, I can say only that there has been no change in the situation, and so far as rumors of a proposed compromise are concerned, which it was said would be made to Senator Hanna by the friends of Senator Foraker and Mr. Kurtz, no offer of compromise had been received up to the hour of my leaving Washington last night. If any are to be made, Senator Hanna has no information concerning them, except what has appeared in the newspapers.

"Before this contest was precipitated Senator Hanna and Gen. Dick held their different conferences in Washington with Senator Foraker, in the hope that so far as the two Senators are concerned any friction among their respective friends regarding the organization of the two houses might be avoided.

"At the first conference Senator Hanna asked only that Mr. Dick be made chairman of the senate. This was but wholly a personal request upon Senator Hanna's part, but was made because he believed it would be good politics for the reason that the Democrats control the delegation from Cuyahoga County in both the house and senate, and Mr. Hanna desired in the interest of the Republican party of Cuyahoga County that there might be a representative party at Columbus who could keep in touch with any proposed legislation affecting the city of Cleveland and Cuyahoga County.

"For this reason he desired the re-elec-

MRS. BONINE

Jury Reaches Verdict Than Five Hour

WILD SCENES IN

Vindicated Woman Overwh Crowd's Demonstrati

Cheered, Kissed, and Caressed W City Hall Escorts Her to Attere Goes to H Street Home with He Children—Will Continue to Lic ington—Closing Hours of the T

"Not guilty."

With the pronunciation of the ill-fated words last evening at a few minutes after 10 o'clock Mrs. Lola Henry Bonine, who had trial since November 15 for the shooting of James Seymour Ayres, jr., in more than early in the morning of October 18, was a free woman. The dread and death was over. The continued cloud in the court room was broken and sent into the crowded street where many men and women had rushed in bracing her, pressing her hand her cheek, overpowered with emotion...

EAR ADMIRAL WINFIELD SCOTT SCHLEY.

MRS. LOLA IDA HEMRY BONINE.

CHILE'S LAST WORD

Argentine Demands Met by Counter Proposals.

PEACE HINGES ON REPLY

Rejection Would Bring Diplomatic Communications to an End.

Brazil Offers to Act as Mediator, but It Is Not Thought that Her Good Offices Will Be Sought in Settling the Quarrel—Great Britain Also Tenders a Similar Service and the United States Is Preparing a Similar Action—Argentine May Accept.

Buenos Ayres, Dec. 13.—Dispatches received here from Santiago de Chile say that Senor Yanez, Chilean minister of foreign affairs, has handed the basis of a new proposition to Senor Portela, the Minister of the Argentine Republic to Chile, to effect the impartial and friendly settlement of the boundary dispute between the two countries. If these bases are refused by Argentine, Chile will make no further propositions. The refusal of Argentina will be taken as indicating that that country desires war.

The Chilean reply has not yet been made known here.

The newspapers here publish bulletins to-day assuring the public that all matters between the two countries will be honorably arranged.

Santiago de Chile, Dec. 13.—The Brazilian government has proffered its amicable mediation in the Argentine-Chile dispute. It would seem here that the action will not be necessary, as both the Argentine and Chilean governments hope to come to terms.

A contingent of the Chilean reserves has been called to arms. It numbers about fifty thousand men. No movement of the military forces under arms has occurred, however. Everything is quiet here.

Believe Argentina Will Accept.

London, Dec. 13.—The Associated Press learns on authoritative source that the Chilean reply to the representations of the minister of the Argentine Republic is expressed by the officials here that the basis for a settlement proposed will lead to a satisfactory arrangement between the two governments.

Paris, Dec. 13.—A dispatch received here from Santiago de Chile, under to-day's date, says:

"The alarm manifested in Argentina is declared in Chilean official circles to be unwarranted. In the opinion of the government the boundary dispute will never justify a rupture."

A news agency here this afternoon received a dispatch from its office at Buenos Ayres, dated it o'clock this morning, confirming the dispatch from Buenos Ayres last night announcing the calling up of the Argentine army reserves and that at the request of the government the chamber of deputies had sanctioned bill setting aside the conversion fund to be used for the national defense.

American Minister Called in.

Continuing, the dispatch from Buenos Ayres says: "The report that the United States will offer its good offices is confirmed. At Chile's request the American Minister has notified the Argentine government. Brazil has offered mediation.

"It was announced here that Chile has called out 15,000 men, but the news is questioned here...

FOR HEAVY EMBEZZLEMENTS.

Officers of Collapsed Debenture Concern Charged with Looting the Assets.

Birmingham, Ala., Dec. 13.—George W. Morgan, president, and George A. Blinn, jr., treasurer of the Continental Security Redemption Company, doing an extensive business in Alabama, Kentucky, and Georgia, and W. L. Dodd, formerly secretary and treasurer of the Birmingham Debenture Company, have been arrested on charges of embezzlement, the amount varying from $500 to $25,000. Four warrants are held against George W. Morgan, the amounts aggregating $5,000. Two warrants are held against Blinn, one charging the embezzlement of $5,000, while the other charges the embezzlement of a check for $2,500.

The Continental Security Redemption Company up to the time its affairs became involved in the courts carried on a debenture redemption business. Its financial troubles were brought to the attention of the public on April 10 last, when a petition was filed in the United States Circuit Court in this city to have the concern placed in the hands of a receiver.

President Washburn Arrives at Sofia to Reopen Negotiations.

London, Dec. 13.—Under Sofia date, the Telegraph publishes a dispatch to the effect that George Washburn, president of the Robert College at Constantinople, has arrived at Sofia on a confidential mission connected with the release of Miss Stone, the captive American missionary.

The dispatch further says that it is rumored the United States will pay the ransom of the brigands in full.

ROTHSCHILD VS. ROCKEFELLER.

London Paper Predicts Victory for Former in Any Fight Over Copper.

London, Dec. 13.—The directors of the Rio Tinto Company have been meeting here daily, though quite informally, since the copper crisis became acute. A representative of the Associated Press was officially informed after to-day's meeting that whatever settlement may be arrived at now lies entirely with the Amalgamated Copper Company. The Rio Tinto Company has made all the propositions which it intends to make, but so far has received no indication of the action the Amalgamated Company proposes to take. A feeling prevails that the conditions will not be altered at present.

The Pall Mall Gazette says that if Mr. Rockefeller has really thrown down the gauntlet to the Rothschilds, which the paper thinks improbable, there can be little doubt of the Rothschilds' victory.

The Pall Mall Gazette adds:

"The Rio Tinto Company is in a position to regard with equanimity a further drop of 30 shillings per ton, but not so the Standard Oil Company, which has to consider the possibility of a general smash of the American market."

Rio Tinto fell three-eighths at the opening to-day, but subsequently regained this and slightly improved on last night's price.

The copper market is still governed by mysterious influences, the details of which event the dealers are unable to fathom. It is said to be remarkable that, in spite of the selling pressure, coupled with the gloomy reports from New York, the price has remained fairly firm only about 3 shillings per ton. The heaviest selling was from a fresh quarter. It is regarded curiously, but no explanation was forthcoming.

It is believed in many quarters that the most important London houses consider the present prices to be justified by close examination and consumption of copper, and that consequently they are willing to lay in considerable stocks in the neighborhood of it, which they would not have done at 6. Thus the market is sustained by quiet absorption of the surplus supplies.

FOR "OLD COMFORT."

Mrs. Bonine was free in time to do her last-minute Christmas shopping. On the evening of December 13th she heard the "not guilty" verdict locked in her husband's arms, with her sons clinging to her skirts and her sisters and brother crying and laughing.

Mrs. Bonine was having her menstrual period at the time of the shooting. This was indicated, naturally, by nineteenth century indirection. As the *Star* recounted, "The greater part of the testimony brought out tended to show that the defendant's physical condition was such that she could have had no impure motive in going to James Seymour Ayres's room."

The bloody palm print, with its perfect but useless set of fingerprints, was rather oddly seized upon by the defense, which hoped to prove that it *was* Mrs. Bonine's print.

They did so because the prosecution, led by District Attorney Gould, had offered as its theory the hypothesis that Mrs. Bonine had come to Ayres's room by way of the fire escape and had shot him without ever entering the room. If that palm print was hers, then obviously this theory was false.

The defense contended, as had been indicated by Mrs. Bonine's earlier confession, that Ayres pointed his gun at her and attempted to force her to do his wicked will. She had, they argued, then wrestled with him and the gun had gone off, dousing her in blood. The blood had gotten on her hand and with that bloody hand she had seized the barrel of the pistol.

In support of this proposition was the fact that the gun barrel was bloody and the handle was not.

In contradiction to it was the improbability of a 92-pound woman successfully wrestling with a young athlete over six feet tall.

District Attorney Gould did his best in a final plea. "Her story is a thing to cause mirth and laughter," he told the jury. "If that story would acquit her, then human life in the District of Columbia is not safe."

He then made a sort of national appeal to protect the frailty not of young women, but of young men.

"How many parents throughout this wide land are asking themselves if their sons are now safe in the capital of the nation?"

The jury, after five hours, decided to string along with Lola and let the sons of the nation look out for themselves.

The Wife Killers

ONE CALM SEPTEMBER NIGHT in 1921 Roger Eastlake and his girlfriend took an axe and gave Mrs. Eastlake 29 whacks.

On August 20, 1952, shortly after midnight, G. Edward Grammer, a plump church usher, tucked his wife's dead body behind the wheel of her almost-new Oldsmobile and sent it rolling down the hill.

Six years later Larry Lord Motherwell, another church usher, held his wife gently but firmly, face down in the bath. Burble, burble.

Then, Robert Ammidown, a star member of the Cherrydale Baptist Monthly Men's Club—who looked enough like Motherwell to be his blood brother—arranged to have his wife murdered and raped.

Husbands kill wives ten times as often as wives kill husbands—or at any rate they get caught ten times as often. The ingenious ones get caught. Not all, but most of them. They get caught because they're ingenious. They do not all have the same motive or skill but there is a thread that loops around them, strong

enough to hang a man. They have much in common, these plump, bland men: Motherwell, Grammer, Ammidown, Eastlake, and even the Air Force sergeant who, in 1952, shoved his pregnant wife out of the car door, backed up and ran her down, and then drove to the Waldorf, Maryland, police and reported that she was missing from the front seat. They were mild, meticulous, church-going men. They all had girlfriends as well as wives, though the girlfriends were seldom the major reason why they killed. They were military men. Ammidown was a career Naval officer; Grammer had been an Army criminal investigation agent; Eastlake was a chief petty officer; even Motherwell pretended to be a Naval officer, varying his rank up to admiral, and he was once arrested for impersonating a lieutenant commander—blue suit, gold braid, and all.

Roger D. Eastlake was a chief petty officer in the Navy's air branch back in 1921. He did his wife in at Colonial Beach, Virginia, and he was less ingenious than some. Which may have been the reason that, although he was caught, he was not convicted. The Chief had a wife named Margaret, a couple of kids, a cottage at the beach, and a girlfriend with the improbable name of Sarah Euphemia Knox. The Chief was not much of a churchgoer but other than that he was one of the boys—mild, chubby, polite, and as devoid of the deeper impulses of kindness as a crab.

Mrs. Eastlake departed the world abruptly on September 30, 1921. Colonial Beach never had much charm but in the twenties it was wet, sandy, and easy to get to. The first big Bay Bridge was decades away and summers in Washington without air conditioning were as humid as a marathon runner's armpit. So everyone went to Chesapeake Beach on the Maryland side of the bay or to Colonial at the mouth of the Potomac, doused themselves in citronella, sat elbow to elbow on the tiny public sand pile at the water's edge, played bingo at night on the pier, and sweated out the long hot nights in ten-by-six crackerbox hotel rooms or in small cottages on dirt roads.

The Eastlakes' cottage was blocks from the beach. By September the nights were cooler, even in Washington. Most of the cottages were closed and the hotels uncrowded.

Miss Knox came to Colonial Beach September 29th with a hatchet in her bag. She and the Chief had shared many a hotel room over the years and at least 85 letters. The letters were both romantic and—in a word chosen later by the trial judge—unprintable. They seemed out of character, for Miss Knox was a graduate nurse from Johns Hopkins and a lady of exemplary reputation.

She had given the Chief money—$700 —as well as herself and she had also exchanged less romantic letters with the Chief's wife, Margaret. In one she had specifically denied trying to "vamp" Roger. In reply Mrs. Eastlake had confided she "dispised" him herself. There were also indications that Mrs. Eastlake had been carrying on a bit herself with, of all people, Miss Knox's brother. That September things came to a head. Miss Knox came down with hatchet and registered at Azeele's Hotel. When darkness fell she headed for the cottage. She spent the night, or most of it, in a shack nearby.

When the multiated body of Dorothy Eastlake was found in a Colonial Beach cottage one autumn morning, the local constabulary jumped to the conclusion that her husband and his girl friend did it. The girl friend had discovered the body, she said, after spending the night hidden in a shed in the cottage's yard.

The Eastlakes' little boy, Roger, Jr., age eight, woke up about 5 AM. He had heard his little sister, Margaret, six, cry. Margaret told him that a man, "who looked like Papa" had shoved her aside and run from the house. He had been wearing a raincoat. Junior put her back to bed, got dressed, and attempted to go into the parlor where his mother was sleeping. The door was blocked. He looked out the window and saw Miss Knox through a gap in the fence. She was emptying a pan of water. He was puzzled. He sat down by his sleeping sister and waited. In a little while he saw a group of neighbors coming down the road with Miss Knox in the lead. Before he could figure out what had happened he and his sister were hustled out of the house and taken to a neighbor's down the road.

Miss Knox had sounded the alarm. She had gone to the neighbor's and reported finding Mrs. Eastlake hacked to bits on the parlor floor. She said she had seen a "dark man" run from the scene and jump the fence. The local constabulary went and fetched the Chief from the launch where he was on duty. The village G. P., Dr. William Carruthers, told him that his wife had been murdered and added, significantly, "That woman is there." Roger asked, "What woman?" and the Doctor replied, "Miss Knox."

Roger went to the cottage. Miss Knox was standing calm amidst the gore. "Oh, Roger," she said, "who can be your enemy?"

Roger went to Detective T. K. Boulware of the Colonial Beach police and told him to arrest Miss Knox. He said that they'd find a pistol and some dope in her possession. Detective Boulware had gotten his training through a correspondence course, but he knew his duty. He

vote on ratification shortly after
...er 11, probably late Saturday
...ng, October 15.

... unanimous consent agreement
blocked by Senator Sterling yes-
... morning because he feared it
...d mean that Congress would ad-
... without taking action on the
...er bill. He was assured by the
...rity leaders that the antibeer
... would be given consideration
... the treaties and tax revision
had been disposed of, and there-
...withdrew his objection when the
...er came up again at 5 o'clock.

Action Pleases Leaders.

...ere was admittedly much anxi-
... among Republican and Demo-
... leaders over the possibility of
dissenting vote blocking the road
... definite date for a vote on the
...ties. Presumably President
...ling and Secretary Hughes were
...ly anxious, especially as news
come that the German reichstag
... ratified the treaty with Germany,
... would have pleased the adminis-
... if ratification here and in
...in could have come approximate-
...at the same time or simultane-
..., but there is some consolation
...nowing that the date for ratifi-
... has been arranged for on the
... day that the German ratifica-
...has been secured.

...e reservations to the treaty,
... the Senate foreign relations
...mittee has favorably reported
... not necessitate resubmission of
...treaty to the reichstag for ratifi-
...on. The reservations merely deal
... procedure which the United
...ea will adopt to avail itself of
...ats granted by Germany, in case
... United States wishes to do so.
... amendments or changes in the
...ty would, of course, negative the
...man ratification if they altered
...terms agreed upon in the process
... negotiation.

Will Speed Formal Exchanges.

...was explained at the State De-
...ment that no delay would be in-
...ved in the formal exchanges of
...fications after the Senate acts and
...President approves, so that the
...nite establishment of peace with
...that it implies to both countries
... to the economic stability of the
...ld will be practically assured
...hin three weeks. The appointment
... diplomatic officers and consular of-
...als and agents to mutually help
...de considerations, &c., will follow
...mediately.

...ere is the unanimous consent
...eement which was slightly chang-
...from the text first drafted so that
... hour, instead of half an hour,
... given to each senator for debate
...er October 14, provided he de-
... it.

...It is agreed by unanimous consent
...t the Senate will continue the con-
...eration of the treaties with Ger-
...y, Austria and Hungary to the
...lusion of any other bill or resolu-
... upon the calendar or that may
...reported from a committee, or the
...sideration of other business that
... not unanimously recognized as
...gent, and will dispose of such trea-
...s in the order named:

Limits Speeches to One Hour.

...That at 11:30 a. m. on the calen-
... day of Friday, October 14, 1921,
... Senate will proceed to the con-
...ation of the said treaties and
...ntinue such consideration until
...y are finally disposed of, and that
...m and after the hour named on
...said day no senator shall speak
...on any or all of said treaties, or
...on any amendments that may be
...ered thereto or to the resolutions
... ratification, for a longer period
...an one hour in the aggregate on
... treaties and not more than ten
...nutes on any reservation.

...Provided, That if within the pe-
...d outlined by the provisions of the
...t paragraph hereof no senator is
...pared to discuss the treaties or
...er of them, then the Senate shall
...oceed at once to the consideration
... H. R. 8245, the tax bill, so called,
...a will give that measure the right
... way to the exclusion of other leg-
...ation until such time as the con-
...eration of the treaties is resumed.
...Provided further, That nothing in
... unanimous consent shall in any
...er interfere with the unanimous
...ent agreement entered into on
...gust 15, 1921, respecting the final
...e on S. 665, the Panama canal tolls

...The date for the vote on the Pan-
... canal...

... of a filibuster, if it is not actually in
the grip at this moment of a deliberately hampering movement. Although much was hoped for when
Congress resumed its sitting after

CONTINUED ON FOURTH PAGE.

MARINES PREPARE FOR HARDING VISIT

Build Tented "White House" as Guns Boom in Mimic War of Wilderness.

REPRESENTATIVE LENDS AID

Summers, of Washington, Sheds Coat to Help Solve Problems of Presidential Housing.

Special to The Washington Post.

Wilderness Tavern, Va., Sept. 30.—
Amid the booming of artillery and
the rattle of machine guns, the last
nails were driven this afternoon in
the canvas White House which the
marines are preparing for the accom-
modation of President Harding, who
is to visit the maneuvers in the his-
toric Virginia Wilderness tomorrow.
As this will be the first time in the
history of the United States that a
President of the republic has spent a
night under canvas with a military
force, no pains are being spared to
make the accommodations to be offered worthy of the distinction of the
occasion.

In their efforts to render the canvas White House worthy of its distinguished occupant the marines were
not alone. Much of the work of de-
signing and planning, and a considerable amount of the actual labor was
done by a member of the House of
Representatives, John W. Summers,
of Washington. Mr. Summers is an
engineer, contractor and builder by
profession. He declared that in his
career he has designed and built
many houses, but never before has he
had an opportunity to build an abode
for a President of the United States.
Although Mr. Summers was with the
marine force in the capacity of a
guest, he declared the opportunity too
good to lose, and taking off his coat
and rolling up his sleeves was soon
plunged in the task of the erection
of the building.

Provide Three-Room Home.

No pains will be spared to render
the canvas White House perfect in
every appointment and fitting. It
will consist of three large rooms,
made from store tents with a bath
apartment, made of a smaller tent.
All of these will be equipped with
hardwood floors and the living room
will be supplied with furniture, much
of which will be that made by the
arts-crafts school of Quantico. The
bath will be equipped with a sunken
tub, supplied with hot and cold running water, electrically heated, and a
shower. To attend the personal wants
of Mr. Harding and to care for the
canvas White House, two typical
Southern colored "mammies" have

CONTINUED ON FOURTH PAGE.

PLANE DROPS WORLD'S BIGGEST BOMB IN TEST

Monster of 4,300 Pounds Blows Up Crater 100 Feet Wide, 25 Feet Deep.

Aberdeen. Md. Sept. 30 (By the Associated Press).—A crater, 100 feet in
diameter and 25 feet deep, was blown
into the earth at the army proving
grounds here today by a bomb weighing 4,300 pounds, dropped from an
altitude of 4,100 feet. This was the
result of the first test of a new aerial
bomb, the heaviest and probably the
most destructive ever constructed. It
was dropped from a Handley-Page
airplane equipped with a device for
carrying and releasing the projectile.

Army and navy officers who witnessed the test from an elevated plat-
form 1,500 feet from the spot chosen
for the trial, expressed satisfaction
with the result. They suffered no ill
effects from the terrific concussion.

Capt. Norbert Carolin piloted the
plane on its perilous undertaking, accompanied by Sergt. Stewart Smink
as bomber.

HELD WITH WOMAN AS WIFE'S SLAYER

Jury Charges R. D. Eastlake and Miss Knox Killed Mrs. Eastlake.

BLOODY HATCHET IS FOUND

Colonial Beach Residents Tell Police of "Triangle"—Left Wife Alive, Husband Testifies.

Special to The Washington Post.

Colonial Beach, Va., Sept. 30.—
Roger D. Eastlake, a petty officer in
the navy, and Miss Sarah E. Knox
were jointly charged this afternoon
by a coroner's jury with the murder
of Eastlake's wife, whose mutilated
body was discovered in her home here
early this morning. The husband and
Miss Knox have been placed in jail
at Montross, county seat of West-
moreland county, to await the action
of the grand jury.

Miss Knox, who claims Baltimore as
her home, aroused residents in the
neighborhood of the Eastlake home
this morning and informed them that
Mrs. Eastlake had been murdered. She
declared that she had spent the night
in a small house about 10 yards from
Eastlake's house in order that she
might see him early this morning and
company him to the naval proving
grounds at Dahlgreen, where he is
stationed. While waiting, she said,
she saw a man run from the house at
about 6 o'clock. Miss Knox declared
she hastened into the house and found
Mrs. Eastlake murdered. Neighbors
quickly sent word of the tragedy to
Eastlake.

Left Her Alive, He Tells Jury.

When informed of the murder, witnesses testified, Eastlake showed no
surprise, but coolly returned to the
house. He told the jury that he arose
this morning at 5 o'clock and left at
5:30, going direct to the wharf, where
the boat was to leave for the naval
proving grounds. He said his wife
prepared breakfast for him and that
she was alive when he left the house.

Mrs. Eastlake's body and head were
badly mutilated when she was found
by neighbors on the floor of the dining room. A sharp hatchet, with
which the police believe the wounds
were inflicted, was found near the
scene of the tragedy. Mrs. Eastlake's
head was almost severed from the
body. A blood-stained revolver also
was found under the step of the house
in which Miss Knox said she spent
the night, and a raincoat covered
with blood splotches, was found in
some undergrowth near the house.

Find Blood Clots in Sink.

Evidence also was found, say the
police, indicating that instruments
used in the murder of Mrs. Eastlake
had been washed at the kitchen sink
which contained clots of blood.

Two children of Mr. and Mrs. Eastlake, Roger, 10 years old, and Cather-
ine, 8, were asleep in an adjoining
room when their mother was murdered. They told the police that they
came out of their room early in the
morning when they were awakened
by noises in the house but were hastened back into the room by their
father who, they said, told them their
mother had been hurt and was being
taken to the hospital.

Wife Unserved, Neighbors Say.

Eastlake and his family came to
Colonial Beach to live about two years
ago when he was first stationed at
the naval proving grounds at Dahl-
gren. Miss Knox, the police say they
have learned, came with them to the
beach at that time and lived in the
same house for several days when she

CONTINUED ON FOURTEENTH PAGE.

FLORIDA—SOUTH—IMPROVED
SERVICE
Will leave Washington 3:15 p. m. ar-
rive Jacksonville 8:05 a. m. Tues.
11:30 P. M. Atlantic Coast Line, 1415
H st. Phone Main 3800.—Adv.

...tribulations. The Smoot bill is a
radical departure from all the prin-
ciples of the measure which the party
in power has sponsored.

CONTINUED ON FOURTH PAGE.

...ference, apparently had been cleared
away by the message of Mr. de
Valera. The reply raised no question
as to the status of the Sinn Fein delegates, and no further correspondence
between the premier and the Irish
leader is expected.

"Our respective positions have been
stated and understood, and we agree
that conference, not correspondence,
is the most practical and hopeful way
to an understanding." said Mr. de
Valera's message in announcing that
the Irish delegates would meet Mr.
Lloyd George on the date the premier
had set. The letter follows:

"We received your letter of invitation to a conference in London October 11 with a view to ascertaining
how the association of Ireland with
the community of nations known as
the British empire may best be recon-
ciled with Irish national aspirations.

"Our respective positions have been
stated and understood, and we agree
that conference, not correspondence,
is the most practical and hopeful way
to an understanding.

"We accept the invitation. Our
delegates will meet you in London on
the date mentioned and explore every
possibility of a settlement by personal discussion."

Surrender by Neither.

The formula of the association of
Ireland with other communities of the
British empire, for which the mind of
Mr. Lloyd George was responsible, has
finally brought together two sides to
the long-drawn-out controversy on
terms which it is considered here in-
volve the surrender by neither side.

The conference is expected to be unprecedented in the history of Great
Britain, if not of Europe. One result
of it will be the cancellation of an

CONTINUED ON FOURTEENTH PAGE.

House Committee Will Consider Kuklux Klan Inquiry Next Wee...

Imperial Wizard William J. Simmons of the Kuklux Klan in a telegram apparently sent to practically
all senators and members of the
House, yesterday urged that they
vote for the resolution of Representative Peter F. Tague, of Massachusetts, providing for a congressional investigation of the klan.

The imperial wizard "demurred" to
the charges set forth in the resolution,
but asserted that "we unreservedly
agree" with the purpose of the bill.
An impartial inquiry, he said, would
"fully exonerate" the klan.

Simmons's telegrams to the senators
and representatives followed similar
messages to President Harding and
Attorney General Daugherty pledging cooperation in any investigation
the Department of Justice should
undertake.

On receipt of the wire from Imperial
Wizard Simmons, Representative P.
P. Campbell (Republican), of Kansas,
chairman of the House rules committee, dictated the following statement:

"I shall call the rules committee
together as soon as the members return to the city next week and lay
before it the resolutions relating to

the Kuklux Klan, and also Mr. Simmons' telegram.

"In connection with the consi...
tion of these measures, we will ...
the proponents of the investigati...
submit to the committee any info...
tion they may have bearing on ...
necessity for the inquiry asked...

In view of the imperial wiz...
telegraphed approval of the pro...
investigation, Chairman Campbe...
of the opinion that it would ...
essential that representatives of ...
klan be given an opportunity ...
press their views on the resolu...
He said:

"If an investigation is order...
Simmons will be notified and be ...
ample opportunity to be present ...
the investigating committee tak...
the matter."

The text of the wizard's tele...
to the senators and representa...
follows:

"The knights of the Kuklux ...
through their founder and chie...
ecutive, respectfully ask and ...
appreciate your vote in favor o...
passage of a bill introduced Se...
ber 21, 1921, by Hon. Peter F. T...

CONTINUED ON FOURTH PAGE

...resents the composite view of
leaders as to the steps necessar...
relieve the unemployment situa...
and then adjourned until Octobe...
Two or three new committees p...
ably will be appointed in the int...
and the steering committee will ...
main in session during the re...
The most important recommenda...
follow:

Calls for Lower Prices.

1. That manufacturers and w...
salers readjust the prices of ...
commodities to replacement value...
terms of efficient producing and ...
tributing cost plus reasonable p...
and that retailers follow this le...
price reduction, so that the confid...
of the buying public may be rest...

2. That the construction ind...
be revived, to reduce the shortag...
homes and to cut down unemp...
ment in the building trades by ...
certed action in the States and ...
those factors, such as "undue co...
and "malignant combinations" w...
have been making proper expa...
impossible.

3. That the Federal, State ...
municipal governments procee...
once with the expansion of ...
school, sewerage and repair work...
with public buildings and road ...
struction.

Adopted Section by Section.

Henry M. Robinson, chairman o...
organization committee, read th...
port which was adopted sectio...
section.

A sharp difference of opinion ...
during the reading of the figure...
when Secretary of Labor Davis ...
lenged the accuracy of the figure...
ported as to the number of un...
ployed persons in the United S...
It was reported that the committ...
unemployment statistics had ...

CONTINUED ON THIRTEENTH PAGE

The Washington Post.

SUNDAY ENTERED AS SECOND-CLASS MATTER POSTOFFICE, WASHINGTON, D. C.

WASHINGTON: THURSDAY, OCTOBER 6, 1921.

COPYRIGHT, 1921, BY THE WASHINGTON POST CO.

TWO CENTS

Weather—Fair today and tomorrow; warmer today; moderate southeast and west winds. Temperature yesterday—Highest, 64; lowest, 46.

30,203 Paid $103,965
To See Opening of Series

Official figures for game played yesterday:

OTHER FIRST GAME FIGURES.		

LEAGUE ASSEMBLY CLOSES SATISFIED

Brazil, Belgium, China, Spain Reelected Nonpermanent Members of Council.

KARNEBECK SEES PROGRESS

Most Delegates Hopeful of Results of Parley Here—Some Fear Rival Organization.

Geneva, Oct. 5 (By the Associated Press)—The second assembly of the league of nations adjourned at 8 o'clock tonight, after reelecting Brazil, Belgium, China and Spain, the four nonpermanent members of the council.

RAPS TRAINING SHOPS

Forbes Calls Placement System for Veterans Near Slavery.

DOUBTS 6,000 GET BENEFIT

Charges 40 or 50 Institutions Operate Simply to Get Money.

Head of Bureau, Back From Tour, Reports Amazing Conditions to President Harding—Finds Government Controlled Shops and Schools—Finds Men in Universities Making Progress.

BY HARRY N. PRICE.

(Copyright, 1921, by The Washington Post Co.)

The system of educating former service men, in the so-called placement training in private shops, was branded by Col. Charles R. Forbes, director of the war veterans bureau, yesterday as nothing short of criminal, and relating to slavery.

WILL ALTER TAX BILL

Republican Leaders of Senate Reach Compromise Agreement.

15 MEET AT CAPPER'S HOME

Lodge Attends After Party Conference With the President.

Plans Adopted, Which Will Be Submitted to the Finance Committee Today, Are Expected to Result in Passage of Measure Without Democratic Vote—Changes Regarded to Popularize Schedules.

BY GEORGE ROTHWELL BROWN.

(Copyright, 1921, by The Washington Post Co.)

In an eleventh-hour effort of grave import to the Republican party to prevent an impending coalition of insurgent Republicans and Democrats against the party's taxation program, the conservation leaders in the senate are ready to consider a compromise.

DIE IN BURNING CARS

Many Trapped by Train Crash in Paris Rail Tunnel.

33 ON LIST OF KNOWN DEAD

Deadly Fumes Balk Firemen From Exploring Blazing Wreckage.

Explosion of Gas Tanks Cause of Fire in Seventeen Coaches—Call Troops—Hole Cut Through Pavement Into Roof of Tube Leading to St. Lazare Station—Hundreds Run Through Dark Passageway.

By the Associated Press.

Paris, Oct. 5.—A rear-end collision of two suburban trains in the half-mile tunnel leading to the St. Lazare railroad station tonight led to terrifying scenes and the death of many persons bound on their homeward journey to Paris.

Seeks "Invisible Force" Behind Delay in School Construction

Vice President Edwards of School Board Caustic in Demand for Reasons for Hold-Up of Eastern High—Ballou Blames Architect's Office.

Inquiry by Daniel A. Edwards, vice president of the board of education, into the delay in pushing the new Eastern High school to completion led to a discussion at the meeting of the board of education yesterday which developed the first statement school officials have made concerning the slow progress made on a few projects of the emergency building program.

CONTINUED ON TENTH PAGE.

POLICE FACE PROBE OF BOND ACTIVITY

Inspector Starts Investigation of Relations of Officers With Bail Deals.

COMMISSIONERS WILL ACT

Judge Mattingly Declares Guilty Merit Quick Punishment—Would Disbar Lawyers Involved.

Reports that some members of the metropolitan police force have been involved in shady transactions with certain professional bondsmen will be thoroughly investigated by the commissioners.

GUNS GUARD PRISON ON FIRE; 3 ESCAPE

Troops Patrol Reformatory in Ionia, Mich., as Flames Destroy Cells.

$500,000 DAMAGE CAUSED

Investigate Rumor That Auto Load of Convicts Used—Soldering Lamp on Roof Cause of Blaze.

Ionia, Mich., Oct. 5 (By the Associated Press)—Michigan national guardsmen and members of the State constabulary this evening were patrolling the outer wall of the Michigan State reformatory here, where fire today destroyed all cell blocks, the administration offices, the chapel, and women's office.

CONTINUED ON NINTH PAGE.

EASTLAKE CHARGES NURSE KILLED W[...]

Confesses Miss Knox [...] Jealous of Slain Woma[...]

DENIES HAND IN CR[...]

Was Not in Love With [...] Husband Tells Police.

SHE IS ANGRY AND DEFI[...]

Admits, Under "Third-Degree" amination, She Believes [...] "Have Strong Case Again[...] Objects to Being Photograph[...] Officially—Finger Prints Re[...] Forefinger Amputated—Ea[...] Suffers Severely Under Or[...] Both Jailed in Richmond.

(By the Associated Press.)

Richmond, Va., Oct. 5.—[...] that Sarah Knox killed my wife that the reason she did it w[...] cause she was jealous of her[...]

Group Hears Statemen[...]

BROKEN SWING HURLS 29 INTO TERRIFIED CROWDS

Eight Children Hurt Severely When Gondolas Fly Through Air at Brockton Fair.

Brockton, Mass., Oct. 5 (By the Associated Press.)—A swing that singed the flight of an airplane sent pieces at the fair grounds here today, sending twelve cars in which were 29 persons, most of them children, spinning into the crowds on the midway.

Stabbed in Fight With Kuklux, Victim Dies From His Injuries

Waco, Tex., Oct. 5 (By the Associated Press)—Louis Crow, victim of the Lorena fight Saturday night when Sheriff Bob Buchanan and two of his deputies attempted to stop a Kuklux Klan parade, died today. He was near the scene of the conflict and was attempting to prevent a clash, it was said, when the disturbance began. He was stabbed in the right breast.

Chicago, Oct. 5.—The Chicago Herald and Examiner today printed a news story saying that 490 men were initiated into the Kuklux Klan here last night and that a lawyer had obtained a secret service report of the administering of the o[...]

HELD, AFTER 11 YEARS, IN DEATH OF DAUGHTER

Testimony in Pardon Hearing of Convicted Man Implicates Girl's Father.

Madison, Wis., Oct. 5 (By the Associated Press)—Martin Lemberger, father of Annie Lemberger, 7, who was killed here in 1911, was arrested today on a warrant charging second-degree murder, marking the climax of a hearing on an application of John A. Johnson for pardon after serving ten years in State prison for the murder of the girl.

"I believe that Sarah Knox killed my wife and that the reason she did it was because she was jealous of me," was the gallant statement Petty Officer Roger B. Eastlake made to police. In time, in a total reversal of the usual procedure, she was indeed found guilty and he was set free.

arrested both Miss Knox and Chief Eastlake.

Dr. Carruthers, the gentle old family doctor, volunteered his expert opinion. Mrs. Eastlake had been hit with a hatchet 29 times, and it was his opinion that it had taken at least two people to do it. He was also of the opinion that it had been done some hours earlier, between 2 and 4 AM. The body was cold and stiff and the blood congealed.

Mrs. Eastlake had grown up near Colonial Beach and she had a lot of relatives living in the vicinity. A strong tide of anti-Roger feeling came rolling up the shore. Detective Boulware hustled the Chief and Miss Knox off to Richmond under heavy guard.

The Chief was tried first. His defense was simple. He said Miss Knox had done the whole thing. He admitted that he'd had a long affair with her, but insisted that he'd broken it off. He suggested that she'd been driven wild with jealousy. He had an alibi, as implausible as a cast-iron life belt. He said he had arisen that morning as usual, had eaten the breakfast his wife had prepared for him, had noticed nothing amiss, had walked down the road to the beach, had heard a scream or two apparently from a neighboring cottage, and had arrived at the Navy launch about 5:40 AM.

Examined at all, the alibi collapses. Dr. Carruthers said flatly that the killing took place in the early, early morn—before 4 AM. If the doctor was right, the Chief would have had to sleep through the prolonged butchery in a cottage in which it would be difficult to swing a large cat. He would have had then to get up and eat a breakfast prepared by his wife at some time prior to her murder. And he would have had to notice no sign of anything amiss.

Even if the doctor were wrong the alibi falls apart. To believe the Chief it would have been necessary to believe that Mrs. Eastlake was alive and sleeping peacefully when the man who "looked like Papa" knocked over her daughter at 5 AM and that she was not chopped up until after the Chief left the premises at approximately 5:30. Then the murderers, working at a pace that would have done credit to senior butchers at the A&P, would have had to do their dirty work before Miss Knox sounded the alarm some time before 6 AM.

The Chief was unbelievable but the jury found him not guilty. He was freed and an understanding Navy promptly transferred him to the Washington Navy Yard. In January he met a Washington girl; in February they became engaged; and in March they married. In April Miss Knox went on trial. The newspapers suggested that she would plead "moral insanity." She didn't. She simply pleaded not guilty and said she hoped the whole affair wouldn't do the Eastlake children too much harm. She expressed surprise when told that Roger had married again. "It is hard to believe he could do such a thing so soon after Margaret's death," she said. She sat crouched in her chair, a middle-aged woman in a blue tailored suit, and when Roger took the stand to testify against her she stared at him hour after hour. He looked in every direction but hers. He had a sorry story but he stuck to it.

When he finished Miss Knox's lawyer tried to switch the blame back to him.

"Could you fly on the wings of the morn," he said, "from the snow-clad peaks of the north to the sunny shores of the south, the winds would whisper and the mountains rumble that he is one of the blackest, most disloyal scoundrels alive."

The courtroom applauded but the jury found Miss Knox guilty. Which she was. As Dr. Carruthers said, it took two to hack Margaret Eastlake to bits. Miss Knox got twenty years and a month. Roger got a bit of unfavorable publicity. It is difficult, looking back, to decide exactly what scenario Miss Knox and Chief Eastlake had in mind when they began. They were the most maladroit butchers since Burke and Hare. They presumably intended to blame the imaginary "dark man" whom Miss Knox reported running from the scene. The Chief was not a great plotter and he got off because he wasn't. A great plotter makes a precise and complicated plan, a plan with hundreds of movable parts. And if one goes bad the plan turns on its maker and chews him up.

G. Edward Grammer was the champion complicated planner of them all. He was officer manager for the Climax Uranium Company, with offices in Manhattan and a home in Baltimore County.

He was a successful office manager making $150 a week, a very good salary for a 35-year-old high-school graduate in 1952. A successful office manager is a fussy fellow who believes in triplicate copies, double-entry bookkeeping, and a single standard of success. He believes a thing should be done systematically if it is done at all. He believes in records—things written down and preserved.

Climax Uranium thought well of him. He ran the clerical staff and in his spare time acted as a courier between Washington and New York. He routinely carried company papers back and forth, and on one occasion the company dispatched him all the way off to Denver.

G. Edward and his wife, the former Dorothy Schmidt, had grown up together in the still bosky lanes of Baltimore County. Dorothy's family thought G. Edward was a great man. Her brothers were big bruisers but they were slightly in awe of their bulgy brother-in-law who spoke knowingly of corporate affairs. The neighbors considered him a man of obvious if dreary virtue. When he wasn't fussing around the office he was fussing around the church or the front yard. When Climax Uranium moved him to New York he took Dottie and the children along, and they all promptly joined their neighborhood Methodist church. G. Edward became an usher. Dottie taught Sunday School. When Dottie's father became ill, G. Edward insisted that Dottie and the kids go home. When Dottie suggested, after a couple of months, that they move back to Manhattan, he said no. He said her place was at her father's bedside. Besides, he was beginning to have fun.

G. Edward Grammer was too clever by much more than half. He concocted a marvelously intricate plan for killing his wife in an apparent auto accident. He did everything wrong. Here, detectives escort him to headquarters.

He started taking the girls in the office out. Particularly the girls with husbands off in the Army. And he joined a bowling team in a league composed of employees of loan companies. G. Edward had been in loans before joining Climax. As fate had it, G. Edward's team bowled on Monday, the same night the teams in the United Nations league rolled. On a certain night in November Miss Mathilda Mary Mizibrocky, a striking 28-year-old UN employee and a native of Canada, was more or less insulted by an uppity pin boy. She looked around and saw this self-important-looking man standing there in his shirtsleeves. She assumed it was the alley manager. It was, of course, G. Edward Grammer himself. He sympathized with her. And for the moment he let her mistaken impression persist. He suggested that since an employee of the house had insulted her she was "entitled to a few drinks at the bar." After a few drinks G. Edward revealed that he was an office not an alley manager, and he proposed that they meet for lunch the next day. Tillie accepted. They met for lunch and then for regular after bowling Monday-night dates. Then they began meeting on weekends as well. He told her all about himself except that he was married and the father of two. Tillie gave him a cigarette lighter for his birthday and she wrote words of endearment on the white ribbon with which it was wrapped. G. Edward, a true sentimentalist, kept the ribbon displayed on his desk, and he told Tillie that her gift was the "lighter of my life." Tillie thought that was funny. She was in love.

Spring came. G. Edward began planning. He bought his wife a new Oldsmobile for their wedding anniversary. She was overwhelmed. He waited a few weeks and took it to a garage for a checkout. He told the mechanic that the accelerator got stuck. The mechanic checked it, over and over. It didn't stick and the mechanic wrote that down on the shop card.

123

Summer came. Climax decided to send G. Edward out to the uranium fields in Denver on a "general educational trip." G. Edward decided to make the education as broad as possible. Back in those golden days people went to Denver by train and the trains always stopped in Chicago. G. Edward invited Tillie to go along as far as Lake Michigan. She blushed and accepted. They went to the Edgewater Beach Hotel and registered as Mr. and Mrs. Grammer. They spent three glorious days. Every time G. Edward lit Tillie's cigarette he made his little joke and Tillie giggled. He went reluctantly on to Denver alone and got a room at the Brown Palace. During the day he played golf with Climax's field manager and at night he looked out the window at the moonlit mountains and wrote letters to Tillie: "It seems like ages since I held you in my arms and kissed you, yet it was only a few short days ago that I saw you. I sure do love you, very much my darling. Please take good care of my Tillie G." Tillie G. stood for Tillie Grammer. G. Edward was hinting that they were married in the eyes of God as well as the desk clerk. The eyes of God squint, however, even when looking down at a church usher. Tillie was a Catholic and G. Edward a Methodist and they had, they both agreed, a "religious problem." Tillie obviously didn't think it was an insurmountable block. G. Edward hinted that love would find a way. He wrote her that he was praying for a solution. "Perhaps Protestant prayers are heard too," he said. It seems clear enough that G. Edward, whatever his faults, was no gay deceiver. He intended to marry Tillie but he had to stall a bit. First he had to unmarry Dottie. Divorces were so messy and besides Tillie, as a Catholic, wouldn't want to marry a divorced man. So time moved on.

Tillie went to visit her folks in Canada and to talk to her father about her "religious problem." She had good news for G. Edward. "He expressed much delight in the news of 'our romance' and has given us his blessing."

It was now August and G. Edward did the next in his series of dumb moves. He wrote two letters, dating them in July. He gave them to his secretary, telling her to deliver them to his wife and to a lawyer

friend in the event of his death. It is impossible to figure out what purpose the letters were intended to serve. Perhaps he intended to fake his own death. At any rate, in one of the letters, the one to the lawyer, dated in July, he enclosed an August hotel bill and asked that it be paid. The letter to his wife closed with the solemn proclamation: "There will never be a finer person on earth than you, my sweetheart."

On August 19, G. Edward went down to Washington on business. From Washington he went to Baltimore, arriving in the afternoon. He spent the evening with Dottie, his wife. About 10:30 PM he said it was time for him to catch his train and he asked her to drive him to the station. He said he wanted to catch the 11:28 to New York.

At 12:40 AM, two Baltimore County policemen were driving up a steep hill on Belair Road. As they drove up, a car came careening down, weaving from side to side. It narrowly missed the cops, turned abruptly and hurtled across the road, sideswiped a telephone pole, shot up an embankment, and turned on its side. The policemen hurried to the scene. The car seemed almost undamaged—the windows were rolled down and intact and the windshield wasn't even cracked. The wheels were still spinning. A woman was inside and obviously hurt. One policeman dived through the back-seat window and pulled her out. Her forehead was slashed with deep lacerations and her skull was caved in. Her body, however, was almost without bruises. An ambulance came and took her to St. Joseph's hospital. She was dead on arrival. She was Dorothy Grammer, age 33, mother of three.

The Schmidt family collapsed. Dottie's brother Harold called G. Edward's apartment first thing in the morning. G. Edward didn't answer. Harold finally got hold of a neighbor and left a message. When G. Edward got it he immediately flew south, arriving in Baltimore County in mid-afternoon. He said he had gone to the office about 7 AM to leave the papers he'd brought up from Washington and so he missed the phone call. He said he'd last seen Dottie at the railroad station and he'd given her four dollars for gas just before she drove away. He said that once 13 years before Dottie had been scared out of her wits when a bee had flown in the car window while she was driving and that ever since then she'd been scared to death of flying insects. He then announced that he was in shock and had himself placed under a physician's care.

On August 29 Dr. Russell S. Fisher, Baltimore's chief medical examiner, announced that Mrs. Grammer had been murdered. He said that she had been dead already when the car came rolling down the hill. He said the murderer, whoever that might be, had made a few mistakes.

A pebble had been found, firmly lodged under the accelerator. It had made the car go, though no one had been stepping on the gas.

Mrs. Grammer had always worn glasses. Her glasses were missing.

Mr. Grammer had said he'd seen her stick the four dollars for gas in her purse. The purse was missing.

Mrs. Grammer had always driven with the windows up. The windows were all rolled down.

Mrs. Grammer's forehead was cut as if by flying glass but there'd been no flying glass. Even the dome light was unbroken.

Mrs. Grammer had obviously been thrown about by the impact of the crash but there were only two small bruises on her body. Dead bodies don't bruise.

Her principal injury—the crushed skull —could not have been caused by the crash since there was no point of possible contact that would have crushed it in the particular way it was crushed. It looked more as if she'd been hit repeatedly with a pipe.

The newspapers immediately began referring to Mrs. Grammer's death as the "almost perfect crime" though it is difficult to see how a crime that missed on seven major points can be considered almost perfect.

Dottie's mother, Mrs. Martha Schmidt, told police that once when G. Edward was away in the Army a man acquaintance had beaten Dottie up. That gentleman was the prime suspect for at least several hours.

G. Edward meanwhile remained in seclusion at the Schmidt home but his brother-in-law Harold was getting suspicious. He began to doubt that G. Edward was as shocked as he said. "He made believe that he didn't want to eat or see the newspapers during the day. Then he'd get up late at night when mother had gone to bed and eat and read the newspapers."

G. Edward also had behaved oddly when he and Harold went up to his New York apartment to get some clothes. Harold had found a purse in the apartment that looked like Dottie's.

"When I said I'd thought I'd seen her purse he turned white, dropped what he had in his hands, and turned toward me. I was afraid to say any more. We didn't talk for 20 minutes after that."

The cops treated G. Edward with a certain discretion. For one thing they knew he'd been sort of a cop himself— a criminal investigation agent in the Army. First they sent one of his boyhood friends out to question him. Sergeant Gordon Holmes of the county police. He was accompanied by Captain Carroll Simmons.

G. Edward told them how his wife had reported the accelerator sticking and how he'd taken the car into the garage to get it fixed. He said it had stuck on him once or twice as well. He said he'd no idea how the pebble had gotten lodged under the accelerator pedal. He admitted it was quite a coincidence. He said he was surprised to hear that the pebble was just like the gravel in his own front yard.

The county cops had two long conversations with G. Edward. Then the city police determined that the actual murder had taken place at the top of the hill, in front of the Maryland State School for the Blind, about a tenth of a mile inside the city limits. So the city police arrested G. Edward and took him off to jail. They took him first to one precinct, then to another, and finally out to the scene of the crime. They kept him riding around all morning and grilled him in the afternoon. At 2:15 PM he was well done. He confessed, sort of.

He said Dottie had not driven him to the railroad station as originally planned. Since they'd had a bit of time they'd

Mayport, pick up | early yesterday afternoon. The hurricane at the time was blowing 100 miles east of Jacksonville.

Way, old son

bright

, Aug. 30.
n tonight distasteful the armed eech rem- Churchill's years.
is no easy ent world ck way to ne.
ortcuts to he said. ortcuts to

n said he not try to

on

'TOP

ches by nd Gov- l be car- iroadcast- emocratic ttee an-

t address om 1 to ill be on

eech in broadcast :30 to 11

ur fighting it, adding: ith in the l them the n to work sacrifices back you only way ".
less than and con- us on the l and tri- s.
time in a presiden- aid some- :; Col. 7

'No Coercion'
Ike Pledges Fair Play For Labor

NEW YORK, Aug. 30 (P).—Dwight D. Eisenhower promised the Nation's workers today he would not seek to "coerce" them with laws if he is elected President, but added that he would try to serve the worthy interests of every group of Americans.

The Republican candidate vowed in a Labor Day "pledge to the working men and women of America" that he would lead the Nation along the "broad middle way" to peace and prosperity without setting off any group of people by class.

His test of every policy, he said, would be: "Is it good for America?"

Also made public today was Eisenhower's message to serv- icemen overseas, recorded for Armed Forces Radio broadcast, in which he told them the rotation system of bringing them home should be continued —and that their pay should not lag behind the inflationary spiral.

Eisenhower's Labor Day state- ment was released through his New York campaign headquar- ters. He said he would spell out his labor policy in detail in a speech here Monday to the Na- tional Association of Letter Car- riers (AFL).

In his pledge, Eisenhower said that if elected, he would conduct the office of President so that at the end of his service every worker could say:

"He has been fair.

"He has been my friend.

"He has not coerced us with laws, nor divided us by class, but has fostered mutual respect, un- derstanding and good will.

"He has led us forward along the broad middle way toward prosperity without war for our- selves and for our children."

Eisenhower said that during his campaign it was his "firm in- tention" to tell the nation his views and thinking on "the great questions which trouble every one of us in our daily lives."

"In reaching those conclu-

See IKE, Page 2, Column 3

Husband Held For Inquiry in Auto Slaying

By Matt McDade
Post Reporter

TOWSON, Md., Aug. 30.—G. Edward Grammer, 35-year-old husband of Towson's "perfect crime" victim, was booked for investigation this afternoon fol- lowing a 4-hour grilling by Baltimore City and County au- thorities.

Although Grammer has had free run of Baltimore County since August 20, when his come- ly wife, Dorothy, 33, was found murdered in a crashed automo- bile, he was ordered held in the jail here for further questioning Sunday.

Asked why the balding father of three children suddenly had been clapped in jail, Frank H. Newell, 3d, deputy State's attor- ney for Baltimore County, said, "I can't disclose that reason."

"We're making a full investi- gation. We're holding Grammer for investigation," Newell re- peated as reporters pressed him for an explanation.

Newell refused to say whether Grammer is a suspect in the 10- day-old murder, and again an- swered, "I can't tell you that," when asked whether the office manager of a New York metals and mining firm had been co- operating in answering ques- tions.

The deputy State's Attorney responded with a crisp "no com- ment" to questions concerning a possible lie-detector test for Grammer, and would not say whether Grammer had offered to take such a test.

Grammer appeared tired, sol- emn and aged beyond his years as he was led from the question- ing room in the Towson Court- house by two detectives at 5:50 p. m.

Although he dragged his heels from fatigue, the detec- tives hurried him to a waiting automobile and rushed him to police headquarters where he was booked, fed and locked up for the night.

County police refused to al- low reporters to speak with Grammer, and photographers

See SLAY, Page 6, Column 5

miles southwest of Charleston. Power lines in the town were down and it could not be reached by telephone.

Power lines also were going down at Charleston where 60- mile an hour winds were re- ported.

The South Carolina Electric & Gas Co. said half the power in Charleston was off and tele- phones were out in some areas.

Charleston's streets were ankle-deep in water and even deeper along the waterfront.

Lights Go out

John A. Cummings, meteorolo- gist for the U. S. Weather Bu- reau, gave this description of the situation as he sat in the Customs House overlooking Charleston Harbor:

"Most of the city now appears to be without lights. The winds are taking down power lines and I can hear windows break- ing. The only light I can see clearly through the sheets of rain is the one in the steeple of St. Michaels Church. The streets are deserted. Across the harbor I can see the ships riding at anchor. The water is getting very choppy."

Officials at Pawley's Island, near Georgetown, ordered all persons to leave the island at once. Baptist and Methodist churches in Georgetown were opened tot evacuees.

Traffic Is Halted

H. E. Hicks, chairman of the Red Cross disaster committee at Wilmington, N. C., asked all residents of nearby Wrightsville and Carolina beaches tto move inland. The chief of police at Wrightsville Beach stopped all

See WIND, Page 6, Column 4

Seminarians Find Doctor Lost 6 Days In Md. Forest

ELDERSBURG, Md., Aug. 30 (P).—Dr. William I. Buppert, 75- year-old Carroll County physi- cian, was found by searchers to- day nearly a week after he dis- appeared while taking a walk through a wooded section near here.

A group of Jesuit students of Woodstock College discovered him leaning against a tree only about a mile from where he be- came lost.

"Hi, boys," Buppert greeted them. "I certainly am glad to see you."

The physician said he had walked into the woods last Mon- day near the home of a son, Doran, and lost his way. He said he had not eaten since then and subsisted only on water he scooped from streams. At night he slept at the base of trees.

"I walked and walked and walked, but it seemed I never could get out of the woods," he added.

s 21 and Over

stopped for a couple of drinks at a bar on Belair Road. He was, unfortunately, unable to remember the name or specific location of the bar. They had quarrelled. Then they'd left and driven up Belair Road to get some gas. When they got to the top of the hill in front of the school for the blind (a perfect place to avoid witnesses), Dottie said, "You love your job more than you love me," and G. Edward was suddenly driven into a wild fury. He stopped the car, he said, got out, saw a pipe lying on the ground, picked it up, and hit her. Then, dazed by drink and emotion, he'd left her there and had gotten, somehow, to the train station where he caught a late train.

It was an impossible story to believe. G. Edward possibly decided that it was asking too much to expect to find 12 men who would. So he asked that he be tried by a judge alone instead of a jury.

The trial was, to a point, a foregone conclusion. G. Edward showed little emotion except when his own mother took the stand. Then a single tear was noted in his eye. Captain Carroll Simmons proved an interesting witness. He told his tale of the early conversations he and Sergeant Holmes had with the accused in his bedroom. G. Edward's lawyer decided to attack Captain Holmes' credibility. He asked the captain if he had not once been convicted of stealing seven kegs of beer from a picnic. The captain denied that indignantly. After a bit he asked the captain if he had not once been convicted of carnal knowledge. It turned out he had. The principal witness was, of course, Tillie Mizibrocky, elegant and austere in a tailored suit with long white gloves. G. Edward stared at her, just the way Miss Knox had stared at Chief Eastlake. And she, like the Chief, avoided her erstwhile lover's eye. She said she didn't know how she then felt about the dashing office manager who'd wooed her in the bowling alley and at the Edgewater Hotel. She said it was hard to decide a thing like that when

the person loved turns out to be a total liar.

Judge Herman M. Mosel handed down his verdict after spending several hours alone in his chambers. It turned out he was composing what he perhaps hoped would become a literary highlight in the annals of jurisprudence.

"Grammer's love for Miss Mizibrocky was the drive that turned a loving husband and kind father and a man apparently at peace with himself and the world into a violator of all those God-given commandments he had heretofore apparently respected."

As the judge droned on and on, G. Edward's left foot began to tap. When the judge began listing the points that showed premeditation he stopped tapping and slumped down limp. He got the chair, fair and square. The only thing unfair was the judge's conclusion that love for Tillie had driven G. Edward out of his respectable head. The G. Edwards of the world, like the Motherwells, are hardly ever driven by passion. They are often driven by greed and by a simple childish desire not to become inconvenienced. People who are obstacles need simply be removed. Motherwell removed his wife, an infant daughter, and a rich old lady who had a lot of money. He did it, probably without ever once losing his temper.

Robert Ammidown, the nastiest of them all, was a singularly unsavory product of the age of affluence. He had been a bureaucrat all his adult life, first 20 mindless years in the Navy, then three as a GS 14 in the Job Corps. Ammidown lived surrounded by easy money. He was a retired lieutenant commander, and the Job Corps paid him some $20,000 a year. His wife had a $130,000 trust fund.

On the eve of Christmas Eve in 1963, he'd made a fevered pass at Vivian Ann Brown at a steamy office party at the old Navy Department on the Mall. Vivian Ann had been his assistant. They began an affair, and Robert naturally screwed it up. Mrs. Ammidown found out about Vivian Ann. There was a negotiated settlement. Robert signed over their Arlington home to Linda, and all his paychecks went into a trust fund for Robert, Jr. Vivian Ann went off and married someone else. That marriage broke up. She came back to Washington and got a job as a budget analyst in the Defense Department. Mrs. Ammidown saw her at Fort Meyer's PX one day and told Robert. He called Vivian Ann, and their romance resumed its dreary way. They got together about three times a year for lunch and an afternoon roll in the hay. Meanwhile Ammidown was out of the Navy and into the Job Corps. In its early days the Job Corps had hired academic types with mildly wild eyes but they made President Lyndon Johnson very nervous. So the Job Corps began hiring the least passionate men around—retired military officers.

In twenty years in the Navy Ammidown had never rocked a boat. He slipped into the Job Corps like a machined replaceable part. The people who worked with him then find it difficult now to say what he was like. He was, or so he seemed, a careful man, circumspect. Mild, polite, fussy. A man who would never forget to salute.

Then he met Tony Lee.

They met on a plane, flying back from the West Coast. Tony was young and black. He had been a pool-hall hustler but he'd graduated into being a private detective. He'd once been convicted of possessing marijuana. They became very close friends. It is easy to suspect that they became more than that. Ammidown was very restrained with Vivian Ann but he let himself go with Tony.

Tony had a bright idea. He had found an ancient hotel at Wicomico on Maryland's Eastern Shore. Ammidown would supply the money and he, Tony, would run it as a combination gambling den and sex palace.

Ammidown took Vivian Ann to Wicomico to show her the place and outline the plan. She was not impressed. His wife Linda wasn't either. She refused to give him the money. Tony had the answer to that. "Bob, you know what the solution to our problem is—to kill her." So Ammidown put his careful mind to work. First they would hire a killer. Tony hired William Preston "Dutch" Johnson, a senior hustler. He gave him $100 down, with $900 to come on execution. It was to be an execution, simple and brutal. Johnson was to wait outside while Ammidown and his son escorted Linda out of the Hecht

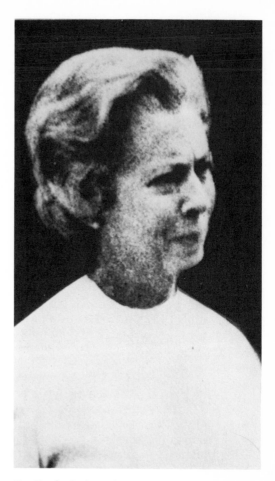

Lt. Cmdr. Robert Ammidown had a wife (left) with money and a scheme to start a sexy night club on Maryland's Eastern Shore. He hired Tony Lee (right) to arrange her rape and murder. Lee couldn't find a willing killer, so he did the job himself.

Co. at the Parkington Shopping Center in Arlington. She would be in the middle. At the last minute Ammidown called the plan off. He told Tony he was afraid that Robert Jr. would have an "emotional attitude" toward all Negroes as a result of seeing his mother killed by a black man.

Plan number two went into effect. This time Tony himself would be the killer. Ammidown had had one last fling with Vivian. They'd gone to the Skyline Inn on South Capitol Street, a hostelry devoid of magic, frequented by troops of visiting Boy Scouts. The summer ended.

Ammidown called Vivian Ann on the morning of October 1, a drizzly day. He said dispiritedly that he had to go home

and put weed killer on his lawn. That evening he drove up to a New York Avenue gas station, slammed on the brakes, and announced breathlessly that his wife had been abducted in the Flagship restaurant's parking lot and was probably being murdered under the East Capitol Street Bridge. She was. Raped and murdered by Tony Lee.

Ammidown told his tale, and everyone apparently believed it. There had been a similar rape-murder some months earlier. The assumption was that the same mad dog had struck again.

To Tony it looked like Bob would soon inherit Linda's $130,000 and they'd be in business in Wicomico. He wouldn't. For one thing Linda had secretly cut Bob out of her will a couple of weeks before. For another Dutch Johnson, the hustler, read of Mrs. Ammidown's death and decided to cut himself in. He decided to hit Ammidown for $50,000.

As he explained later, he had no choice. "I had three alternatives. I had to kill Tony, blackmail him, or inform on him." He was not the sort to stoop to killing or informing.

"I just couldn't walk around the streets, happy-go-lucky," he said enigmatically. "I knew too much—Tony knew that I knew."

He saw his duty and he did it.

Dutch began calling up Ammidown at work. Ammidown wasn't there. He was at Disney World with Junior. Dutch grew threatening. Ammidown's co-workers grew suspicious and called the cops. One cop, Sergeant John J. Moriarory, pretended to be Ammidown. He met and nabbed Dutch and two hustling accomplices. Then he went out to see Ammidown at his wife's family home at Locust Grove, Virginia.

Ammidown confessed—up to a point—over a cup of coffee. He had, he admitted, arranged for Tony Lee to abduct his wife and himself as they left the Flagship. He had arranged for Tony to take them out to the East Capitol Street Bridge and rape Linda. He had not, he insisted, arranged for Tony to kill her. He had intended, he said, merely to frighten her into giving him and Tony the money for the sex club in Wicomico. It was as plausible as a moth-ball necklace.

Tony got the chair—but the Supreme Court subsequently ruled out capital punishment.

Ammidown got two life terms—one for murder in the first and one for felony murder, a murder while committing another felony such as rape. At one point the jury asked Judge John J. Sirica if it could recommend life on one count and the chair on the other.

They apparently thought of sentencing him to life and death, both of which he deserved.

Vivian Ann was a key witness against him. She said in the course of her testimony that she had never loved Robert, not for a moment. Life had just been dull at the Navy Department.

And she had given a sort of epitaph for Linda.

"I found her to be a very gracious and ladylike person."

Wives who are murdered by the likes of Ammidown apparently always are.